Whatever It Takes

Whatever It Takes

Geoffrey Canada's Quest to Change Harlem and America

Paul Tough

Houghton Mifflin Company

BOSTON · NEW YORK

2008

For information about permissions to reproduce selections
from this book, write to Permissions, Houghton Mifflin Company,
215 Park Avenue South, New York, NY 10003.

www.houghtonmifflinbooks.com

Library of Congress Cataloguing Data
Tough, Paul.
Whatever it takes : Geoffrey Canada's quest to change Harlem
and America / Paul Tough.
p.   cm.
Includes bibliographical references and index.
ISBN 978-0-618-56989-2
1. Poverty — New York (State) — New York — Prevention. 2. African
American children — Education — New York (State) — New York.
3. African American children — New York (State)—New York —
Social conditions. 4. Poor — New York (State) — New York — Social
conditions. 5. Harlem (New York, N.Y.) — Economic conditions.
6. Canada, Geoffrey. I. Title.
HC79.P63T68 2008   362.74'8097471 — dc22   2008013303

Printed in the United States of America

Book design by Robert Overholtzer

DOC 10 9 8 7 6 5 4 3 2 1

A few brief portions of this book first appeared
in the *New York Times Magazine*.

For P. and G.

Contents

1. The Lottery 1

2. Unequal Childhoods 21

3. Baby College 53

4. Contamination 98

5. Battle Mode 126

6. Bad Apples 155

7. Last Chance 174

8. The Conveyor Belt 188

9. Escape Velocity 213

10. Graduation 234

11. What Would It Take? 257

   Acknowledgments 271
   Notes 276
   Index 286

1   The Lottery

By the time Geoffrey Canada arrived at the Promise Academy lottery, the auditorium was almost full. He had expected a modest turnout—he figured the rain would keep a lot of parents away—but by 6:00 P.M. more than two hundred people had crowded into the back of the hall, and there were dozens more still streaming in the front door. Here and there, members of Canada's staff were consulting clipboards and calming anxious parents. His director of education hurried past him, shouting into her cell phone. It was April 14, 2004, a cool, wet night in Harlem. The hand-lettered sign out front of PS 242, streaked with raindrops, said "Welcome to the Promise Academy Charter School Lottery," and inside, past the sign-in table set up in the school's front hallway, a tall, bull-chested young man named Jeff was handing a rose to each woman as she walked in. "These are for the moms," he said with a smile. "Welcome to the ceremony."

Canada, a tall, thin black man in a dark blue suit, surveyed the crowd. From what he could see, the parents taking their seats in the auditorium were the ones he had hoped to attract: typical Harlem residents, mostly African American, some Hispanic, almost all poor or working class, all struggling to one degree or another with the challenges of raising and educating children in one of New York City's most impoverished neighborhoods. In many ways, their sons and daughters were growing up the way Canada had, four decades before, just a few miles away in the South Bronx: cut off from the American mainstream, their futures constrained by substandard schools, unstable families, and a segregated city.

Five years earlier, frustrated by Harlem's seemingly intractable problems, Canada had embarked on an outsized and audacious new endeavor, a poverty-fighting project that was different from anything that had come before it. Since 1990, he had been the president of a well-respected local nonprofit organization called the Rheedlen Centers for Children and Families, which operated a handful of programs in upper Manhattan targeted at young people: afterschool drop-in centers, truancy prevention, antiviolence training for teenagers. They were decent programs, and they all did some good for the kids who were enrolled in them. But after Canada had been running them for a few years, day in and day out, his ideas about poverty started to change.

The catalyst was surprisingly simple: a waiting list. One Rheedlen afterschool program had more children who wanted to enroll than it was able to admit. So Canada chose the obvious remedy: he drew up a waiting list, and it quickly filled with the names of children who needed his help and couldn't get it. That bothered him, and it kept bothering him, and before long it had him thinking differently about his entire organization. Sure, the five hundred children who were lucky enough to be participating in one of his programs were getting help, but why those five hundred and not the five hundred on the waiting list? Or why not another five hundred altogether? For that matter, why five hundred and not five thousand? If all he was doing was picking some kids to save and letting the rest fail, what was the point?

Canada became less and less sure of what his programs really added up to. Each one was supported by a separate short-term grant, often on a contract from one city agency or another, and in order to keep the money flowing, Canada was required to demonstrate to the foundations and agencies that paid for the programs that a certain number of children had participated. But no one seemed to care whether the programs were actually working. In fact, no one seemed to have given a whole lot of thought to what, in this context, "working" might really mean.

Canada began to wonder what would happen if he reversed the equation. Instead of coming up with a menu of well-meaning programs and then trying to figure out what they accomplished and how they fit together, what if he started with the outcomes he wanted to achieve and then worked backward from there, changing and tweaking and overhauling programs until they actually produced the right results? When he followed this train of thought a little further, he realized that it wasn't the outcomes of individual programs that he really cared about: what mattered was the overall impact he was able to have on the children he was trying to serve. He was all too familiar with the "fade-out" phenomenon, where a group of needy kids are helped along by one program or another, only to return to the disappointing mean soon after the program ends. Head Start, the government-funded prekindergarten program for poor children, was the classic example. Plenty of studies had determined conclusively that graduates of Head Start entered kindergarten ahead of their inner-city peers. And plenty of studies had shown that a few years later, those same graduates had slipped back to the anemic achievement level of neighborhood kids who hadn't attended Head Start. A few years of bad schooling and bad surroundings were powerful enough to wipe out all of the program's gains.

Canada wanted to find a way off the treadmill. So he asked himself a series of questions, and gradually his thinking took shape.

Who did he want to help?

He wanted to help poor children.

What was his goal for them?

He wanted them to be able to grow into fully functioning participants in mainstream American middle-class life.

What did they need to do to accomplish that?

They had to survive adolescence, graduate from high school, get into college, and graduate from college.

And what did he have to provide in order to help them accomplish that?

Well, that was where the questions got interesting, and difficult to answer.

He concluded, first, that his efforts couldn't be as diffuse and haphazard as they had been. He would need to select a single geographical area and devote all of his energies to that one place. He would have to start intervening in children's lives when they were young, at birth or even earlier. The support system he provided would need to be comprehensive, a continuous, linked series of programs. It wasn't enough to help out in just one part of a child's life: the project would need to combine educational, social, and medical services. And he wanted serious numbers. He wasn't interested in helping just a few kids, the ones who were already most likely to succeed, the ones whose parents had the resources and foresight to seek out aid and support for themselves and their children.

It was partly a gut feeling, a personal thing: he had always hated the idea of picking and choosing, helping some kids and letting the rest fail. But it was also practical. He believed that in troubled neighborhoods there existed a kind of tipping point. If 10 percent of the families on a block or in a housing project were engaged in one of his programs, their participation wouldn't have much influence on their neighbors, and the children who did enroll would feel at best like special cases and at worst like oddballs. But if, say, 60 percent of the families were onboard, then participation would come to seem normal, and so would the values that went with it: a sense of responsibility, a belief that there was a point to self-improvement, a hopefulness about the future. Canada's theory was that each child would do better if all the children around him were doing better. So instead of waiting for residents to find out on their own about the services he was providing, his recruiters would seek out participants by going door-to-door in housing projects and low-rent high-rises. They would create programs that were well organized and even fun to attend, and they would sweeten the deal by offering incentives—everything from a free breakfast to Old Navy gift certificates—to break down any lingering resistance.

At the end of the 1990s, Canada dedicated himself to making his idea a reality. He chose as the laboratory for his grand experiment a twenty-four-block zone of central Harlem, an area that contained about three thousand children, more than 60 percent of whom were living below the poverty line and three-quarters of whom regularly scored below grade level on statewide reading and math tests. He and his staff developed an array of new, integrated programs that followed the life of a child: a parenting class for Harlem residents with children three and under, an intensive pre-kindergarten for four-year-olds, classroom aides and afterschool instruction for public school students, and a tutoring center for teenagers. Canada's objective was to create a safety net woven so tightly that children in the neighborhood couldn't slip through. It was an idea both simple and radical, and he gave it a name to match: the Harlem Children's Zone.

A FEW YEARS into the life of the Zone, Canada hit a snag. The problem was the schools. His original plan had called for his staff to work closely with the principals of Harlem's local public schools, providing them with supplemental services like computer labs and reading programs. In some schools the collaboration had worked well, but in others it was a disaster. To Canada's surprise and displeasure, principals sometimes resisted the help, turning down his requests for classroom space or kicking out the tutors that the organization supplied. Even in the schools where the programs were running smoothly, they didn't seem to be producing results: the neighborhood's reading and math scores had barely budged.

In the dozen years that he had been in charge of the organization, first as Rheedlen and then, after he changed the name in 2002, as the Harlem Children's Zone, Canada had worked with five consecutive New York City schools chancellors. And while each one had come into office with new reforms and lofty promises, in the end none seemed to make much of a difference in the lives of Harlem's schoolchildren. Still, Canada felt unusually hopeful about the latest chancellor, Joel Klein, a product of the New York City public schools who had gone on to serve in Bill Clinton's Justice Department, most notably as the lead prosecutor in the federal government's sprawling antitrust case against Microsoft. Klein was appointed by Mayor Michael Bloomberg, a billionaire technocrat with no previous political experience who was elected in the aftermath of the terrorist attacks on New York City in 2001. Once in office, Bloomberg persuaded the state government in Albany to restructure the city's education bureaucracy, centralizing power under the mayor's control. Together, he and Klein succeeded in pushing through a series of significant reforms, often in the face of stiff opposition from teachers' unions and city officials.

One of Klein's early strategies was to recruit private groups, both nonprofits and corporations, to contribute in a variety of ways to the public school system. The Harlem Children's Zone was an obvious candidate, and soon after Klein arrived in New York, in 2002, he called Canada, and the two men met to discuss how the school system and the Harlem Children's Zone could work better together.

Canada brought with him a complex proposal that had his group and Klein's Department of Education working hand in hand to administer a few schools in Harlem. "Great idea," Klein said. "But it will never work." It would take forever to get parents, principals, and teachers to agree to that kind of power-sharing system, Klein explained; by the time they had the details worked out, he would probably be out of office and back in the private sector. But he suggested to Canada that there was a faster and easier way for the Harlem Children's Zone to get involved: charter schools.

In 2002 charters were still fairly rare. There were more than two thousand nationwide, but they were mostly small and new, operating off the public's radar screen. The charter idea was born in Minnesota in the early 1990s: publicly funded schools run by independent organizations, usually nonprofits, outside the control of the local school board. In education circles, there were bitter disagreements over charter schools, and the debate was politically charged. Teachers at charter schools were usually nonunionized, and many conservative policy groups touted the schools as a free-enterprise solution to the nation's choked educational bureaucracies. Liberals were more likely to oppose charters; many suspected that the Right's sudden interest in inner-city education was nothing more than a cloak for a campaign to weaken unions and undermine the public school system.

Nationwide, charter schools had a mixed record. Early advocates claimed the schools would raise test scores across the board, and that hadn't happened; nationally, scores for charter school students were the same as or lower than scores for public school students. But by another measure, charter schools had succeeded: by allowing educators to experiment in ways that they generally couldn't inside public school systems, they had led to the creation of a small corps of schools with new and ambitious methods for educating students facing real academic challenges. One of the best known and most successful was a fast-growing national network of charters called the Knowledge Is Power Program. KIPP schools targeted low-income minority students, the demographic that in most school districts was mired at the lowest academic levels, and yet KIPP students were for the most part thriving, consistently earning above-average scores on state tests. Canada knew KIPP well. He had visited one of KIPP's flagship schools, the KIPP Academy in the South Bronx, and he had become friendly with David Levin, the young Teach for America graduate who had helped found KIPP and now ran the organization's New York schools. Chancellor Klein had encouraged KIPP and other successful charter-management organizations from around the country to apply for charters in New York City, and KIPP had plans to open two new schools in Harlem.

Although Canada was himself somewhat skeptical of the charter school movement—he believed that the only way to successfully educate poor children in significant numbers was to improve, not replace, the public school system—Klein's offer was too attractive to pass up. If Canada could open his own schools in Harlem, the pipeline he had been trying to create would be complete. Instead of reaching kids here and there, for a few hours a day, he would have them under his care for eight or ten or twelve hours a day, enough time, he hoped, to let him bring order to even the most chaotic young life. So in 2003 the Harlem Children's Zone submitted its three-hundred-page application to the New York City Department of Education. With Klein's support, it was approved, and as parents arrived for the lottery that rainy night in April 2004, the opening day of Promise Academy was less than five months away. The school would start with just two hundred students—one hundred in kindergarten and one hundred in sixth grade. Each September, as those students progressed through the school, they would be joined by a new kindergarten and sixth-grade class, and over the course of seven years, the academy would expand into a single, continuous school, educating thirteen hundred students, from kindergarten through the twelfth grade, in the center of Harlem.

Like every charter school in New York, Promise Academy was free of tuition and open by lottery to students from anywhere in the city's five boroughs. But the only students Canada really wanted in his school were from central Harlem, especially the lowest-performing students, exactly the ones whose parents were least inclined to apply to send their children to a different school. So in the days and weeks leading up to the charter school lottery, the organization's outreach workers solicited applications from the parents of children in every one of its programs, and they knocked on doors all over Harlem. By the evening of the lottery, they had received 359 applications—almost twice as many children as the school had room for. Now, here at PS 242, every seat in the auditorium was filled with a hopeful parent or a potential student or a patient sibling, and late arrivals were standing in the aisles. They weren't all model parents—Canada recognized some of them from the organization's substance- and alcohol-abuse programs—but they all wanted something better for their children. Multicolored helium balloons were tied to the end of each row of seats, which gave the room a festive air. More than anything, though, the place felt nervous.

AT A FEW MINUTES after six, Canada stood at the front of the hall, next to the stage, conferring with a tall, stocky white man in a gray suit: Stanley Druckenmiller, a legendary Wall Street hedge-fund manager who for the last six years had been the chairman of the Harlem Children's Zone's board of directors. Druckenmiller was extraordinarily wealthy; his personal fortune of $1.6 billion landed him that year at number 356 on *Forbes* magazine's list of the richest individuals on the planet. In person, though, he was restrained and stoical, with the stilted body language of Al Gore. At public events like this one, he often gave the impression that he would rather be poring over a balance sheet or sitting behind a Bloomberg Terminal. But Druckenmiller was deeply committed to Canada and to the Harlem Children's Zone; next to Canada himself, Druckenmiller had done more than anyone to build the organization into the nonprofit powerhouse it had become.

In the 1990s Druckenmiller sat on the board of the Robin Hood Foundation, a well-funded and high-profile charity that gave grants to various organizations dealing with poverty in New York City. Rheedlen was one of the foundation's biggest recipients, and it was at a Robin Hood board meeting one morning in 1994 that Druckenmiller first met Canada. At the time, a vision was just beginning to form in Canada's mind of an alternative to the traditional social service agency: something bigger and more efficiently run, an organization that would bypass the sentimental you-can-save-this-child-or-you-can-turn-the-page appeals to donors and instead offer, in exchange for substantial financial commitment, results—measurable, quantifiable outcomes that even the coldest-hearted capitalist would appreciate. It was exactly the kind of non-profit that Druckenmiller, a Republican who believed in lower taxes and smaller government and the wisdom of the market, was looking to support. The way Druckenmiller saw it, the tools of corporate America—management consultants, long-range plans, marketing data, quarterly targets—had created the strongest economy in the history of the world, but in the charitable sector, those tools were being ignored in favor of guesswork and good intentions.

At Canada's invitation, Druckenmiller joined the Rheedlen board, and with Druckenmiller's help Canada began to remake his organization along the sleek, efficient lines of a modern corporation. He hired a team of management consultants to help him write a ten-year business plan, and over the next several years the Harlem Children's Zone grew quickly, its budget expanding from $6 million to $58 million. Construction began on a brand-new building on 125th Street, Harlem's main boulevard, that would serve as the organization's headquarters. The annual fundraising dinner became a glittering event held in a cavernous restaurant across from Grand Central Terminal. Even as the donations increased, though, Druckenmiller remained the organization's largest benefactor. He personally contributed many millions of dollars a year, and he paid for about a third of the cost of the new headquarters himself.

There were two other Harlem Children's Zone board members at the lottery: Mitchell Kurz, the treasurer, who had retired early from a successful career as an advertising executive to become a high school math teacher in the South Bronx, and Kenneth Langone, a wealthy investor who had helped found Home Depot and now served as the chair of Promise Academy's board of trustees. Canada had invited the three men up to Harlem to witness what he had hoped would be a celebration, the culmination of months of hard work behind the scenes. But as the crowd swelled, he began to get an uneasy feeling about the way the evening might turn out. He knew that for half these parents, the night would indeed be celebratory, full of hope and promise. But the others, he realized, were going to leave disappointed. There was no requirement for charter schools to hold their lotteries in public; legally, Canada could have drawn the names behind closed doors and simply mailed out acceptance letters. But he had decided to make it a big show. It seemed like a good idea at the time. Now he wasn't so sure.

"COULD I HAVE everyone's attention?"

Canada had mounted the stage, and he stood behind a lectern, leaning over the microphone. The room was loud, a steady din of chatter pierced by an occasional wail from a child, and Canada waited for the noise to recede. On a long table next to him, a gold drum held a jumble of index cards, each one printed with the name of a prospective student.

Canada had turned fifty-two the previous January. When he joined Rheedlen, two decades earlier, as the organization's educational director, he carried an intimidating physique, a broad chest and thick biceps, the legacy of an adolescence spent in school-yard brawls followed by years of black belt training in karate. Now, in middle age, he still had the look of an athlete, but he had grown leaner with the years, tall and rangy, his arms long and his wrists narrow. His hair was going gray, and he wore it shaved close to his scalp. A sparse mustache and goatee, also graying, framed his mouth. These days, Canada divided his time between the streets of Harlem and the boardrooms of corporate America, and when you looked at him you could see the two sides of his personality reflected. Tonight, as always, his downtown uniform was flawless:

his dress shirt was monogrammed and his cuff links were gold. But there was something about the smooth, loping way he moved—or even now, the way he stood curled over the lectern—that was straight from the streets of the South Bronx.

When the hum in the auditorium died down, Canada began. "We are calling our school Promise Academy because we are making a promise to all of our parents," he said. "If your child is in our school, we will guarantee that child succeeds. There will be no excuses. We're not going to say, 'The child failed because they came from a home with only one parent.' We're not going to say, 'The child failed because they're new immigrants into the country.' If your child gets into our school, that child is going to succeed." The curriculum at Promise Academy would be intense, he said: classes would run from 8:00 A.M. to 4:00 P.M., five days a week, an hour and a half longer than regular city schools. Afterschool programs would run until 6:00 P.M., and the school year would continue well into July. There would be brand-new facilities, healthy lunches, a committed staff. "If you work with us as parents, we are going to do everything—and I mean everything—to see that your child gets a good education," Canada said. "We're going to have the best-quality education that parents can imagine."

From their narrow wooden seats, the parents watched Canada and considered the promises he was making. It was a complicated time to be raising a school-age child in Harlem. For as long as anyone could remember, the neighborhood's public schools had been uneven at best and downright dangerous at worst. Parents traded rumors about a promising new principal or a decent afterschool program, but their options had always been limited: Catholic school, if you could afford the tuition, or whatever the city was offering. In recent years, though, Harlem had become home to a growing number of educational alternatives: small, narrowly focused academies, selective public schools, and brand-new charters. The new schools meant more possibilities, but also more risk: how were you supposed to know which promises to believe?

For some in the auditorium, the choice was obvious: they had

decided on Promise Academy the moment they heard it was opening. There were forty children currently enrolled in Harlem Gems,
the Harlem Children's Zone's prekindergarten program, and all
forty of them had entered the lottery for the Promise Academy
kindergarten. Yasmin Scott was one of the true believers. She was
here with her daughter, Yanice Gillis, who was about to turn five.
About a year earlier, an outreach worker had stopped Scott on the
street and invited her to attend Baby College, the Harlem Children's Zone parenting program. Scott signed up. She was young
when she had Yanice, just fifteen, and she felt like she needed all
the help she could get. For Scott, Baby College turned out to be
a great experience — nine Saturdays in a row, four or five hours a
day, discussing immunization schedules and asthma prevention
and the importance of reading and singing to your baby. The discipline classes, especially, were real eye openers, where she learned
about time-outs and alternatives to corporal punishment. After
Scott graduated from Baby College, she wanted more, so she enrolled Yanice in Harlem Gems, an all-day pre-K with a 4:1 child-to-
adult ratio. After half a year in the program, Yanice was shining,
learning the basics of reading and math, singing songs in French,
coming home armed with words like "astronomy" and "meteorol-
ogist." Scott hoped Promise Academy would mean more of the
same. She couldn't stand the thought of sending Yanice to a regular
Harlem public school after this.

In the second row, right next to the aisle, Wilma Jure sat wearing
an "I Love New York" T-shirt and a red nylon jacket, her head
bowed in an anxious prayer. Jure wasn't here for her own child. She
was praying for her niece, Jaylene Fonseca, a four-year-old who
was a classmate of Yanice's in Harlem Gems. Jaylene's mother,
Jure's sister, was living in the city's shelter system for homeless
families, and most nights, Jaylene slept with her mother in a shelter on Forty-first Street, then spent the day in Harlem Gems. Jure
sometimes felt that the Gems program was the only thing keeping Jaylene alive.

In the front row, Virainia Utley sat with her daughter Janiqua.

Utley was something of a model parent in the Harlem Children's Zone. Janiqua was in the Fifth Grade Institute, an academic club that the organization ran here at PS 242, and her three younger siblings—Jaquan, Janisha, and John—were all enrolled in the afterschool computer-assisted reading program. Utley was the vice president of her tenants' association, which was part of Community Pride, the Harlem Children's Zone's community-organizing division, and she was a regular presence at Zone events. She had been talking for months about Janiqua going to Promise Academy.

Onstage, Ken Langone, the board member, was reaching into a plastic bucket filled with ticket stubs. As at many Harlem Children's Zone events, one of the lures Canada had used to pack the house tonight was a raffle. Langone, an owlish, balding man in his late sixties, read the winning numbers into the microphone like he was calling a church bingo night, and one by one, parents came to the front to display their tickets and collect a twenty-five-dollar gift certificate from Old Navy, the Gap, or HMV, the music store. The winners looked happy, and there was mild applause for each one, but the audience was beginning to grow a little restless, and the noise level was rising again. It was approaching 7:00 P.M., and not a single child's name had been called.

But Canada still wasn't quite ready to spin the drum. He called up one last guest: Rev. Alfonso Wyatt, a friend of Canada's since the early 1980s and now a minister on the staff of the Greater Allen Cathedral in Queens. Wyatt was on the school's board of trustees along with Langone and Druckenmiller and Kurz, but not because of his fundraising acumen. He was there for less tangible reasons—a moral authority, maybe, or maybe it was just that unlike the businessmen, all of whom were white, Wyatt shared a culture and a history with Canada: the peculiar joys and sorrows of inner-city black activism in the post–civil rights era. Wyatt and Canada were a decade or two younger than the men who had marched with Martin Luther King Jr., the generation that now made up the nation's civil rights establishment; their perspective was shaped not by Selma and the March on Washington but by what followed: Black Power and busing riots, drugs and AIDS and hip-hop.

Wyatt pulled the microphone from its holder and walked to the front of the stage. He wore a white turtleneck under a dark suit jacket, a modified version of a clerical collar. A stylized cross hung around his neck. "Some people don't believe that there are folks in Harlem who really care about their children," he began, his voice a sonorous baritone, his cadence deliberate, straight from the pulpit. "They don't believe that on a day when it was raining all day, that they would come out and that they would sit and that they would wait. People don't believe that there are folks who don't mind being inconvenienced." As he warmed up, the attention of the crowd, which had been wandering, was pulled back to the front of the auditorium. "But I know that the people here in this room don't mind waiting. Because if they can wait a *little* while tonight, they can change their children's life over the *long* while." Wyatt began pacing the stage, and suddenly even the people who did mind waiting didn't mind waiting. "So I want to salute you," he said. "We're going to show people all over the world that with a good staff, with dedication, with teamwork, that we can turn out first-rate scholars." There was a loud burst of applause. "Oh, you *better* clap," Wyatt continued. "We're not cutting no corners. We're going to *do* this." He pulled out one of his favorite stories, one he often used in front of a crowd like this one. "I want to tell you something that maybe you don't know," he said, his voice rising. "The people who run prisons in this country are looking at our third-graders. They look at their test scores each year to begin to predict how many prison cells will be needed twenty years from now." Some scattered murmurs of disapproval were heard. "And so I want the people in this house to tell them: You will not have our children!" The applause was louder now, a Sunday-morning feel on a wet Tuesday night.

"Let me hear somebody say it," Wyatt called out, and he led the crowd in a chant: "You! Will! Not! Have! Our! Children!"

"Let me hear somebody else say it," Wyatt cried, and the parents shouted again, louder:

"You! Will! Not! Have! Our! Children!"

"Let's make some noise in this place!"

AND THEN THE drawing began, starting with the kindergarten class. Doreen Land, the academy's newly hired superintendent, read the first name into a microphone: "Dijon Brinnard." A whoop went up from the back of the auditorium, and a jubilant mother started edging her way out of her row, proudly clutching the hand of her four-year-old son. Land smiled and took the next card: "Kasim-Seann Cisse." Another whoop, some applause, and then, a few seconds later, "Yanice Gillis." Yasmin Scott clapped her hands and leapt to her feet.

At the front of the auditorium, Canada congratulated each mother (or, occasionally, father) and child. Proud parents shook his hand and introduced their children, beaming on their way back to their seats. In the front row, Wilma Jure was praying harder than ever, her eyes shut tight, her lips moving, reciting one supplication after another. And then Land read out, "Jaylene Fonseca," and Jure's eyes flew open, and the next thing she knew, she was on her feet, hugging Canada, tears brimming in her eyes, and then running out of the auditorium to call her sister with the good news.

As the evening wore on, though, the mood in the auditorium started to shift. The kindergarten lottery ended, the chosen students trooped out to the cafeteria for a group photo, and the sixth-grade lottery began. In the front row, Virainia Utley sat with her daughter Janiqua, listening to the names and trying not to worry. But the lottery numbers were rising—fifty-four, fifty-five, fifty-six—and Janiqua hadn't yet been called.

After Land read out the one hundredth name, Canada took the stage again and explained to Utley and the other remaining parents that it wasn't likely there would be room for their children in the sixth grade. Land would read out the rest of the names and put them on a waiting list, he said, but this part wouldn't be much fun. He encouraged everyone to go home. Land went back to reading names, and Utley and Janiqua sat and listened, still in their seats, as the waiting list grew and the number of cards in the drum dwindled. By the time Land got to the eightieth place on the waiting list, they were just waiting to make sure Janiqua's name was called. Maybe her card got lost or stuck to another card.

The room was thinning out, and the only remaining parents were angry ones. They were lining up to let Canada know how they felt. One by one, the parents came up to him to find out what could be done to get their children into the school, and he had to tell each one the same thing: nothing. Nothing could be done. One disappointed woman spat out her complaint to anyone who would listen. "I think it's not fair, and I want someone to know," she said, her voice loud and bitter. "It's *very* unfair. Drag people out and they sit here all day, half their night is gone—they can't cook dinner, they can't do nothing—because they said that our child's going to get in here, and then our child don't get in here. But we're still sitting here, waiting to do what? On a wait list? It's not fair, and I don't like it."

Finally, at number 111 on the waiting list, Janiqua Utley's name was called, and her mother rose, took her by the hand, and started up the aisle to the back door.

AS WORKERS BEGAN sweeping up coffee cups and deflated balloons, I sat down next to Canada in the front row of the auditorium, off to the side. I had by this point been reporting on his work for almost a year, following him to meetings and speeches and events around the city. But I had never seen him look so exhausted; he was overwhelmed, it seemed, not only by the emotion of the evening but also by the enormity of the task ahead of him.

"I was trying to get folks to leave and not to hang around to be the last kid called," he said. "This is very hard for me to see. It's very, very sad. People are desperate to get their kids into a decent school. And they just can't believe that it's not going to happen." His eyes were watery, and as we talked he dabbed periodically at his nose with his folded-up handkerchief. "These parents really get it," he said. "They understand that if the school is good, the odds that your child is going to have a good life just increase exponentially. So now they just feel, 'Well, there go my child's chances.'"

Canada often spoke of a "competition" that was going on in New York City, and by extension in the nation, between the children he called "my kids," the thousands of children who were growing up in Harlem in poverty, and the kids living below 110th Street, mostly white, mostly well off, with advantages visible and invisible that shadowed them wherever they went. The divisions between these two populations had grown more stark than ever. The average white family in Manhattan with children under five now had an annual income of $284,000, while their black counterparts made an average of $31,000. Growing up in New York wasn't just an uneven playing field anymore. It was like two separate sporting events.

"For me," Canada said, "the big question in America is: Are we going to try to make this country a true meritocracy? Or will we forever have a class of people in America who essentially won't be able to compete, because the game is fixed against them?" Canada's voice sounded raspy and solemn. "There's just no way that in good conscience we can allow poverty to remain the dividing line between success and failure in this country, where if you're born poor in a community like this one, you stay poor. We have to even that out. We ought to give these kids a chance."

The creation of the Harlem Children's Zone had brought Canada to a strange new moment in his life. He had known since he was a child that this was the work he wanted to do. In college, he was a political activist, and he led angry demonstrations against the injustices that he and other black students saw on campus and in the nation. He went to work as a teacher after graduation, and for thirty years now he had been a passionate advocate for children. It was a very emotional business he was in, and the approach that he and many of his peers had always taken was an intensely personal one: if you could reach one child, touch one life, your work was worthwhile. But the old way of doing things wasn't working for Canada anymore, or at least it wasn't working fast enough. He had seen it happen over and over: you reach one child and ten more slip past you, into crime or substance abuse or just ignorance and indolence, menial jobs, long stretches of unemployment, missed child-support payments. Saving a few no longer felt like enough.

"We're not interested in saving a hundred kids," Canada told me. "Even three hundred kids. Even a thousand kids to me is not going to do it. We want to be able to talk about how you save kids by the tens of thousands, because that's how we're losing them. We're losing kids by the tens of thousands."

In starting the Harlem Children's Zone, Canada was asking a new set of questions: What would it take to change the lives of poor children not one by one, through heroic interventions and occasional miracles, but in a programmatic, standardized way that could be applied broadly and replicated nationwide? Was there a science to it, a formula you could find? Which variables in a child's life did you need to change, and which ones could you leave as they were? How many more hours of school would be required? How early in a child's life did you need to begin? How much did the parents have to do? How much would it all cost?

The questions had led Canada into uncharted territory. His new approach was bold, even grandiose: to transform every aspect of the environment that poor children were growing up in; to change the way their families raised them and the way their schools taught them as well as the character of the neighborhood that surrounded them. But Canada had come to believe that it was not only the best way to solve the relentless problem of poverty in America; it was the only way. Across the country, policymakers, philanthropists, and social scientists were carefully watching the system that Canada was building in Harlem. The evidence that he was trying to create, they knew, had the potential to reshape completely the way that Americans thought about poverty.

Canada realized that if he was going to make this new approach work, he couldn't take each child's success and failure as personally as he used to. Promise Academy was a crucial new step, but it was just one link in the chain that Canada was constructing, and he knew he needed to stay focused on the big picture. It wasn't easy for him, though, especially on nights like this one. For all his attempts to be cold-hearted and analytical, when he looked into the eyes of the parents he was turning down, he still felt the pain in their lives viscerally. At the end of what was supposed to be a triumphant event, he couldn't shake the feeling that he wasn't doing enough, that he had failed.

"What I'm going to remember about tonight," he said, "is how those mothers looked at me when their kids didn't get in." It made him think about his own young son, Geoffrey Jr., who was at home with his mother, Canada's wife, Yvonne. "When I go home tonight to my own kid, whose life is pretty much secure," Canada said, "it's not going to make me sleep well knowing there are kids and families out there that *don't* feel secure. They just are terrified that their child is not going to make it, and they think this is another opportunity that slipped by."

It was a waiting list that had started him on the path to the Harlem Children's Zone a decade earlier. And now, despite everything he had accomplished and all the millions he had spent, here he was, still setting up waiting lists. "We've got to do more," he said with a sigh. "We've got to give these people a chance for hope."

2   Unequal Childhoods

THE SERVICES were always held at the same place: the Century funeral home on Amsterdam Avenue, a modest storefront in a mostly Dominican neighborhood, next to a discount liquor store and a coin laundry. For Geoffrey Canada, each funeral meant the same sad rituals: the cramped vestibule where men in dark suits stood staring while mourners filed past the condolence book; the parlor, where another grieving mother wept in the front row; the open coffin where another Harlem child lay, the wound from the gunshot that killed him carefully concealed beneath his Sunday suit. In the second half of the 1980s, it became almost routine for Canada: another shooting, another funeral. In the worst year, 1989, seven children in his organization's programs were killed.

Harlem had the highest mortality rate of any neighborhood in the city in those days. One notorious study in the *New England Journal of Medicine*, in 1990, found that the life expectancy for young men in Harlem was lower than that of young men in Bangladesh. Heart attacks and cirrhosis were part of the cause, but it was the murder statistics that stood out: the homicide death rate in the neighborhood was fourteen times the city's average. That year, two police precincts in Harlem together recorded 107 murders, most of them linked, in one way or another, to the trade in crack cocaine.

Things were bad in Harlem, but Harlem wasn't alone. Across the country, young black men were killing one another in startling numbers. In just three years, from 1986 to 1989, the homicide rate among black males between the ages of fourteen and seventeen had doubled, and it kept rising into the 1990s. By 1991, gunshot wounds had become the leading cause of mortality for black American males between fifteen and nineteen, accounting for almost half of all deaths.

It was a draining and depressing era for Canada. He felt each morning as though he were going to work in a burning building, as though his job was simply to rescue as many kids as he could from the flames. "It was almost primal," Canada told me, looking back. "We were literally just trying to keep our children alive." There were plenty he couldn't save; for many kids, the pull of guns and drugs was impossible to resist. For years, he offered martial arts lessons to a small group of young men and women from the neighborhood, mentoring them, hoping to show them an alternative to the violence of the streets, and he became closer to them than to any other children in Rheedlen's programs. And then two of his top students told him that they had decided to go into business selling cocaine.

In the mid-1990s, Canada wrote a book, *Fist, Stick, Knife, Gun: A Personal History of Violence in America,* that chronicled his own violent childhood and decried the brutality he was witnessing in Harlem. "It really is getting worse," he wrote. "Too many guns, too much crack, too few jobs, so little hope." He cautioned that the United States was approaching "one of the most dangerous periods in our history," and warned that young urban African Americans were forming "a new generation, the handgun generation. Growing up under the conditions of war." He spoke out, writing op-eds and lobbying Congress for stronger gun-control laws. Unless the violence stopped, he told audiences, there was no way that the youth of Harlem could ever escape the trap of the ghetto.

And then, remarkably, miraculously, the violence did stop—or most of it, anyway. Beginning in 1993, crime statistics in New York and in Harlem began to drop off sharply. Burglaries, robberies, homicides: the numbers all went down. Those two Harlem precincts where 107 people were killed in 1990 recorded just 14 murders in 1998. The kids in Canada's programs stopped dying, and his visits to Century funeral home came to an end.

Canada had always figured that it was the guns and the drugs that were the big problem in Harlem. Solve that crisis, he thought, and the neighborhood's youth could do as well as anyone. But as the tide of violence receded, Canada was able to look more deeply into what was going on among Harlem's young people. And below the surface, things were worse than he expected. Poor children were still failing in school, poor families were falling apart in record numbers. A few kids seemed to be getting ahead, but they were the exception. Most of them seemed as stuck as ever. Canada was baffled. If it wasn't the gun violence that was holding back the children of Harlem, what was it?

Canada had come up against one of the simplest and yet most nettlesome questions in all of social science: Why are poor people poor? And by extension: Why do they stay poor? And what would it take for them to get out of poverty? These were questions that had long perplexed and divided American politicians and scholars—and as I spent time reporting in Harlem, it became clear to me that they were questions I would need to explore more deeply if I wanted to truly understand the significance of Canada's project.

In recent years, the debate over poverty has taken what many people in the field feel is an important turn. From universities and policy centers and experimental programs across the country, new ideas and new scholarship have emerged that challenge some of the most basic assumptions of the past. Some of these new theories are still unproven, and they are mostly unknown outside of academic circles. But now, for the first time, many of them are being put to the test in the Harlem Children's Zone.

And so during the years that I was following Canada's work, sitting in on parenting workshops and early-morning math classes, I also traveled the country, visiting schools, attending conferences, and interviewing social scientists from Houston to Chicago to Tennessee. Understanding their research and the ongoing debate over poverty, I came to feel, was essential to understanding what was under way in Harlem.

FOR MORE THAN a century, the conventional wisdom on the question of American poverty has swung back and forth, depending on the tides of politics and the economy, between two poles. One explanation blames powerful economic and social forces beyond the control of any one individual. This belief holds that it is the very structure of the American economy that denies poor people sufficient income, and so the appropriate and just solution is to counter those economic forces by providing the poor with what they lack: food, housing, and money. The opposing explanation for American poverty is that it is caused by the bad decisions of poor people themselves and often perpetuated by the very programs designed to help relieve its effects. If this theory is correct, what the poor need is not handouts, but moral guidance and strict rules.

As Susan Mayer, a public policy professor at the University of Chicago, explains in her book *What Money Can't Buy*, each era of state-sponsored generosity toward the poor in American history has been followed by an era in which government aid was judged to be part of the problem, not part of the solution. At the beginning of the nineteenth century, local public agencies offered poor families "outdoor relief," an ad hoc system that provided the poor with aid at home, whether it was food, clothing, or cash. In the middle of the nineteenth century, though, outdoor relief came to be seen as encouraging idleness and dependency among poor families, and new restrictions were put on aid in order to promote the moral fiber of the poor. If the destitute wanted help, they were required to enter poorhouses, harsh, unpleasant institutions where they were expected to work in exchange for food and other assistance.

During the Great Depression, public opinion softened again. Poverty descended on so many families, including many that had been stable and middle class before the economic upheaval of the 1930s, that Americans came to accept that any family could become poor: it was bad luck, and not bad character, that created the need for government aid. There was widespread public support for the robust safety net provided by the programs of the New Deal. Through the 1940s and 1950s, those public assistance programs remained mostly intact. Individual states occasionally applied restrictions, such as kicking mothers off welfare when they were judged to be of questionable character; when, for instance, their children were born out of wedlock. For the most part, though, poverty retreated from the public's consciousness during the postwar boom, as the American middle class grew strong, affluent, and complacent.

With the election of John F. Kennedy in 1960, the dominant ideas on poverty began to shift again. Early in his presidency, Kennedy appointed a top-level committee, chaired by his brother, Attorney General Robert Kennedy, to investigate the newly discovered crisis of "juvenile delinquency," a phrase used to cover everything from truancy and torn blue jeans to the fighting gangs that Leonard Bernstein and Stephen Sondheim romanticized on Broadway in *West Side Story*. It was a big moment for committees, an era marked by what Daniel Patrick Moynihan, then a leading intellectual in the federal government, later referred to as "the professionalization of reform." Kennedy's election, Moynihan wrote, "brought to Washington . . . a striking echelon of persons whose profession might be described as knowing what ails societies and whose art is to get treatment underway before the patient is especially aware of anything noteworthy taking place." These government reformers, who called themselves "the guerrillas," were looking for big solutions to big problems, and the President's Committee on Juvenile Delinquency and Youth Crime became a vehicle for their efforts. Delinquency, the committee soon concluded, was not an isolated crisis with a single solution. It was a result of poverty, and it could only be solved by "a total attack on the problems of disadvantaged youth." Why are poor people poor? The reformers had found an answer: because the government wasn't helping enough.

IN THE WAKE of Kennedy's assassination, President Lyndon B. Johnson helped turn the ideas of the reformers into federal policy, declaring what he called the War on Poverty and pledging billions of government dollars to aid the nation's poor. It was a hopeful moment, but it didn't last long; by the end of the decade, most observers concluded that the war had been lost, done in by a variety of factors—the war in Vietnam, which sopped up much of the extra funding that had been allocated to social programs; the riots that seemed to spread from one American inner city to the next in the late 1960s, enraging blacks and intimidating whites; the political radicalization of many black American leaders, who by the time of Martin Luther King Jr.'s assassination in 1968 wanted not community job programs but full-scale revolution.

Also contributing to the disintegration of the reform effort were two government reports, issued in 1965 and 1966, that inflamed and later suppressed public debate over poverty by challenging some long-held liberal beliefs. The first was a confidential internal memorandum by Daniel Patrick Moynihan, then an analyst in the Department of Labor. Its full title was *The Negro Family: The Case for National Action,* but after it was leaked to the media in the summer of 1965, it quickly became known as the Moynihan Report, and just as quickly became famous (and infamous) for arguing that "at the heart of the deterioration of the fabric of Negro society is the deterioration of the Negro family." In the report, Moynihan took pains to emphasize that what he defined as the "pathology" of many ghetto families, including high rates of illegitimacy, divorce, and single motherhood, was the direct result of slavery and racism, and he said it was the responsibility of the nation as a whole to address the situation. But his report was condemned by many civil rights leaders, who felt that it was simply the latest manifestation of the white desire to see African Americans as inferior, irresponsible, immoral, and sexually irrepressible.

The second report, *Equality of Educational Opportunity,* was a public finding of the U.S. Office of Education, though the department tried to bury it by issuing it on a holiday, July 4, 1966. It, too, became known colloquially for the name of its lead author, the sociologist James S. Coleman, as the Coleman Report—and it, too, met with an unhappy response from some quarters, though nowhere near as virulent as the one provoked by Moynihan's work. The report, mandated by the 1964 Civil Rights Act, was explicitly intended to demonstrate that educational opportunities in the United States were racially unequal. Instead, it concluded the opposite: while just a decade earlier, predominantly black schools were indeed underfunded, black students and white students now received approximately equal resources. Just as surprising, Coleman and his coauthors determined that a school's financial resources were not the main contributing factor to a child's educational success. It was the child's family background, they said, that made the more significant difference.

Together, these reports pointed toward the importance of the home environment in the negative outcomes experienced by many poor children. They also demonstrated the political danger in reaching such controversial conclusions. The Coleman Report was greeted mostly with silence or dismissals, the Moynihan Report with angry denunciations. And as William Julius Wilson, a leading black sociologist, later wrote, "the controversy surrounding the Moynihan report had the effect of curtailing serious research on minority problems in the inner city for over a decade, as liberal scholars shied away from researching behavior construed as unflattering or stigmatizing to particular racial minorities." Government aid kept flowing into ghettos, in substantial amounts, but many of the thinkers who had helped turn on the taps didn't want to have to think any more about where exactly it was going or what effect it was having. For many years, the debate over poverty had been a thoroughly liberal conversation, with the only disagreements coming from the different stations of left-leaning thought. Now liberals mostly recused themselves altogether from the uncomfortable question of the disappointing condition of the country's poor minorities.

Into the vacuum came a new generation of conservative scholars, led by Charles Murray, a social scientist who was then a fellow at the Manhattan Institute. Murray's book *Losing Ground,* published in 1984, offered a counterhistory of poverty in America, as well as a new look at this question: why are poor people poor? Murray's answer: because government is helping too much. He argued that the Great Society programs that grew out of the War on Poverty, like Aid to Families with Dependent Children (AFDC), didn't only fail to help poor people, they actually *hurt* poor people. He conceded that overall poverty figures had fallen sharply since Kennedy's inauguration, from 22 percent of Americans living below the poverty line in 1961 to 13 percent in 1980. But all of that progress, he pointed out, had come in the 1960s, and Murray contended that serious expenditures on Great Society programs only began in the 1970s, at exactly the moment the drop-off in the poverty rate stalled. Beyond those top-line poverty numbers, though, Murray was able to provide some powerful and disturbing statistics about the way the lives and prospects of poor people, and especially poor minorities, had changed since the War on Poverty began, during a period when total government spending on social welfare programs increased sharply, from 11 percent of the gross national product in 1965 to 19 percent of the GNP in 1980.

In 1965, he showed, a third of poor African Americans were living in households headed by a single mother. In 1980, two-thirds of them were.

In 1965, the unemployment rate among black teenagers stood at 20 percent. In 1980, it had climbed to 33 percent.

Nationally, violent crime rates almost tripled between 1965 and 1980.

Murray argued that the existing system of aid to the needy provided an array of perverse incentives that encouraged poor people not to work, not to marry, and to have children at an early age and out of wedlock. His solution to this growing crisis was a drastic one. He proposed "scrapping the entire federal welfare and income-support structure for working-aged persons, including AFDC, Medicaid, Food Stamps, Unemployment Insurance, Worker's Compensation, subsidized housing, disability insurance, and the rest." This, he wrote, "would leave the working-aged person with no recourse whatsoever except the job market, family members, friends, and public or private locally funded services." What Murray was proposing was a kind of radical social Darwinism. "Some people are better than others," he starkly concluded. "They deserve more of society's rewards, of which money is only one small part. A principal function of social policy is to make sure they have the opportunity to reap those rewards. Government cannot identify the worthy, but it can protect a society in which the worthy can identify themselves."

LOSING GROUND FINALLY awakened the liberal thinkers who had been reluctant to draw attention to the disaster that was brewing in the nation's ghettos. Chief among them was William Julius Wilson, who in 1987 published *The Truly Disadvantaged,* in many ways a response to Murray's book. Wilson, then a professor at the University of Chicago, identified many of the same symptoms of urban decay that Murray did, but he diagnosed a very different root cause and prescribed a very different cure.

It was true that there had been a "sharp increase in social pathologies in ghetto communities," Wilson wrote. But government aid wasn't to blame. Instead, African Americans in the inner city were the victims of a series of tectonic shifts in society and the economy since the end of World War II. The first blow to communities like Harlem, Wilson wrote, was actually a result of a positive social change: increased mobility for middle-class blacks. At the beginning of the twentieth century, Harlem was an affluent white neighborhood. Then blacks began to move in and whites began to move out, a process that accelerated during the 1920s and the Depression, until the neighborhood was virtually all black. Yet even as Harlem became racially segregated in the middle of the century, it remained economically integrated. There were plenty of poor people, but there was also a healthy proportion of working-class and professional families. But then as official and unofficial restrictions on where African Americans could live eased after World War II, the neighborhood's wealthier residents began to leave. By the 1960s, the trickle of departures had become a steady stream—and this phenomenon was occurring not just in Harlem but in black urban neighborhoods across the country.

At the same time, the American manufacturing economy was experiencing a rapid decline, and the kind of low-skill jobs that had sustained many urban African American families in the middle of the century were disappearing. They were replaced with white-collar jobs, which for many years black Americans had been constrained from holding; what's more, the new jobs often required a level of education that for many years black Americans had been discouraged from achieving. Between 1970 and 1984, Wilson reported, New York City lost 492,000 jobs that required less than a high school education, and gained 239,000 that required more than a high school education. As a result, and for the first time, a gap opened up between African American and white employment figures, especially among young adults, and it quickly grew. In 1965 the national employment rate for black men in their early twenties was 82 percent, slightly higher than the corresponding figure for young white men, at 80 percent. Nineteen years later, in 1984, the employment rate for young white men had dipped just slightly, to 78 percent—while the number for young black men had fallen off a cliff, to 58 percent. A 2 percent advantage for African Americans had turned into a 20 percent shortfall.

These twin forces led to a self-perpetuating concentration of poverty in many American cities. In the five largest American cities, the number of poor people living in what Wilson called "extreme-poverty areas," neighborhoods where the poverty rate was at least 40 percent, almost tripled from 1970 to 1980. And to a striking degree, the isolation of the poor was a problem that affected blacks much more than whites. In 1980, two-thirds of all poor whites in the five largest cities still lived in mixed-income neighborhoods, but only 15 percent of poor blacks did. The rest lived in a brand-new kind of urban ghetto, almost all poor and all black, with very low employment rates and very high poverty rates. Other social dysfunctions followed: large numbers of recipients of government aid, high crime rates, high teenage-birth rates, low marriage rates.

The exodus of middle- and working-class families from neighborhoods like Harlem, Wilson wrote, had removed a "social buffer." In poor neighborhoods, during economic downturns, the presence of middle-class families once provided "mainstream role models that help keep alive the perception that education is meaningful, that steady employment is a viable alternative to welfare, and that family stability is the norm, not the exception." But in a ghetto neighborhood where those families have left, there would be instead "a ripple effect resulting in an exponential increase in related forms of social dislocation." Wilson described a spiral of decay in such neighborhoods, where "the chances are overwhelming that children will seldom interact on a sustained basis with people who are employed. . . . Joblessness, as a way of life, takes on a different social meaning. . . . Teachers become frustrated and do not teach and children do not learn."

Wilson's proposed solutions to the problem were as broad and radical as Murray's, though in more or less the opposite direction. In the short run, he supported the continuation of the kind of remedial and targeted programs that Murray wanted to do away with: job training, education, and public assistance. But Wilson had become convinced that over the long term, programs targeted at poor people were no longer politically palatable. The real solution to ghetto dysfunction, he wrote, was an overall transformation of the American economy through a "program of economic reform designed to promote full employment and balanced economic growth." Under Wilson's plan, policies to improve the country's employment situation would be combined with "a nationally oriented labor-market strategy, a child support assurance program, a child care strategy, and a family allowances program," all of which would be universally available. Such a concerted (and expensive) government effort would improve the economic situation of the ghetto underclass, and that in turn would lead to "changes in cultural norms and behavior patterns."

Both Murray and Wilson believed that the way to fix the broken lives of the country's ghetto poor was for the government to work the policy levers in Washington—and not to tinker around the edges, but to overhaul the national economy completely. Wilson wanted a European-style social democracy in which the federal government would guarantee a wide range of financial supports to every American family. Murray wanted a system in which vast swaths of the social welfare system simply ceased to exist. Although neither man's proposal showed much evidence of being politically acceptable as it was written, their two books essentially established the parameters for the next fifteen years of public debate over poverty. Murray's book provided intellectual support for the Reagan-era cutbacks in government aid for the poor, and it helped inspire the reforms of the welfare system that were eventually passed in the mid-1990s. Wilson's formulations underlay much of the Democratic social policy agenda of the late 1980s and early 1990s.

Despite their many differences, the two books both rested on a series of assumptions about human nature—and especially about the nature of poor Americans in ghetto neighborhoods—that were as yet untested. Murray and Wilson agreed that lives in Harlem were deeply affected by decisions made in Washington, D.C. If the right set of incentives and disincentives and opportunities were dangled in front of poor ghetto residents, they would respond in predictable ways: they would get jobs, they would become better educated, they would be more likely to marry, and they would raise their children more conscientiously. The two men acknowledged that the dysfunction of ghetto families was the result of decades—generations—of discrimination, isolation, and cultural decay, as well as one of the most cataclysmic shifts in the economy in American history. But they shared a faith that the problems those forces had produced could be fixed simply by the passage (or the dismantling) of the right federal laws.

ODDLY, THE FIRST public cracks in that consensus came with the publication, in 1994, of another book by Charles Murray: *The Bell Curve*, which he wrote with Richard J. Herrnstein, a Harvard psychologist who died just before the book's publication. In *Losing Ground*, Murray had included in his list of the negative consequences of government aid the fact that the scores that black children received on achievement and aptitude tests trailed significantly behind those of white children. Now, with Herrnstein, he returned to that phenomenon, though with a new explanation: the cause of the persistent achievement gap between rich and poor children and black and white children was not federal welfare policy, it was deep-rooted differences in intelligence. It was intelligence, Herrnstein and Murray argued, that was the critical factor missing from discussions of social policy, and especially from discussions of poverty.

The book's thesis was based on three observations: The economy had changed in a way that had caused intelligence to be more highly valued than ever before. The IQ of wealthy people tends to be higher than the IQ of poor people. And the IQ of children is closely related to the IQ of their parents. These observations were relatively uncontroversial. What *was* controversial, deeply so, was the set of conclusions Herrnstein and Murray drew: that intelligence was inherited, and probably genetic; that there were significant inherent racial differences in IQ; and that it was better for society to accept this state of affairs than to try to change it. Attempts to compensate for cognitive differences through affirmative action or extra help for disadvantaged children, Herrnstein and Murray argued, simply didn't work. Rather than trying to level a playing field that was biologically uneven, the government should devote its energies to creating a society where people of different abilities were all valued and all treated with "dignity."

Mostly because of its claims and insinuations on matters of race, *The Bell Curve* produced a tidal wave of criticism; entire anthologies of refutations were published. Writing in the *New Republic,* the journalist Mickey Kaus filleted the book's purported evidence that racial differences were most likely genetic and not environmental. In the *New Yorker,* the scientist Stephen Jay Gould made short work of the authors' statistical methods, accusing them of ignoring or downplaying the considerable evidence for the malleability of IQ.

One of the more intriguing responses—and, arguably, one of the most significant—was a short article by James Heckman, a professor of economics at the University of Chicago, whose critique was made more meaningful by the fact that he was the first person thanked in the book's acknowledgments. Murray had consulted with Heckman while compiling his research, and before publication, Murray had given him the manuscript of the book to read and comment on. Heckman told Murray privately what he later wrote publicly, in the *Journal of Political Economy:* Three-quarters of the book was insightful and groundbreaking, and the other quarter was completely off the rails.

Although most critics found little to redeem *The Bell Curve,* Heckman argued that the book had one great merit: it demonstrated in a coherent and thorough way how important results on standardized tests had become. Other observers, including Robert Reich, then the secretary of labor, had written about the ongoing development of a meritocratic cognitive elite in the United States, increasingly powerful and increasingly isolated from the rest of the country. But Herrnstein and Murray applied a new scrutiny to those observations, and they focused on the effect the change was having on the bottom of the cognitive scale, rather than the top.

The authors used as a measure of intelligence the Armed Forces Qualification Test (AFQT), a military aptitude test that, in one richly detailed nationwide survey of youth, had been administered to twelve thousand Americans between the ages of fifteen and twenty-three. The authors showed that young people's scores on the test corresponded closely to a variety of eventual outcomes in their lives, from high school graduation rates to adult income level. Those who scored poorly, who were in what Herrnstein and Murray called the lower "cognitive classes," were more likely to drop out of school, to experience long-term unemployment as an adult, to become chronic welfare recipients, and to have children out of wedlock. Moreover, their test scores were even better predictors of these various outcomes than their socioeconomic class was: growing up poor predicted all of those negative outcomes, too, but low cognitive skills predicted them even more closely.

Where the authors went wrong, Heckman wrote, was in conflating IQ, which he agreed was a mostly immutable quality, with overall cognitive ability and achievement, which are subject to manipulation by all sorts of outside forces. Herrnstein and Murray based their entire argument on the premise that the quality the AFQT was measuring was some kind of genetically determined, unchangeable "intelligence." In fact, the AFQT was more similar to an achievement test like the SAT than to a pure IQ test. It measured a variety of cognitive and noncognitive abilities, many of which were affected by education and family background. As

Gould had done in his review, Heckman pointed to studies that showed that children who were born into a disadvantaged family and then adopted by a wealthier family scored better than their disadvantaged peers on tests similar to the AFQT, which would of course be impossible if the quality those tests measured was truly inherited. Whatever you called that quality — intelligence, IQ, ability, aptitude — it appeared to be much more malleable than Herrnstein and Murray had assumed.

This revelation turned the conclusions of The Bell Curve upside down. Where the book was intended to demonstrate that class stratification was inevitable and impervious to change, in fact it showed that a child's chances of success in life depended at least in part on something tangible, measurable, and, most importantly, teachable. In the ongoing debate over poverty in America, this was big news. It was a new answer to the central question: Why are poor people poor? They are poor, this evidence suggested, not because of government aid, not because they are genetically flawed, and not because the system denies them opportunities, but because they lack certain specific skills.

In some ways, this seemed obvious. Of course poor people lack many skills, and of course people with skills do better in life. But the close connection between abilities and outcomes was something new, especially where poor minorities were concerned. Christopher Jencks, a professor of social policy at the John F. Kennedy School of Government at Harvard, had published in 1972 a book titled Inequality, which concluded that the variance in cognitive skills between black and white Americans was not in fact a major reason for racial inequality in the United States. At that time, black American men on average earned about 58 percent of what white American men earned, and black American men who scored above average on the AFQT earned about 65 percent of what whites earned. Clearly, there wasn't much incentive for African Americans to develop the abilities the test measured; they were going to earn about the same lousy wages no matter how smart and educated they were. But in 1998, in the wake of *The Bell Curve,* Jencks took a look at more recent data, and he concluded that "the world has changed." Black men overall were now earning 68 percent of what whites earned, a modest increase. But higher-skilled black men, those who scored above average on the AFQT, were earning 96 percent of the white average, a big jump. This meant that opportunities had increased considerably for certain African Americans—the ones with the kind of abilities that were measured on standardized tests. If you were a black man in the 1950s, it didn't matter much how skilled you were; you were still likely to wind up in a menial, low-paying job. But if you were a black man in the 1990s, your abilities suddenly mattered very much indeed.

For people who cared about the fate of poor children, and particularly poor black children, the news of this meritocratic realignment was both exciting and daunting. It was daunting because, as Herrnstein and Murray had exhaustively demonstrated, the reality was that black kids and poor kids weren't doing very well on tests like the AFQT. If that didn't change, the gap between the classes and races would never shrink. But at the same time, this new evidence suggested that solving the problems of poverty might not require the kind of overhaul of the nation's economy and politics that Murray and Wilson had recommended, each in his own way. Instead, reformers might be able to directly improve the lives of poor children simply by raising their skill level.

THE EXTENDED ECONOMIC recovery of the 1990s buttressed Wilson's belief that a booming economy and a healthy job market would do much to alleviate poverty, but it also revealed the limits to those macroeconomic solutions. Beginning in 1991, the American economy entered into the longest expansion in its history. By the time it ended, in 2000, the United States seemed to be approaching the state of full employment and balanced growth that Wilson had wished for. The unemployment rate had fallen to 3.9 percent, a thirty-year low. Real wages went up during the decade for most workers, and the national poverty rate dropped from 15 percent in 1993 to 11.3 percent in 2000. And to a certain extent, Wilson's prediction that a national boom would help inner-city areas like Harlem was borne out. Across the country, the intense concentrations of poverty that Wilson had chronicled began to reverse. In Harlem, as Katherine S. Newman reported in her 2006 book *Chutes and Ladders,* the poverty rate fell from 38 percent in 1990 to 26 percent in 2002. But in many ways, the most remarkable economic statistics out of Harlem at the turn of the millennium were the ones that showed how much things *hadn't* changed, especially for those at the bottom. There were almost forty thousand people living below the poverty line in Harlem in 1989, and about the same number in 1999, at the height of the boom. Fifty-one percent of Harlem's working-age population was employed in 1989; in 1999, the figure had actually dropped, to 49 percent. If this was the best that the strongest economy in history could accomplish for Harlem, then some other solutions were going to be necessary.

The generational cycle of poverty in neighborhoods like Harlem was well known: poor parents raise children with poor resources and abilities, who therefore can't make it out of poverty and thus raise their own children with the same problems. Before, the assumption had been that the most effective way to break the cycle was to raise the income level of the parents; the abilities and prospects of children, it was believed, would improve along with their parents' income. Now some economists began to argue that policymakers were trying to affect the wrong part of the cycle. Let's not worry so much about the income level of the parents, they said. Yes, let's provide enough of a safety net to prevent them from falling into extreme poverty; let's make sure they have enough money to give their children food and shelter and decent medical care. But then let's aim all of our serious resources and attention at the children themselves. We know, anecdotally, that some children of poor families turn out successfully, despite their deprived upbringing—Geoffrey Canada himself was a perfect example. Why not try to systematize that process, so that poor children are regularly growing up with the resources they need to become successful middle-class adults?

Economists use the term "human capital" to refer to the skills and abilities and qualities and resources that each individual possesses. And in the late 1990s and early 2000s, human capital became an increasingly popular way to look at the problem of poverty. No one had all the answers yet, but they had, at least, a new set of questions: What specific resources did middle-class children have that allowed them to succeed at such higher rates than poor children? What skills did poor children need to help them compete? And most important, what kind of interventions in their lives or in their parents' lives could help them acquire those skills?

One advantage of this new perspective was that it took the poverty debate out of the realm of morality, where it often got bogged down, and into the realm of science. Political opinions on poverty had always seemed to be based mostly on gut feelings: Seeing poor children without enough to eat made middle-class voters feel sad and guilty. Seeing poor parents who were using welfare checks to buy steaks and big-screen TVs made them feel indignant and resentful. Poverty policies tended to grow out of those two conflicting emotional reactions, with the result that they were often haphazard and contradictory and poorly thought through. The human-capital perspective, by contrast, said, Forget for a moment how different policies make you *feel*. Instead let's examine what different policies and interventions actually accomplish.

Ever since the days of the Moynihan Report, anyone who tried to look for causes of poverty inside the lives and homes of poor people, instead of in the broad structures of the economy, would hear a very specific criticism from some on the left: they were promoting a "deficit model," blaming the victims of poverty by claiming that their situation was due to some personal shortcoming. The human-capital perspective did an end run around that criticism. Of *course* poor people have deficits, researchers could now reply. That's what poverty is: a lack of resources, both internal and external. But those deficits, whether they were in income or knowledge or even more esoteric qualities like self-control or perseverance or an optimistic outlook, were not moral failings. The appropriate response was not to deny them or excuse them, nor was it to criticize them and cluck about them and wag a finger at them. It was to solve them.

GEOFFREY CANADA mostly tried to stay out of academic and political debates. But he found himself, at the turn of the millennium, right in the thick of this one. The ideas that he was proposing to test out in the Harlem Children's Zone were precisely the ones that the human-capital advocates were suggesting. He believed that children in Harlem were exactly like children anywhere else; they were just missing certain specific resources, knowledge, and skills. "When I meet these kids at age three or age four," he told me, "I just don't see any reason they should not be successful." Canada didn't underestimate the size of the problem. The missing resources were crucial, and there were a lot of them—but that didn't mean he couldn't provide them. He believed that he could find the ideal intervention for each age of a child's life, and then connect those interventions into an unbroken chain of support. Woven together, the programs would provide poor children with every advantage that middle-class children had—except money itself.

For Canada, it went without saying that a poor child in Harlem had countless obstacles to success that a middle-class child elsewhere in the city did not have: worse schools, worse living conditions, worse nutrition, fewer books, fewer educational toys, fewer Raffi CDs, as well as, in all likelihood, parents who were less well-educated, younger, less healthy, and more overwhelmed. The question for Canada became: which of those obstacles could the child cope with, and which did Canada need to try to remove?

While Canada was asking this question in the field, in Harlem, social scientists around the country were embarking on a similar and related quest into the causes of and potential cures for the nation's two overlapping achievement gaps, the one between black students and white students and the one between poor students and middle-class students. One fact stood out in all the academic research: the gap began when children were very young. By the time they started kindergarten, there was already a large and disturbing difference between the scores that poor and minority students received on various tests of cognitive abilities and the scores that middle-class white students were receiving on those same tests. This didn't let schools off the hook altogether, of course, but it did mean that schools couldn't possibly be the whole problem. Something was going wrong early on, in the homes and families and neighborhoods of poor children, before they ever set foot in a school building.

In 1998 Christopher Jencks, the social policy professor from Harvard, along with a colleague, Meredith Phillips, compiled a collection of scholarly papers on the subject of minority underachievement into a book titled *The Black-White Test Score Gap*. It marked the first serious and comprehensive effort to engage the achievement gap as a subject of scientific inquiry. Jencks and Phillips, in their introduction, considered a wide variety of possible explanations for the problem, and they concluded that while many factors were certainly at play, the most promising avenue for researchers to investigate was home life—and specifically, the parenting practices of poor families. "Indeed," they wrote, "changing the way parents deal with their children may be the single most important thing we can do to improve children's cognitive skills."

RESEARCHERS BEGAN PEERING deep into American families, investigating up close the interactions between parents and children. The first scholars to emerge with a specific culprit in hand were Betty Hart and Todd R. Risley, child psychologists at the University of Kansas who had been studying the intellectual development of young children for many decades. In the early 1980s Hart and Risley had recruited forty-two families with newborn children in Kansas City, from a variety of races and economic backgrounds, and then spent more than two years visiting each family once a month. Each visit lasted an hour, and for that hour, the researcher would record every word that was spoken in the home. The researchers transcribed the recordings and then analyzed each child's rate of language acquisition and each parent's communication style. They divided the families into three classes—parents on welfare, working-class parents, and professional parents—and compared the statistics for each group.

They found, first, that vocabulary growth differed sharply by class and that the gap between the classes opened early. By age three, the children of professional parents had vocabularies of about 1,100 words, and the children of parents on welfare had vocabularies of about 525 words. And the children's IQs correlated closely to their vocabularies. The average IQ among the professional children was 117, and the welfare children had an average IQ of 79.

When Hart and Risley then addressed the question of just what caused those variations, the answer they arrived at was startling. By comparing the children's vocabulary scores with their own observations of each child's home life, they were able to conclude that the size of each child's vocabulary correlated most closely to one simple factor: the number of words the parents spoke to the child. And that varied greatly across the homes they had visited, and it varied by class. In the professional homes, parents directed an average of 487 "utterances"—anything from a one-word command to a full soliloquy—to their child each hour. In welfare homes, the children heard 178 utterances per hour. By age three, Hart and Risley concluded, welfare children would have heard 10 million words addressed to them, on average, and professional children would have heard more than 30 million.

What's more, the *kind* of words and statements that children heard varied by class. The most basic difference was in the number of "discouragements" a child heard—prohibitions and words of disapproval—compared to the number of encouragements, or words of praise and approval. By age three, the average professional child would hear about 500,000 encouragements and 80,000 discouragements. For the welfare children, the ratio was reversed: they would hear, on average, about 80,000 encouragements and 200,000 discouragements. Hart and Risley found that as the number of words a child heard increased, the complexity of that language increased as well. Every child heard a similar number of words and phrases that related to what Hart and Risley called "the necessary business of caring for and socializing little children": basic instructions and directions. Poorer children didn't hear much else. But the children from more wealthy families were exposed to millions of extra words on top of those basics, and those words tended to be more varied and rich. As conversation moved beyond simple instructions, it blossomed into discussions of the past and future, of feelings, of abstractions, of the way one thing causes another—all of which stimulated intellectual development in a way that "Put that down" or "Finish your peas" never could.

Hart and Risley were able to demonstrate strong correlations between the amount and kind of language that children heard in infancy and their IQs and abilities later in childhood. They found that a child's experience of language mattered more than socioeconomic status, more than race, more than anything else they measured. Hearing a relatively large number of prohibitions and discouragements had a negative effect on IQ, and hearing more affirmations, questions, and complex sentences had a positive effect on IQ. The wealthier parents were giving their children an advantage with every word they spoke, and the advantage just kept building up.

THE ONE PROBLEM with Hart and Risley's study was that it was small. Their methods were so intensive that it took them six years to evaluate forty-two families—and although their overall results were persuasive, a sample size of forty-two meant that it was difficult to break out more subtle demographic effects. So psychologists and other social scientists went looking for some new approaches.

In the 1960s an early-childhood researcher named Bettye Caldwell had developed a method for evaluating parental behavior called the Home Observation for Measurement of the Environment, or the HOME inventory. In the 1990s, it became newly popular as a research tool. To complete the inventory, a researcher conducted an interview in the home with a child's primary caregiver and observed some interactions between the caregiver — usually the mother — and the child. The researcher then scored the home environment on forty-five different measures, from whether there were toy musical instruments for the child to play with to whether the parent expressed "overt annoyance with or hostility to the child." Researchers found that the parent's score on the HOME inventory corresponded closely to the child's level of cognitive ability, especially after the age of two.

Another, similar test that social scientists began to employ was the Three-Bag Assessment. A mother and her child would be videotaped playing together for ten minutes. They were given three different sets of children's items — a book, a puzzle, and a toy kitchen — each in its own bag, and the mother was instructed to have her child play with them one by one. The play sessions were videotaped and then, later, coded according to a matrix of parental behaviors. The parents were judged on "sensitivity," "intrusiveness," "stimulation of cognitive development," "detachment," and the amount of positive and negative feedback they delivered, with each factor scored on a precise seven-point scale.

Whether they used the Three-Bag Assessment or the HOME scale, researchers consistently found a strong three-way correlation between socioeconomic status, high scores on parenting scales, and child outcomes. In other words, children from more well-off homes tended to experience parenting that was more sensitive, more encouraging, less intrusive, and less detached, and they also did better on standardized tests. This brought up two complicated questions. The first was whether the middle-class parenting methods were really the cause of those improved outcomes, or if they were simply coincidental. Maybe it was something else in middle-class homes that boosted children's performance, and parenting methods were in fact irrelevant. Researchers believed they could answer this question by doing statistical regressions, analyzing the data closely enough that they were able to ascertain the small variations between how parenting style correlated with wealth and how wealth correlated with test scores and how parenting style correlated with test scores. Their conclusion was that wealth mattered, but parenting mattered more.

The second question was more philosophical: could you really quantify a practice as subjective as parenting? Theories and attitudes about raising children varied greatly among cultures, eras, and individual homes, but these two tests employed a rigid and unchanging definition of which parenting practices are better and which ones are worse. Who's to say that frequent praise is "good" and a detached attitude toward children is "bad"? (Your average parent in upper-class Victorian England, for instance, might have disagreed.) The researchers' answer was that, in fact, they *were* able to make those judgments; their data on child outcomes, they said, proved that their scales were accurate, at least for the contemporary United States. Children whose parents took an intrusive or detached approach to child raising consistently did worse in school and on a wide variety of tests—IQ, achievement, behavior. Using those statistics, the researchers said, they could now be definitive about which parenting methods were best. And those methods, it turned out, were the ones that middle-class parents favor.

This conclusion would have been more persuasive if psychologists had had some explanation of just how the cause and effect worked. Social science is notorious for attributing social ills not to the inequities of society but to the moral failings of the poor.

Just how did each of the tiny parental behaviors on the HOME test—hugs, conversations, toys, praise—affect the development of a child's brain?

A researcher named Martha Farah, the director of the Center for Cognitive Neuroscience at the University of Pennsylvania, set out to answer those questions—and in doing so, she added a new level to the achievement-gap debate, and to our understanding of how poor children develop and why. Farah began her career in the laboratory, where most neuroscientists dwell, studying vision disorders caused by brain injuries. She was initially skeptical of the relevance of cognitive neuroscience—a fairly novel hybrid field that combines psychology and psychiatry with neuroscience to study the ways in which the physical processes of the brain become the intellectual and emotional processes of the mind. As she wrote in a 2006 paper, she originally viewed the field "as an ivory tower pursuit, whose potential applications were few and far between." That changed, she said, when her daughter was born in 1995, and she began to hire babysitters who were mostly poor and not well educated. As she spent more time with the babysitters and their children, she became more and more curious about the process of brain development. Was her daughter's brain developing differently from the brains of her babysitters' children? If so, why, and what did it mean?

Farah knew that cognitive neuroscientists generally divided the higher mental functions into five different systems, each of which they had located in a different region of the brain. And neuroscientists had developed tests to measure the strength of each of these systems in any individual. When Farah gave the tests to several different groups of children in Philadelphia and New York City, she found that middle-class children scored higher than poor children, on average, on the tests as a whole. But there were four specific areas where the poorer children lagged most significantly: language; long-term memory; "working memory," which allows us to hold lots of information in our brains temporarily so that we can manipulate it; and "cognitive control," the ability to resist obvious (but wrong) answers and find unexpected ones.

Already, Farah had broken new ground. She had deduced precisely which mental abilities seemed to correlate most strongly with socioeconomic status. But she still didn't know why that correlation existed. What was it about growing up in a poor household that hindered the development of those four systems? To answer that question, Farah turned to the HOME inventory. She divided the HOME data into two subcategories. One included the HOME measurements that have to do with cognitive stimulation, like "Mother uses correct grammar and pronunciation" and "Child is encouraged to learn colors." The other collected the questions around "social/emotional nurturance," like "Parent holds child close 10–15 minutes per day" and "Parent has not lost temper with child more than once during previous week." Farah then compared each family's HOME score with the child's scores on the various neuroscience tests. The result? For the first time, Farah was able to ascertain exactly which systems in a child's brain are affected by which parental behaviors. Children's scores on the language tests were predicted by parents' cognitive stimulation. Children's scores on the memory tests were predicted by social/emotional nurturance. In other words, a child with loving but not particularly educationally oriented parents would be likely to do well on memory tests and poorly on language tests. A child with smart, cold parents who gave out plenty of books and few hugs would do better on language tests and worse on memory tests.

The specifics of Farah's findings may turn out to be practically useful—perhaps they will give scientists a way to develop targeted interventions to address cognitive disadvantages in poor children—but the more lasting benefit is likely to be more conceptual. Her research has provided a valuable reminder that the process of child raising, which has such a powerful effect on the life chances of poor children, is not some mysterious force that inevitably perpetuates poverty through the generations. It is a physical, mechanistic process in which specific inputs lead to specific outputs. Parental nurturance, Farah found, doesn't affect children in a vague, unknowable way—it stimulates the medial temporal lobe, near the base of the brain, which in turn aids the development of memory skills.

STILL, IT SEEMS unlikely that brain chemistry is the only way that advantage or disadvantage is transmitted from one generation to the next. And indeed, as Farah was approaching the question from the perspective of neuroscience, other researchers were considering the sociological angle. Was it possible, they wondered, that of all the things we inherit from our parents—genes, economic resources, language skills, or even beneficial neurochemicals—the most important one was that hard-to-define thing called culture? What effect did the attitudes and beliefs and values passed down by families have on academic success?

This was the question that a sociologist named Annette Lareau set out to answer in 1992. Over the course of several years, Lareau and her research assistants followed eighty-eight families from a variety of backgrounds—urban and suburban; white and black; rich and poor—and later whittled that group down to a representative sample of twelve. Then Lareau and her researchers invaded, basically moving into each home for three weeks of intensive scrutiny, performing an ethnographic study as if these modern American families were a lost tribe of pygmies: observing meals and soccer games and trips to the doctor and fights and conversations, and recording detailed notes on every interaction between parents and their children.

Lareau's study was distinguished by the sheer doggedness of her field research. But she also stood out because of her ideas about class. Most of the economists and sociologists and psychologists studying the issue of achievement gaps looked at class as a continuum. They would calculate an index of socioeconomic status and then try to discern how things differ for families and children at various points on that scale. Lareau, by contrast, didn't see gradual variations among her eighty-eight families. She found instead that they divided into three separate classes—middle class, working class, and poor—and that the middle class had its own particular strategy of child raising, quite distinct from the one used in poor and working-class homes.

The middle-class families she observed followed a strategy that she labeled "concerted cultivation." The parents in these families considered a child's development to be a parent's responsibility, and so they planned and scheduled countless activities to enhance that development—piano lessons, soccer games, trips to the museum. They engaged their children in conversations as equals, treating them like apprentice adults, and encouraged them to ask questions and challenge assumptions and negotiate rules. They taught them how to navigate institutions and get what they needed from professionals like doctors and teachers.

The working-class and poor families did things very differently. They allowed their children much more freedom to fill in their afternoons and weekends as they chose—playing outside with cousins, inventing games, riding bikes with friends—but much less freedom to talk back, question authority, or haggle over rules and consequences. Children were told to defer to adults and treat them with respect. Their schedules were less hectic than the middle-class children, and the kids were much better at entertaining themselves. They spent more time with family and less time with instructors and professionals. In every way, there was a sharp and distinct boundary in their lives between the world of adults and the world of children. This strategy Lareau named "accomplishment of natural growth."

In her book *Unequal Childhoods,* published in 2003, Lareau described the costs and benefits of each approach. Unlike the analysts using the HOME scale, who concluded that certain parenting styles were simply better and others decidedly worse, Lareau saw advantages and disadvantages to each strategy. Concerted cultivation, she wrote, "places intense labor demands on busy parents, exhausts children, and emphasizes the development of individualism, at times at the expense of the development of the notion of the family group. Middle-class children argue with their parents, complain about their parents' incompetence, and disparage parents' decisions." Working-class and poor children, she wrote, "learn how to be members of informal peer groups. They learn how to manage their own time. They learn how to strategize."

Every child learned the skills and attitudes that are valued by their own class culture. But outside of the family unit, all skills were not considered to be equal. Modern American culture, Lareau wrote, valued the qualities that middle-class children were developing over the ones that poor and working-class children were developing. "Central institutions in the society, such as schools," Lareau wrote, "firmly and decisively promote strategies of concerted cultivation in child rearing. For working-class and poor families, the cultural logic of child rearing at home is out of synch with the standards of institutions." In one poor household Lareau studied, for example, family members didn't look each other in the eye when they spoke—an appropriate response in a culture where eye contact can be interpreted as a threat, but ill-suited to a job interview where a firm handshake and a steady gaze are considered assets, and a failure to make eye contact can make a candidate seem shifty.

Most of the advantages of concerted cultivation are less direct. Middle-class parents get involved in (and occasionally obsessed with) their children's activities and recreations much more than less well-off parents do. According to Lareau, in poor and working-class homes, "children's leisure activities are treated as pleasant but inconsequential and a separate world from those of adults," but in middle-class homes, "things that are important to children can easily become major events for their parents as well." As a result, Lareau wrote, middle-class children get used to adults taking their concerns seriously. They grow up with a sense of entitlement, rather than a sense of constraint, and that gives them confidence in academic settings. Likewise, the emphasis on reasoning and negotiation in their homes gives middle-class children a natural advantage when dealing with institutions, whether banks or hospitals or schools. Middle-class children look at their teachers as a resource from whom they can demand attention, help, and praise; poor children are taught by their parents to see teachers as authority figures to be deferred to in person and resented at a distance. All of these cultural differences translate into a distinct advantage for middle-class children in school, on standardized achievement tests, and, later in life, in the workplace.

One surprising finding in Lareau's research was that middle-class parents seemed mostly to be unaware of the advantages they were conferring on their children. The benefits of concerted cultivation, she wrote, do not "seem to be fully understood by parents." There was a close fit, she wrote, "between skills children learn in soccer games or at piano recitals and those they will eventually need in white-collar professional or technical positions"—but ask a suburban mom why she was chauffeuring her daughter to an 8:00 A.M. soccer game, and she would say it was because soccer was fun, or good exercise. The transmission of class advantage often took place without notice. Lareau pointed out that the middle-class parents she studied all grew up like the poor or working-class children in her survey, with a lot of unstructured and imaginative play, interacting much more with children than with adults. And yet when it came time for them to raise their own children, they followed a different path.

TAKEN TOGETHER, the conclusions of these researchers can be a little unsettling. Their work seems to reduce a child's upbringing, which to a parent can feel something like magic, to a simple algorithm: give a child x and you get y. Their research also suggests that the disadvantages that poverty imposes on children aren't primarily about material goods. True, every poor child would benefit from having more books in his home and more nutritious food to eat, and money certainly makes it easier to carry out a program of concerted cultivation. But the more significant advantages that middle-class children gain, these researchers argue, come from more elusive processes: the language that their parents use, the attitudes toward life that they convey.

However you measure parenting, middle-class parents tend to do it very differently from poor parents — and the path they follow, in turn, tends to give their children an array of advantages, both cognitive and noncognitive: a bigger vocabulary, better brain chemistry, a more assertive attitude. As Lareau pointed out, kids from poor families might be nicer, they might be happier, they might be more polite — but in countless ways, the manner in which they are raised puts them at a disadvantage in the measures that count in contemporary American society.

To Canada, this research was both a cause for alarm and a call to arms. The lifelong race that he saw going on—the one between the children he worked with in Harlem and the middle-class children downtown—looked more lopsided than ever. His kids and the middle-class kids might start out, at birth, from the same spot. But from the very first days of life, the middle-class children received extra stimulation and support, an ever-present helping hand that allowed them to develop and hone exactly those skills that they would need to succeed in school and as adults. If Canada wanted his kids to come out ahead in the race, he knew, he would need to find a way to counter each one of those advantages—and he would need to start very, very early.

3 Baby College

GEOFFREY CANADA has a unique appreciation for the way the practices and philosophies of American parenting have evolved, and for a good reason: he has experienced parenthood twice, in two separate generations—and from the perspective of two different socioeconomic classes. When Canada first became a father, he was young and unprepared, unmarried, just turned twenty, part of a small, militant band of black students at Bowdoin College, an exclusive, mostly white school in a small town in rural Maine. The previous summer, after his freshman year at Bowdoin, Canada had been living with his grandparents in Wyandanch, a working-class, mostly black suburb on Long Island, working at the local A&P and dating a girl named Joyce Henderson, the older sister of a friend from high school. Things never grew too serious between them, in Canada's mind, anyway, and when he left for school that fall, he didn't know when he might see her again. And then one night there she was on the other end of a phone line, delivering the news that she was pregnant. Canada was devastated. He wasn't in love with Joyce. She already had one child, a daughter named Melina, and Canada didn't feel ready to raise a family.

Would he have to drop out of college? Was he going to wind up working at the A&P his whole life? "I thought my world had ended," he told me. "I was absolutely not set up to take care of children."

Still, he knew he could never abandon a child the way his father had abandoned him and his brothers. His mother would never let him get away with it, for one thing. Her rule was unambiguous and nonnegotiable: if you got a girl pregnant, you married her. It was something of a family legacy, in fact. His oldest brother, Dan, had married the girl that he'd made pregnant, and John, his second-oldest brother, had done the same. Now it was Geoff's turn. So he proposed to Joyce, and she accepted.

In February 1972 Joyce gave birth to twins, Jerry and Geoffrey Jr. That winter, Canada continued his studies in Maine while Joyce cared for the boys in Wyandanch. And then came another phone call from home with terrible news: Geoffrey Jr. had died in his sleep: crib death, a shock, a mystery. For the next year and a half, Canada was an absentee father and an absentee fiancé. Even when he was at home in Wyandanch in the summer and on holidays, living with his young family in Joyce's small apartment, he barely seemed to be there.

Geoff and Joyce were married the summer after his junior year—by his grandfather, in the backyard in Wyandanch, with everyone wearing African kente cloth—and that fall, Joyce and the children came up to Bowdoin for a visit, and they never left. The four of them lived for the rest of the school year in Canada's tiny dorm room in a suite in the senior tower, in contravention of school rules. "There was a stretch of about three or four months that was idyllic," Canada recalled. "But there is nothing more stressful on relationships than being poor." Canada was working seven days a week in the dorm's dining hall, but there wasn't enough money for babysitters or daycare—there was barely enough money for food. The family's needs eclipsed their resources, and slowly the shortfall ate away at the marriage.

Canada applied to the Harvard Graduate School of Education

and was admitted to the one-year master's program. His family moved with him from Maine to Somerville, Massachusetts, to another cramped apartment and another year of not enough money to go around. The marriage survived the year at Harvard and the beginning of Canada's career as a schoolteacher in Boston, but it didn't last much longer than that. Geoff and Joyce separated in 1978, and Joyce took Jerry and Melina back with her to Wyandanch. For the next few years, the children shuttled back and forth between Boston and New York on holidays and long weekends, but most of the time they were far away, and Canada hated being apart from them. He moved back to New York in 1983, took the job at Rheedlen as the organization's educational director, and found a new home in Freeport, on Long Island, close to his children. Canada spent the next few years trying to make up for lost time with his kids. He felt relieved, downright lucky, that they had turned out as well as they had. He knew he hadn't been able to provide them with the stable childhood they had deserved.

And then, surprisingly, Canada got a second chance at fatherhood. A decade after the breakup of his marriage, he met a woman named Yvonne Grant, an administrative assistant for the two nonprofits that shared the ramshackle building on the upper reaches of Broadway where Rheedlen had its headquarters. She had grown up in Harlem, and she was warm, beautiful, and kind. Canada asked her to the movies, and then, a few years later, he asked her to marry him. By the time they were engaged, in 1994, Geoff was forty-two and Yvonne was thirty-five, and neither of them had any intention of starting a new family. They both had grown children by this time; in fact, Geoff had just become a grandfather.

But one afternoon, a few weeks before their wedding, Geoff was watching Yvonne play with his granddaughter, and he saw something different in her eyes. That night, she asked him whether he would consider having another child. After a few weeks of wondering if they were crazy even to think about starting all over again, they spent the next eighteen months trying to get pregnant, until the day that Yvonne shouted to Geoff from the bathroom that the home pregnancy test had come out positive. ("She starts yelling and dancing," Canada said. "She's like, 'Oh, it's a plus, it's a plus!' There we were like two fools in the middle of the living room, jumping up and down.") And so in 1997, at the age of forty-five, Geoff Canada became a father again. He and Yvonne had a boy, and they gave him the same name as the son Canada had lost twenty-five years earlier: Geoffrey Jr.

When Canada talks about his son now, it's clear that the boy is at the center of his life; his smiling face fills the only frame on Canada's desk. And in addition to all the usual joys a child brings, Geoffrey Jr. provides his father with something else: an object lesson in the vast divide between two different kinds of contemporary American childhood. When Jerry and Melina were young, Canada and his wife were barely out of their teens, stressed out, poor, moving frequently, often quarreling, always struggling to make ends meet. When Geoffrey Jr. was born, Canada's situation was much different. He and Yvonne were comfortable and settled, living in a pleasant co-op in Queens and about to move to a four-bedroom house in Valley Stream, a mixed-race community in suburban Long Island where they still live.

Parenthood had changed, too, in the intervening decades, at least for a certain cohort of Americans. Geoffrey Jr.'s birth coincided with a nationwide groundswell of interest in early childhood. In 1994 the Carnegie Corporation of New York published *Starting Points: Meeting the Needs of Our Youngest Children,* a groundbreaking study on the importance of the first three years of life in the cognitive development of a child. "Across the United States," it began, "we are beginning to hear the rumblings of a quiet crisis." The study drew on new research that neuroscientists were doing on the infant brain, and it concluded that because of inadequate early-childhood stimulation (partly due to the rise of single-parent families and working mothers), too many of the country's youngest children were "entering school not ready to learn."

The word spread quickly through middle-class and especially

upper-middle-class America: if you want to be a successful parent, you've got to start early, and from day one, everything you do matters. An industry was spawned. Publishers and educators produced "zero to three" books, activity kits, and workshops; *Newsweek* put out a special issue on "Your Child from Birth to Three"; startup companies sold Baby Einstein videos and brain-building activity gyms. In April 1997 Bill and Hillary Clinton held a conference at the White House on early development and learning; Rob Reiner, the actor and director, gave the keynote address. Unlike previous educational trends, this one looked as though it had staying power; it seemed more like a cultural shift than a passing fad.

Like many other striving middle-class couples, the Canadas became hyperattentive to every new discovery in the field of child raising. A doctor told Geoff to talk to his child in the womb, and so every night of Yvonne's pregnancy, he would have a little chat with his unborn son. The music of Mozart was said to stimulate a baby's cognitive development, so Geoffrey Jr. received a daily dose—despite the fact that neither of his parents much cared for classical music. Whatever the experts said Geoffrey Jr. needed—flashcards, books, mobiles—he got.

Valley Stream, and suburbs like it, felt like the center of a baby revolution in those days. Every parent the Canadas met at the local playground had new tips about time-out strategies, infant-yoga classes, and "Ferberizing" techniques to train babies to sleep through the night. Geoff Canada traded advice and stories just like the rest of his neighbors, but all the while he was thinking about Harlem. Were parents there having the kind of conversations that these suburban parents were having? He asked Caressa Singleton, one of his program directors, to canvass the various government and nonprofit social service agencies in the neighborhood to see what the zero-to-three movement looked like from the streets of Harlem. What she found shouldn't have surprised him, he knew, but it did anyway: above 110th Street, the revolution was completely invisible. There wasn't a single program that helped parents in Harlem understand the importance of the first years of life or gave them any advice on how to guide their children through that critical early period.

"It was so clear that there was this body of information out there," Canada recalled. "Everybody agreed on the best practices. If you have a child who is three months old, we know exactly what you ought to be doing with that child. When your kid is nine months old, we know that, too—no debate, we don't need any more research, we don't need any more studies. But in our community, no one was talking to our parents about this body of knowledge."

Canada had already concluded that if he wanted to change the lives of Harlem's poor children, then starting at kindergarten was too late. So he turned to the Robin Hood Foundation, and program managers there put him in touch with T. Berry Brazelton, a renowned pediatrician and child psychologist who had helped propel the zero-to-three movement. Canada, Singleton, and Canada's deputy, George Khaldun, met with Brazelton, and with his help they put together a bare-bones curriculum for a new parenting-skills program in Harlem. They decided to call it Baby College.

Since the first class of forty-four parents graduated from Baby College in 2000, the program has grown steadily. Marilyn Joseph, the director of Baby College, now has an annual budget of $1.2 million and a staff of sixty full- and part-time workers, including a dedicated team of outreach workers who spend much of their time recruiting participants door-to-door. She holds five "cycles" of Baby College a year, each one lasting nine consecutive Saturday mornings and enrolling about eighty expecting parents and parents of children up to the age of three. In the years since its creation, Baby College has become an essential part of Canada's vision, perhaps *the* essential part; in many ways, it was the pilot program for the entire Harlem Children's Zone.

THE TWENTY-FIRST cycle of Baby College took place in the fall, from September through November, which meant that the outreach teams had to spend all summer recruiting parents. It took more than two months of door knocking and flyer passing to collect the number they needed.

They got Sharnea Lewis at 132nd Street and Fifth Avenue. Jasmine Tumma just walked right up to her and smiled and said, "Can I talk to you for a minute?" Shauntel Jones got her flyer on 129th Street. Another outreach worker stopped her and went into his rap: "We've got a free nine-week program for parents. It's a discussion," he said, "a chance to share your expertise. Plus, there's free breakfast and free lunch, nine Saturdays in a row." And with that, Shauntel was in, too. Leroy Saxton heard about the program from Natasha Welsh, his girlfriend, who was five months pregnant. Cecilia Davis dutifully filled out the form after Jasmine and Mark Frazier knocked on her apartment door, but it didn't really seem like her heart was in it. So right in front of her, Jasmine bet Mark a case of Pepsi that Cecilia wouldn't show up for the first day of class. "All right," Cecilia said with a smile, "I'm going to prove you wrong."

Cheryl Waite was walking past Harlem Hospital, at Lenox Avenue and 136th Street, on her way to pick up a prescription, when she ran into Anthony Santiago and Francisca Silfa, two of Baby College's twelve outreach workers. Lenox was full of people—it was early September, a warm, sunny day—and Anthony and Francisca were stopping couples with strollers, women who looked like they might be pregnant, anyone who would take one of their flyers. Cheryl was seventeen, and she was three months pregnant, just starting to show. A week earlier, a friend had told her about Baby College, and Cheryl had been thinking about it ever since. She was feeling scared and unprepared, not ready to take care of the new life that was growing inside her, and she figured she needed some help. She hadn't found the time yet to make the call to the Baby College office, but now here were Anthony and Francisca, right in front of her, like destiny, handing out flyers.

"I was actually looking for you guys," Cheryl said, and Francisca started filling out her paperwork: name, address, age, due date.

"Do you have a partner you can bring with you?" Francisca asked.

Cheryl thought about it. "Maybe," she said.

She did have a partner: Victor Boria, her boyfriend. They had been together, on and off, for four years, since she was thirteen and he was fifteen. She loved Victor—they had fun together, and he always made her laugh. But lately, things had been very rocky, ever since the day they found out Cheryl was pregnant. Victor's best friend had been whispering in his ear, saying he was too young to commit to just one woman, and Victor would sometimes sneak around and see other girls on the sly. He and Cheryl were fighting every day now, it seemed; before the pregnancy, they never used to fight. Cheryl didn't know if they'd still be together when the baby was born. Twice, they had been to what she called "the mean-danger-zone place"—an abortion clinic—but each time they couldn't go through with it. Now Cheryl kept waiting for the morning when she'd wake up and feel good about her baby; instead, every morning, she woke up feeling depressed and worried, and at night she sometimes cried herself to sleep.

When she asked Victor if he would come to Baby College with her, he said no. He had been kicked out of more schools than he could count, usually for fighting—one time, after he slugged a school security guard, they called it "inciting a riot"—and finally he had just given up and dropped out altogether. So there were plenty of things he'd rather do than get up early on a Saturday and sit in a public school classroom while someone lectured him about being a better parent.

Cheryl said she wanted them both to know the same things, and she said she thought it might bring them closer together.

Victor said he'd think about it.

When the first Baby College event came along, though—a baby shower for all the expecting mothers in the program—Victor refused to go. Cheryl felt sad and trapped and depressed that night, but she decided to go anyway. When she walked through the doors of PS 197, the public school where the shower was being held, her eyes were wet with tears.

The baby shower was much bigger than Cheryl expected. It was bigger than anyone expected, in fact. The shower was a regular feature of Baby College, a get-to-know-you event that took place a few days before the first class. Usually there were just a couple dozen pregnant mothers at the shower, but this time, on a Thursday night at the end of September, more than sixty showed up, and when you added in the fathers and grandmothers and friends who were accompanying the pregnant women, there were more than a hundred people, almost all of them from Harlem, and they filled up the gymnasium in the school's basement. When the chairs ran out, the outreach workers ran upstairs to the classrooms to get more.

Cheryl found a seat and started talking to the young women on either side of her, sharing pregnancy stories. After a little while, she realized that for the first time in weeks, she was actually enjoying herself. There was no teaching at the shower, just fun — chicken and rice and salad and cake on plastic plates, a wisecracking MC running raffles and guessing games, organizing group photos and handing out prizes. At the end, someone pulled out a boom box and there was dancing, all the grandmothers doing the Electric Slide, even the ones with canes.

Two days later, the twenty-first cycle of Baby College began.

PS 197 WAS A LOW, white brick building on the corner of Fifth Avenue and 135th Street, across from a sprawling high-rise housing project. That first morning, parents started arriving at the school before 9:00 A.M., pulling toddlers and pushing strollers, dressed mostly in T-shirts and basketball jerseys, jeans, and running shoes. By 10:00 A.M., more than 120 had appeared, along with about 100 children, and they were all crammed into the cafeteria, sitting at the long white scratched-up tables they remembered from school, listening to the fluorescent lights hum. They lined up for breakfast and shushed their kids and tried to recall why they'd agreed to get up early on a Saturday. Once everyone had had a little fruit and cereal and juice, Marilyn Joseph, the director of Baby College, welcomed them all and explained that they would be assigned to classrooms according to the age of their youngest child—the expecting parents were in room 107; the zero-to-eleven-month class was in room 109; and so on up to the parents of three-year-olds in room 129. There was a separate class for "young adults," meaning teenage parents and parents-to-be, plus a sizable class in Spanish and a smaller one in French, for the handful of parents who had immigrated to Harlem from West Africa.

Each session of the nine-week course was dedicated to a particular subject. The first week was an orientation session, and once all the children were safely down in childcare, finger painting and playing with balls and books, and the parents had all found the right room and gathered their chairs into a circle, the instructors talked about the weeks ahead and asked everyone to say what had brought him or her to Baby College.

Most of the parents were still feeling shy or skeptical, and they were reluctant to go too deep. But in the three-year-old class, a young mother named Stridiron Clark spoke up. "What I want to know," she said, "is why is it so hard for us to get information that will take us to the next level of society?" Stridiron was thirty-three, slender and soft-spoken, fashionably dressed in a black T-shirt and jeans and expensive-looking shoes, an elegant, streetwise look that was topped off by an olive-drab military-style cap. She leaned forward in her chair, which was in the back of the classroom, next to a bubbling fish tank. "I have a seventeen-year-old daughter," she explained. "I was too young when I had her. Now I have a three-year-old daughter, and I know how I want to raise her: I want her to turn out the opposite of her seventeen-year-old sister."

Russell Oliver, the instructor, was a giant, six foot two and bulky, with a tiny hoop earring on each side of his huge, dark, almost-shaved head. During the week, at his regular job, he was a drug counselor. Here at Baby College, he liked to wander the room during classes, throwing out observations and wisecracks and questions. "The opposite?" he said to Stridiron. "In what way?"

"I don't want to sound all uppity, but the bottom line is I don't want her to be an ignorant teenage parent. I don't want the cycle to continue."

Even on the first day, it was clear that there were some mothers in the twenty-first cycle of Baby College who saw the program as a second chance — a way to correct mistakes that their parents had made with them or that they had made themselves early on. Stridiron, or Stry, as she was known, was one of them. After class, I sat down with her in an empty classroom, and she told me her history: She grew up in Harlem in the 1980s, at the beginning of the crack boom, and when she was a little girl, her mother became addicted to drugs and lost control of her life. At the age of twelve, Stridiron was removed from her mother's home and entered the child-welfare system, and for the next six years she bounced around between upstate and the city, in and out of foster homes, group homes, and residential treatment centers.

Somehow, Stry managed to piece together a decent education. She was smart and creative, and most of the schools she landed in were pretty good. But then, at the age of sixteen, she got pregnant, and when her daughter arrived, Stridiron didn't really know what to do with her. She was living in a group home, and she had no family to help out. She did her best those first years, she said, and she wasn't a terrible mother. But she was neglectful: she'd go out at night with her friends instead of staying home with the baby. Stridiron held her little two-person family together for seven years, but then her life took a couple of bad turns, and the city wound up taking her daughter away. When a family in the Bronx said they wanted to adopt the girl, Stry didn't contest it, though she made sure it was an open adoption, which meant that she was able to remain a part of her daughter's life.

Over the next few years, in her mid- and late twenties, Stridiron found within herself a new resourcefulness. She enrolled in theater classes at City College and wound up graduating from the Katharine Gibbs School, a technical college, with an associate's degree in fashion marketing. At thirty, she got pregnant again, and this time she was ready.

For her teenage daughter, though, those years didn't go so well. She had always told Stry, "I'm not going to turn out like you," and then that's exactly how she did turn out: pregnant at sixteen, a mother at seventeen, living with her own baby boy in a group home for teenage mothers, just like the one she had lived in as a baby girl sixteen years earlier.

"The cycle continued," Stridiron said. Her voice was a mixture of disappointment and wonder, like she couldn't believe how difficult it could be for a family to break its patterns. "I was like, Oh, no! I don't want this again."

Stridiron said she was still trying to help her older daughter as much as she could, but her real focus now was on her new little girl, Adonya. After our talk, she and Adonya were reunited in the childcare room along with the other three-year-olds and their mothers. Watching them together, singing "I'm a Little Teapot" with the other children and parents, it was plain to see how much Stridiron loved her daughter. To me, it was striking that someone who had grown up neglected and rejected was now able to be as attentive and patient and supportive and gentle as Stridiron was with Adonya. At home, she told me, she read to Adonya all the time, and they played and sang together and watched educational programs on PBS. She said she felt like she had finally broken the cycle that had plagued her family for so long.

When Stridiron left with Adonya after that first day of Baby College, she seemed happy and excited, and she said she'd be back the next Saturday. But then she didn't show up, not that day and not for any of the eight remaining classes. Jasmine, her outreach worker, called the three phone numbers Stridiron had given her, even went to her apartment and knocked on the door, but she never found her.

What did it mean?

Jasmine thought the most likely explanation was that Stry lived outside of the boundaries of the Harlem Children's Zone and didn't want anyone to find out that she wasn't really eligible for the program. That was Jasmine's theory, but in fact she had no idea what had happened, and it drove her a little crazy. Baby College was like that for everyone who worked there—highs alternated with lows, lost causes turned into success stories, hopes were raised and then dashed. On the first day of class, no one could say for sure who would graduate and who would drop out, which parents would take the message of Baby College to heart and which ones would drift through the classes, grab their plaques at graduation, and then do everything exactly the same way they always had.

Jasmine's frustration was particularly acute because she and the other outreach workers at Baby College prided themselves on always getting their woman. Their goal—their quota, really—was to ensure that 80 percent of the mothers and caregivers of young children in Harlem were graduates of the program. That number was not only very high, a level of market penetration that was far above that of any other social service program in any neighborhood in the country, but meeting it was made even more challenging by the fact that the number was a moving target: new babies were always being born, and new mothers were always moving into the neighborhood, so the outreach workers' labor was never complete. Like everyone on the outreach team, Jasmine was extraordinarily resourceful. She patrolled housing projects, knocking on every door, taking the stairs from floor to floor; she haunted Laundromats and daycare centers and check-cashing outlets; she cajoled, she encouraged, she threatened; she called some reluctant mothers a dozen times, until they finally showed up at Baby College just to get her off their backs. And once a mother was in, Jasmine tried to ensure that she was in to stay. She knew that her bosses would go to great lengths to retain the parents they had enrolled, whether that meant rescheduling a home visit four or five times or paying for a taxi for someone to get to class or placing a half-dozen wake-up calls every Saturday morning. Whatever it took.

And now Stridiron, the model mom, had slipped through her fingers.

WHEN CANADA AND HIS staff first met with T. Berry Brazelton, the pediatrician, to discuss what Baby College might look like, Brazelton told them that it was most important to talk to parents about brain development and discipline; the two subjects, he said, were intricately intertwined. It was agreed that those would be the two tent poles; they would each take up two weeks of the nine-week cycle. And then, to that mix, Canada decided to add a few basic instructional units to protect the children's bodies at the same time as he was helping their parents cultivate their minds: a class on home safety, which would cover window guards and sudden infant death syndrome and socket plugs; a class on the prevention of asthma, which was becoming near-epidemic in Harlem homes; and a class on immunization, which would enable his staff to monitor the vaccination records of all of the children enrolled in the program.

Baby College first began to take shape just as Canada was putting together his plan to change Rheedlen into the Harlem Children's Zone, and Canada saw an additional benefit in the program: it would serve as a means for him to start the agency's relationship with Harlem's parents early, to connect them with the many new services that he was planning to offer in the neighborhood.

And so throughout cycle 21, project managers from around the Harlem Children's Zone trooped one by one through PS 197's auditorium, where the parents gathered each Saturday morning after breakfast. There was Linda Gardner, the administrator of Harlem Gems, the prekindergarten; Amber Cartwright, who ran the Harlem Children Zone's Head Start program; Mona-Lisa Tolbert, in charge of the organization's fitness program for adults and teens; Kaaryn Nailor, the head of Community Pride, which encourages residents to form tenants' associations and block associations. Each woman gave a brief talk to the parents, and the message was always the same: come and check us out; we're here for you, and our services are free. The idea was to entangle these parents in the Harlem Children's Zone web in any and every way possible. There were other visitors, too: a few volunteers from a charity called Eastern Star, who were donating children's books to the parents; a woman from Harlem Hospital, inviting newly expecting parents to enroll in a federally sponsored home-visiting program for poor mothers called the Nurse-Family Partnership; another from the New York Public Library, signing parents and children up for library cards (if Baby College parents had accrued fines that were keeping them and their children away from the library, the Harlem Children's Zone offered to pay them off).

Each parent responded differently to these offers and entreaties. Some were enthusiastic, eager to catch up and determined to connect their children with every program they were eligible for. Others sat in silence, slouched in their seats, never raising their hands.

At the top of the enthusiasm scale were Darryl Reaves and his wife, Damita Miles-Reaves. Darryl had first come to Baby College in cycle 17, two years earlier, as a guest. He was a new father then, and a friend from his building who was also a new father had enrolled in Baby College. Halfway through, he told Darryl how he was spending his Saturday mornings, and Darryl figured he might as well tag along; Damita worked on weekends, and he didn't have anything else to do with his infant son, Darryl Jr., on Saturdays. From his first visit, Darryl loved Baby College, loved everything about it, and he enrolled officially in the next cycle, starting from the first class and retaking the ones he had attended with his friend. He bonded with the other parents in his zero-to-eleven-month class, and even now, two years later, he and Damita had close friendships with six or seven of them, all of them with children born just a few days apart, the kids all going to one another's birthday parties and trading sleepovers. For the last two years Darryl had been waiting for Damita to get pregnant again so that he could come along with her for his third dose of Baby College. Damita was due to deliver just before Baby College graduation.

Darryl was born into poverty and grew up living in a housing project in inner-city Trenton, New Jersey. As a four-year-old, in 1967, he was part of one of the first classes of Head Start, the federal government's preschool program for poor children. He grew into a champion athlete, and he was admitted to the University of Virginia on a football scholarship. He excelled on the playing field, and in the classroom he worked hard to catch up, trying to wring from the school every benefit and bit of knowledge he could. After graduation, he told me, he played a year of professional football for the Miami Dolphins, mostly warming the bench, and then spent a few years in the Marine Corps. The words "U.S. Marines" were tattooed on his right forearm, but he carried himself more like an athlete than a military man. He was muscular and easygoing, comfortable in his frame, and his manner was confident and gregarious. By the end of cycle 21 every parent in Baby College knew his name. He had the gleam in his eyes of a man who had been to a motivational workshop or two, or perhaps had even led a motivational workshop or two. He worked in Morris County, New Jersey, as a level-two human services specialist for Medicaid, and when he told me about his job, he took pains to emphasize that he was a level-*two* human services specialist, just a step away from supervisor, and not a lowly level one. He was well respected at his job, he said, and it wasn't hard to imagine that if you were applying for Medicaid benefits in Morris County and you found yourself in front of Darryl's desk, you would thank your lucky stars. "I'm the master at getting information," he said. "I must have fifty letters from clients saying how much they appreciate what I did for them. I do cases in one day that the normal worker will spend ninety days on."

Darryl's overachieving bent extended to fatherhood. During his first full cycle of Baby College, two years earlier, he and his son, Darryl Jr., had come to class each Saturday dressed exactly alike, in matching football jerseys and caps, right down to their identical running shoes. Marilyn Joseph had taken him aside and spoken to him about it, in fact; she knew his challenge as a parent would come the day that Darryl Jr. brought home a subpar report card, or announced that he didn't like football. Darryl responded well to Marilyn's nudge—he took seriously everything that the instructors at Baby College said—and now he and Darryl Jr. dressed alike only occasionally. He was clearly a devoted husband and a loving father; he announced to anyone who would listen that he had never spanked his son. He was also a born leader, helping out in class, saying supportive things to other parents, recruiting the young men in the program to join the Baby College fathers' group that met every Thursday night in a classroom at PS 197 for an hour of discussion and male bonding (no women allowed).

Most mornings, Darryl and Damita and Darryl Jr. arrived at Baby College early, almost an hour before class started. But they were rarely the first parents there. That distinction usually went to Shauntel Jones, an expecting mother who seemed to inhabit the opposite end of the parenting spectrum. Shauntel's life was complicated and confusing and hard, and every week there was something new. She was thirty-two, and this was either her third or her fifth pregnancy; she told me different things about her family history on different days. Her other children had been taken away from her by the Administration for Children's Services, or ACS, New York City's child-welfare agency. She still had regular contact with her older son, who was being raised now by relatives, but her younger son was in North Carolina, she said, and she rarely saw him.

Her new pregnancy didn't seem to be built on a very strong foundation. The father was a man named Leroy. Shauntel was very fond of him, even if she wouldn't go so far as to call him her boyfriend. He had moved to Harlem recently from North Carolina, and the woman he had left behind had followed him and brought along their four children. Shauntel wasn't happy about this situation—she referred to the woman as Leroy's "stinking baby mother" or his "fat-ass baby mother"—and the way she told the story, Leroy wasn't happy, either. He wanted to be with Shauntel, not the other woman, but he didn't have the heart to send the other woman back to North Carolina. Shauntel was a small woman with a wandering eye and two missing front teeth. Her face was pretty despite those flaws, and she ducked her head into a shy grin whenever anyone said something funny. She grinned a lot when she talked about the baby girl she was expecting, whom she had already named Treasure Lee, the Lee being short for Leroy.

Shauntel had an uneasy relationship with her obstetrician, and one Saturday morning she told me that at the doctor's office that week, everyone had been yelling at her, cursing her out for missing an appointment. When her doctor conveyed various concerns to her—that her baby might be born prematurely, that she might need a C-section, that he wanted to inject her womb with a dye that would let him check whether there was enough amniotic fluid around her baby—Shauntel heard what he said as threats, like the doctor was going out of his way to try to scare her. "I'm not going to take the needle," she said, "'cause the needle is a lawsuit. They stick a needle in me, Treasure would be dead."

Shauntel and Damita sometimes seemed like they were from different planets—Shauntel, compact and closed in on herself, was born in Harlem Hospital, just a block away from the school where Baby College was held, and she had lived in public housing in Harlem all her life. Damita, who was long-limbed and laid back, grew up in Washington, D.C., in what she described as an upper-middle-class family; her father had been the commissioner of officials for the National Football League. But the two women got along well, and some mornings, before the other parents arrived, they would sit at a table together, over corn flakes and orange slices, and while Darryl chased Darryl Jr. around the cafeteria, they would talk about Braxton Hicks contractions and whether it was easier to sleep on your back or your side as your belly grew larger and more uncomfortable.

It was important to Marilyn Joseph that Baby College be able to offer something to both Damita and Shauntel. She did her best to "customize" the experience, she said, so that Damita and Darryl might get from the program the sense of community and connectedness they wanted, and Shauntel might get more immediate and specific assistance: visits from a social worker, connections with social service agencies, counseling, and financial help, as well as the kind of instruction in discipline and brain development that could enable her to have a better relationship with Treasure Lee than she had been able to have with her other children. Shauntel told her outreach worker, Shanta Chapman, that she wanted to make sure ACS didn't take this child away. And already, things seemed different. She talked to Treasure in the womb, like her instructors suggested, and at night, when she couldn't get to sleep because of Treasure's kicks, she lay in bed and sang "The Itsy-Bitsy Spider" and "Twinkle, Twinkle, Little Star" until her baby calmed down.

IT WAS DIFFICULT to tell just where Victor Boria and Cheryl Waite fell on the spectrum of parents at Baby College. There were, it seemed, plenty of strikes against them: Victor a high school dropout with a criminal record, living with his single mother in a housing-project apartment; Cheryl an unmarried teenage mom-to-be taking the bus in from her mother's home in Englewood, New Jersey, to see Victor and go to school. But after missing the baby shower and the orientation class, Victor had finally showed up for week two, and when he and Cheryl were together now, they seemed happier and more hopeful and enthusiastic than most parents in similar circumstances. They had big plans, and Victor, especially, could get excited when he talked about them, even if they changed somewhat each week.

Over breakfast on the morning of the third week of Baby College, Victor told me that he probably wouldn't be around when cycle 21 ended. In another week or two, he said, he'd be going down south, to Wilmington, North Carolina, where he had lived till the age of five and where his mother still owned a modest house out-side of town.

"My mom signed the house over to my name," Victor said. "She knows that I'm expecting. She said: 'You look like you have your head on. Let me try to help you. But you mess it up, it's on you.'" Victor still had plenty of family down in Wilmington, lots of cous-ins who lived just a short walk away from the house. "So I'm going down in two weeks," he said. "It's all arranged. I'm going to get a job. My cousin is a hiring manager for a construction company. So I get down there, and next day I'm on work. Cheryl's going to stay up here and finish her degree, and I'll go back and forth. When she's finished"—she was due to graduate from high school three months later, in January—"she can come on down, house all set up, baby room painted."

"It's a little scary," Cheryl said. "I've never been down there. I heard there are wild turkeys." She laughed. "I'm already scared of pigeons!"

Victor wore his hair in short cornrow braids tight against his scalp. There was a tuft of beard on his chin and a wispy mustache on his upper lip. He was small, about five foot seven, and he wore all his clothes a few sizes too big. His thin frame often looked like it was going to disappear inside his leather jacket, which was of a style that had become popular in Harlem that year: it was covered with intricate stitching that spelled out a collage of words and pic-tures. The theme of Victor's jacket was the movie *Scarface*. From a distance, it looked like a plain black jacket, but up close, you could see scenes and phrases everywhere, a thin, wan Michelle Pfeiffer on one arm, Al Pacino with a machine gun on the back. Victor could look like a gangster when he needed to, folding his face into a scowl and narrowing his eyes, and when he did, he could almost con-vince you he was a public enemy. But more often, his eyes were wide and eager, and he laughed and grinned a lot, especially when Cheryl was around.

Cheryl had a broad face and a warm smile, with glossy straight hair that fell to her shoulders. Her outfits were always well matched, and her eyebrows were always well plucked. Cheryl's mother was a union construction worker, big and brawny, and her father was a reggae musician, an albino Jamaican with blond dreadlocks and blue eyes who had separated from her mother and lived now down in Florida. Cheryl was more responsible and practical than Victor, more of a realist, and although Victor had the bigger personality, it seemed that Cheryl made a lot of their decisions. Even telling the story of her relationship with Victor, she was serious. "We met at his house four years ago," she said. At the time, Victor was in Job Corps, a federal job-training program for poor teenagers and young adults, living in a dorm somewhere in upstate New York, studying for his GED. "I would see him every holiday," Cheryl said. "And then two years ago he stopped going to Job Corps, and we became a lot, lot more serious. And now we're here with the baby. And hopefully we're looking at another, I don't know, nine years or five years after that."

Victor looked a little hurt. "*I'm* looking at eternity," he said.

"Oh, yeah," Cheryl said with a bit of a smile.

"It's not a long time," Victor said. "It's not. Forever is not a long time. It all depends who you spend it with. I'm happy with who I'm with."

"Yeah, we get along good," Cheryl said. Ever since Victor had agreed to come to Baby College, the fights that they had endured early on in her pregnancy had mostly evaporated. "We have our basic little arguments," she said. "It's just little things."

"*So* little," said Victor.

"We mostly have fun with each other instead of argue."

"I get mad at her for eating too many sweets. She says she wants to eat healthy, and then I see her eating Oreos."

"I get cravings," Cheryl said with a shrug. "I'm still waiting for my cheesecake."

"I *brought* you your cheesecake."

Cheryl laughed. "I don't eat *everything*," she said.

"You clean the refrigerator out if it got snacks."

"Yeah, certain snacks," Cheryl admitted.

"I just keep swiping, keep swiping," Victor said, playing the harried boyfriend with a credit card and a huge grocery bill. "'Charge it, ma'am, charge it.' It's like, 'Feed me, Seymour, feed me.'"

"I like cheesecake. I like ice cream a lot. I like yogurts a lot. It's all about the snacks right now. He doesn't understand that."

"I don't like it. You need nutrition. Sit down and eat a bowl of lettuce. Let me see you do that."

"Yeah," Cheryl said with a little roll of her eyes. "He's the nutritionist."

After she finished with high school, Cheryl planned to get a job working with kids and then, when her baby was a bit older, to go to college. Victor's plans were more fanciful. He was the CEO of what he described as an underground record company, which had, so far, signed up four artists: Victor; Victor's teenage nephew; Cheryl's twin sister, Chiffony; and the security guard in Victor's building. Victor could get excited when he talked about it, his eyes even wider than usual. "All of us together," he said, "and with my mind power, and who I know inside Universal/Def Jam, it could all go through."

He was a regular performer at a hip-hop open-mike night in the East Village, and over lunch at Baby College one day he recited in low tones one of his raps, called "Too Many Women," a funny and catchy lament about the difficulty of staying committed in a world full of gorgeous distractions. One Saturday morning he said that he and Cheryl's sister were both signed up as opening acts for a concert that Lil Wayne and the Clipse were giving at Radio City Music Hall, but that fell through. The big plan, the "down south plan," as Victor called it, also took some unexpected turns as Baby College went on. First, his mother changed her mind about handing over the house. She was ill, and she decided she needed Victor to stay around to take care of her at night, when her home health aide was gone. For a while, Victor said defiantly that he was going to just go down to the house in Wilmington anyway—maybe get a key from his older sister, maybe just jimmy open a window—but then that plan fell apart, too.

None of these setbacks seemed to discourage Victor much. He

was an optimist, and the thing he really cared about was being with Cheryl. Although he'd been reluctant when she had first mentioned Baby College, he quickly became a big fan, paying attention and asking questions. When a social worker came through the cafeteria, giving out children's books, Victor asked for an extra one, and he got Dr. Seuss's *The Foot Book* to take home to his unborn daughter. Cheryl's prediction—that going through the course together would bring them closer—seemed to be coming true.

In fact, one morning in the cafeteria, when Cheryl wasn't around, Victor told me that he had a "little surprise" planned for her: he had decided to propose. He just wasn't sure when. "It's kind of hard to set it up," he said. "The right moment, the right timing—and then do I have the ring on me?" As for the wedding itself, he said, "I was thinking maybe when the baby is three, so she can walk down the aisle with us, holding the ring." He smiled. "Besides, that's enough time for me to save up, financially wise, and set everything up, as far as down south and the house and everything."

CHERYL COULDN'T MAKE it to class on the fourth week of Baby College—she had things to take care of in New Jersey—so Victor came alone. "I have to take notes for both of us," he explained at breakfast. The topic of the day was discipline, generally one of the more contentious issues at Baby College, and it was a topic that Cheryl and Victor had already spent some time discussing.

"Cheryl says, 'You know, they're going to ask you questions about hitting the kid, and it's going to change your mind,'" Victor told me. He was open to hearing the Baby College case on discipline, he said, but then he grinned and leaned in, a bit conspiratorially. "Me and Cheryl have this little system going on already," he said. "It's called Beat Ass Early. That's the name of it. It's not really beating, it's pinching. Just a little pinch to chastise them instead of whipping them." To Victor, the problem with abusive parents was that they hit too hard, hard enough to do damage to their children. His plan was different. "Especially when they're in the toddler stages," he said, "I feel like the pinching substitute will really work."

The young adults met in room 125 with their instructor, Carol Grannum, a powerful-looking woman with broad shoulders, a razor-short haircut, a denim shirt, and big dangling earrings. There were eight young women and two young men in the room, all teenagers, all in jeans, and they sat in a circle on folding chairs, all more or less facing Carol. During the week, the room they were in was full of third-grade students, which meant that the walls were covered with vocabulary words and crayon drawings of suns and stars. On a stumpy little grade-school desk, Carol had set up an oversized easel pad on which she occasionally made notes with a black marker.

"Today's class discussion is discipline," she began, "and this is a time when we get to talk about exactly how we were raised, and if we intend to parent our children the same way that our parents or guardians parented us. It may get emotional. We know that everyone's parents did different things." She looked at the young parents and parents-to-be. "How comfortable are you feeling right now? What if I was to go around the room and talk about what kind of discipline and rules and regulations you had to follow in your household? Do you feel comfortable about that? Who would like to go first?"

Angelique Vasquez raised her hand. She was nineteen, small, with a radiant smile and a three-month-old baby girl named Bria in a deluxe-looking Graco stroller parked next to her chair.

"Okay," Carol said. "In your household growing up, as a child, what were some of the rules, and what were some of the punishments that were given to you?

"It was too abusive," Angelique said. "Even if I did something good, I used to always get in trouble from my mother. I didn't have no rules, to be honest. It was just, if you did something bad, Pow!"

"Describe the 'Pow,'" Carol said.

"You get hit."

"By what?"

"Anything. If there's a shoe on the floor, you get hit by a shoe."

Leroy Saxton, who was sitting next to his pregnant girlfriend, Natasha Welsh, went next. "I was raised by my mom," he said. "She always wanted me to set an example, keep the house cleaned up. If I didn't listen, she'd pluck me in the neck or forehead or pull my hair. Unless I did something over the line. Then she'd get a belt and smack me with it."

"And was that punishment or discipline?" Carol asked. The distinction was a critical one at Baby College. Punishment, as Carol Grannum and the other Baby College instructors saw it, was anything physical, from hitting to spanking to shouting to shaking, and all of it, they believed, was the wrong approach. The preferred alternative to punishment was discipline: a consistent, coherent system of rules that was enforced through talking. But the kids in the young-adult class—the men, anyway—didn't see those boundaries the way Carol did.

"It was discipline," Leroy said, answering Carol's question about his mother's use of her belt. "It doesn't make me dislike her. I understand why she did it. The way her mother raised her was a lot worse. And my father wasn't there. As long as my mother was there, that's all that matters."

Victor spoke up. "My mom never really beat me, neither, but boy, oh boy, when she did! It wasn't no *hard* whipping. It was enough to leave a welt on your arm, though. It wasn't abuse. As a mom, I give her an E for effort. She tried really, really hard."

Carol asked Victor the same question she asked Leroy: "Was it punishment or discipline?" The correct answer, to Carol's way of thinking, was "punishment," but Victor didn't agree.

"What my mom did wasn't punishment," Victor said. "It was discipline. See, I didn't have a father, so when she used to get the belt, I used to think, 'What would my father be doing if he was here? He'd man up and think nothing of it. She's not hitting me hard at all.' I never got a whole lot of scars. Maybe one scar."

Leroy said, "You need a dad there. Dad's supposed to wear the pants."

Victor and Leroy were sitting at opposite sides of the circle, but

Carol had a question for both of them: "Are you going to be different than your father?"

"Yeah," Victor said quickly. "I'm going to be there. My father wasn't there."

Leroy agreed. "I feel like the only way to get my father back is to show that I can be a better man." Victor sat forward in his chair, but Leroy slouched backward, a gray Yankees cap on his head and his oversized jeans loose on his waist. He spoke in a low voice, but his eyes were shining. "Sometimes I get to thinking, like, it's messed up how when my mom was pregnant, he begged her, 'Don't kill the baby, keep him'—and then a couple of months after I was born, he just left, told everybody, 'That's not my child, he doesn't look like me.'" The room was silent. "The only reason he used to come around is that he wanted to get back with my mother. It didn't matter if I was there."

"This is very painful," Carol replied. She sounded sympathetic. "And, Leroy, even though you're the one sharing your story, what you're describing might be common to all of us here. So I want to thank you for putting that all out on the floor." She turned to the rest of the class. "And all of this, your understanding and your acceptance of how you were raised as children, will determine what you're going to do with *your* child. Because you're going to make mistakes as parents. You're going to feel like leaving. But we want you to stay focused. Remember that even with all the challenges, you still will be able to get support. I don't think our fathers or our mothers had the support to be the best parents they needed to be. This is your opportunity to do things differently."

The young-adult class was always one of the most important at Baby College. Statistically, teenage parents are more at risk for all kinds of problems, from child abuse to substance abuse to homelessness, and they are less likely than other parents to provide their children with enough educational stimulation. In most of the other classes in cycle 21, there was a mix of working-class and poor parents, with the occasional middle-class couple thrown in. But in the young-adult class, just about everyone was from a family that was on the low end of the socioeconomic scale, and many of the new parents had faced real problems growing up. Leroy, who was abandoned by his father as an infant, dropped out of high school in the tenth grade. When Angelique was a girl, her mother was not only abusive, she was also a drug addict, and Angelique was eventually removed from her home by the city's child-welfare agency. She was now raising her baby daughter in a homeless shelter in the Bronx, waiting for her name to come up on a list so that she could move into a city apartment.

The very fact that they and the other young parents had come to Baby College was a promising sign; it meant that they knew they needed help raising their children, and they were open to new ideas and new strategies. But their children were beginning their lives with grave disadvantages nonetheless. A large part of the mission of Baby College—and, really, it was a problem the entire Harlem Children's Zone organization faced—was to figure out what advice and support to give these parents so that their children would have a better chance at success. If Geoffrey Canada had his way, Angelique's daughter Bria and the child Cheryl and Victor were expecting would, in a few years, be enrolled in kindergarten at Promise Academy. If, between now and then, those kids had the typical experience of children of teenage parents in Harlem—few books, too much TV, insufficient language exposure, a chaotic home life—they would arrive in school already way behind. The point of Baby College was to alter that situation as much as possible. Even a little improvement in Bria's formative years would make her prospects that much brighter.

THE DISCIPLINE CLASS was a critical place for the instructors to try to effect those changes. Almost every parent at Baby College arrived believing that some form of corporal punishment was necessary to keep children in line. Almost all of them had been spanked or hit themselves as children, and many of them believed that discipline could only work if it was backed up by the threat of violence. Many parents in the neighborhood saw strict discipline as the only thing that could keep their children away from the dangers they saw around them; they felt that parents who never spanked their kids were essentially telling them that there were no rules, no limits, and the result was that those children would be easy prey for all the snares and temptations of the streets.

Geoffrey Canada says he understands and respects the long cultural history behind these discipline practices. But he thinks there is a better way to do things, and he believes it is his job, and his agency's job, to explain that to Harlem's parents. "Culture is very strong around child-rearing practices," he told me as cycle 21 was getting under way. "A lot of the families we work with believe good kids are quiet kids. If you're a good parent, your child listens to you, and if you're a bad parent, your child doesn't. Well, the problem is that *no* two-year-old listens to a parent. But no one has ever explained that to a lot of our parents. So you see parents smacking a two-year-old's hand and saying, 'Didn't I tell you not to do that?'

"But the reality is that he's not disobeying you because he's a bad boy; he's not being willful; he's not being mean-spirited; this is just what two-year-olds do. And if you tell that to the parents, then they get it. In fact, hearing this message liberates a lot of our parents: When your mother tells you that your two-year-old son is just a bad little boy, she's simply wrong. It helps to understand how much of what you're doing is just custom. We want our parents to have the same information the rest of America has."

When the Baby College instructors made their case for a different approach to discipline—one that replaced physical punishment with a system of rules enforced by talk, negotiation, rewards, the withdrawal of privileges, and time-outs—they used two arguments with the parents. The first one was a threat: ACS, the city agency that was empowered to remove children from their parents' homes if they were being abused. In the course of cycle 21, parents saw a movie and were given pamphlets describing the city's official definition of child abuse, and many of them were surprised at how low the bar was set. Spanking, tweaking, slapping: all of it was against the law, and "mandated reporters," including teachers and doctors, were required to tell ACS if they thought any of it was going on. ACS was then required to investigate, and often the case would conclude with the children being removed from the home and put into the foster-care system. And although it was true that foster care was better than staying in an abusive home, it was, the Baby College staff knew, a lousy result for everyone involved. Children in the foster-care system had greatly diminished chances for success in life, and they posed one of the biggest challenges to the staff in programs like Promise Academy.

The second argument against corporal punishment was a promise. It was a more subtle argument, but in many ways it was, to the instructors, more significant. As Dr. Brazelton taught, discipline was intimately connected with cognitive growth. The middle-class style of discipline—negotiation, explanation, impulse control— was intertwined with the middle-class style of brain development. There was simply more talk in middle-class discipline, and thus more verbal stimulation; encouraging a child to understand the reasons for a prohibition, and to take part in choosing an alternative, was a powerful cognitive stimulus. If you follow that path, the instructors told the parents, your child will be smarter and happier and will make better decisions later on.

Many of the parents in Baby College responded positively to these arguments, and some of them changed their approach to discipline almost overnight. In Carol Grannum's young-adult class, though, there was resistance, and Victor was leading the resistance. It started when he tried to explain his pinching scheme.

"Me and Cheryl have a little process, a little system, called Beat Ass Early," he announced to the class. "It wouldn't ever really evolve into hitting. It's more of a pinching thing, like, if you do get fed up to the point where you feel like you want to hit your child, instead of hitting him you can pinch him."

Carol looked unhappy. "Is pinching abuse?" she asked the class.

"Yes," Angelique said. She was on Carol's side.

"For the record," Carol said, "hitting, pinching, kicking, spitting, tapping, poking, plucking, beating, stomping, and slapping—it's *all* abusive, and Harlem Children's Zone Baby College discourages it."

Victor seemed taken aback. He had expected Beat Ass Early to go over better. "Oh," he said, a little sarcastically. "I see."

"It's unacceptable," Carol said. "And it can warrant a report to ACS. Are we clear? You cannot hit your children."

"So you think beating changes the person that the baby is growing up to be?"

"What do *you* think?" Carol asked.

"No," Victor said. "I don't."

Angelique spoke up. "I think beating changes a *lot*," she said. "'Cause when your child grows up, he can't talk to you, he can't run to you, because he is going to be scared that you're just going to beat him."

Leroy disagreed. "It all depends on the individual," he said. "I used to be a sneaky kid. I would take a whole box of cereal and pour it out on the floor. My mother would say, 'Don't do that,' and I'd do it again. So I'd get hit. I didn't look at it as abuse. You listen. You stop doing things over and over."

Carol allowed that some parents might, in theory, be able to employ corporal punishment in a way that wouldn't do lasting physical harm. But it didn't matter, she said. "In certain households, you have parents who really have control, so that when they're doing the spanking or tapping, they're not harming their child. But there are other parents who go overboard. So the standard of the state and the city is that you don't participate in any of those behaviors at all." Aside from Angelique, none of the young adults seemed receptive to Carol's message, and as she spoke, none of them were making eye contact with her. She kept going anyway. "As children, we're supposed to be able to be spoken to, and then be able to learn through our mistakes and our experiences. If you practice speaking with your child, and you bond with them because you're reading, singing, touching, listening, you'll know your child's temperament."

Victor raised his hand. "OK, what if you never beat your kid, and you just say, 'Hey, stop doing this.' That's all they know, their mother or their father going, 'Stop doing this.' They think, I could get away with *murder* if I want to. Then your child be walking around mad cocky: 'I do whatever I want!'" He tried to imagine a nonviolent confrontation between a parent and a child. "'Sit down.' 'No, I don't gotta sit down, I know you're not going to hit me.' So now what? Now you've got a kid that's just bouncing off the wall, and I can't control him because they told me not to hit my kid."

"Victor, Victor," Carol said. "You're not just telling him, 'Stop doing this.' You're telling him, 'I *want* you to stop doing this, because here's what can happen to you.'"

"But basically what y'all are saying is: never hit your kid. Never hit your kid!" Victor's voice was rising, as though he'd never heard anything crazier in his life. "That's what you're saying. That's what y'all are saying. Never hit your kid. Never spank him, never pop him, because it's all abuse, it's all abuse."

"Victor, I'm hearing and feeling the energy with you," Carol said. "A lot of parents have a lot to go through. We're talking about creating a nurturing environment. You said that you and Cheryl have this Beat Ass—whatever ugly thing that you-all named it." Victor stared at her. "Not that your thoughts are ugly," Carol clarified, "but your concept, right?"

"It's just a title," Victor said. "I like to say it."

"I would like for you to discuss this class with Cheryl."

"Of course! I'm taking down notes." Victor made one last effort to explain the plan. "It's just, hey, if you're beating, then you could get out of hand. You could get out of hand if you're throwing something. But if you pinch, you can say, OK, boop"—he mimed a little pinch on a child's arm—"'Hey, don't do it again.' They be like, 'Ow, OK.' You ain't hit this kid with an extreme amount of force."

"And then when you go to that child to sit with them to read, and you happen to touch their arm where you pinched them, they're now flinching and running from you."

"You want to tell your child, I'm the parent!"

"Your child is going to *know* that you're the parent!"

DESPITE THE FIREWORKS, despite the fact that Carol called his plan ugly, Victor loved the fourth week of Baby College. When Cheryl looked back later on the whole course, she said that the fourth week was a turning point for Victor—not only in terms of Baby College, but in their relationship. Maybe it was the fact that Cheryl wasn't there and Victor was responsible for both of them, or maybe it was just that Carol took his ideas seriously, even if she disagreed with them. But somehow, that class was the moment when he became a real parent, and after that, Cheryl and Victor were tighter and happier.

There were other parents who went through major changes at Baby College. Take Cecilia Davis. Jasmine lost her wager with Mark about Cecilia—she did show up on the first day with her three-year-old son, Jason, and she had made it to every class since. (Jasmine was delivering Mark's winnings gradually, one Pepsi a day.) In one early class, Cecilia let slip that at Jason's last birthday party, she had served alcohol to the adults, and Russell, her instructor, rode her about it every week. Children's birthday parties are about children, he reminded her, not about drinking. Cecilia really took the message to heart. In one of the brain-development classes, the parents in Russell's room sat around a table strewn with magazines, scissors, crayons, and glue and made little books for their children out of blank luggage tags. Cecilia's was a series of promises to Jason, including a page with a bottle of Absolut vodka cut out of a magazine ad, next to the words "And no drinking at your birthday parties."

Jasmine was Cecilia's outreach worker, which meant that she visited Cecilia once a week in her home to go over the previous Saturday's lesson, to observe and guide her interactions with Jason and to talk about anything else Cecilia wanted to talk about. When

Cecilia arrived at Baby College, Jasmine told me, she was spanking Jason regularly, but by the fourth week, she had stopped altogether. Cecilia was twenty-six, and she lived with her mother, who had adopted two children when Cecilia was a teenager, which meant that Cecilia not only had Jason around, but also an eleven-year-old sister and a thirteen-year-old brother. She had a hard time keeping her temper with Jason and with her young siblings. So Jasmine gave her a challenge: not only was Cecilia not supposed to hit any of the kids, she also couldn't yell at them for an entire week. This was no small thing: Cecilia's was a home where there was usually a lot of yelling. But that week, every night, after the kids had gone to bed, Cecilia called Jasmine on her cell phone and said, "I did it. I made it through another day."

Shauntel was making progress, too, but hers was an uphill struggle. One week, she told me with a shy smile that she had run into Treasure Lee's father, Leroy, on the street, and he had told her that he had had a big fight with the woman from North Carolina, and that he was trying to get rid of her: "He said, 'Shauntel, I'm so sorry about the way I was acting toward you. I didn't mean to do the things I did.'" Shauntel smiled, remembering. "He grabbed me up, started hugging me and kissing me." The fight between Leroy and the girl, she said, was about Shauntel herself. "The girl was like, 'Oh, are you going to stay with Shauntel?' He said, 'Yeah, I'm moving in with Shauntel. When you're gone, Shauntel's still going to be here.' Which I am. Where am I going to go?"

The next Saturday, though, Shauntel looked depressed and withdrawn. She wore more or less the same thing every week—jeans, a worn sweatshirt, and a headscarf, usually a blue one printed with images of hundred-dollar bills—but this week, as she ate her breakfast, she looked like she wanted to vanish inside her clothes, her head down, her voice quiet. "My baby father got in some shit," she said. "He got into a mess."

The story she told was a little hard for me to follow, but it seemed that the previous Saturday night, Leroy and another man got into a fight in Leroy's apartment. Leroy was furious because he thought the other man had touched his sister, and in his rage, he stabbed the other man with a kitchen knife. The man wound up in the hospital, and now detectives were looking for Leroy, and Leroy had disappeared. He had asked Shauntel to come with him before he left, she said, but she had told him no. "It's crazy," Shauntel said, sad and aggrieved. "I have a daughter that's going to be born." Wherever Leroy was now, it seemed the woman from North Carolina was with him, and Shauntel's dream for some kind of stable father figure for Treasure Lee was dashed.

There were moments when Shauntel's life, and Treasure Lee's prospects, seemed hopeless. Shauntel was poorly educated; she lacked many cognitive skills, including the ability to read fluently. She didn't work. Her home life was in disarray, and she seemed unable to deal well with institutions like hospitals, doctors, courts, and schools. If it was true that in Harlem, even children with fairly stable parents were at a disadvantage in the race with middle-class children, then what chance would Treasure Lee have?

Geoffrey Canada believed that parents like Shauntel were not beyond help, and children like Treasure Lee were not beyond saving. But he admitted it wasn't easy. "There's a core group of our parents who have issues that are not going to be resolved by our just having a conversation with them," he told me. "Mental-health issues or substance-abuse issues or I'm-a-lousy-parent issues. They need additional support just to manage themselves—forget managing the child. And they're just not going to be good parents. They're not going to be the kind of parents who are going to sit down and read to their kids and take that extra step." This cohort, Canada guessed, made up about 10 or 15 percent of the parents in the neighborhood.

And he felt he had them covered. "Our theory encompasses that group, also," he said. "We think that we should be able to get that group of children performing on grade level by ensuring all of these other supports are working in the community." Canada said he knew that a lot of people disagreed with him on this point. "People think that in the end, if the family home is chaotic and disruptive, the child can't make it out of that," he said. "And I reject that, partly because I've seen it happen. I've seen plenty of kids who've come from pretty dysfunctional families who get pretty beat up and damaged, but they can still make it, and they can still be successful. I admit it's much harder if the parents are not with you, but I don't think that it's at all impossible."

And if Geoffrey Canada wasn't giving up on Shauntel, then Shauntel, for her part, wasn't giving up on Baby College. She came early, she stayed late, she was able to explain the difference between discipline and punishment, she talked to Treasure Lee every night before going to sleep.

From Shauntel's point of view, Baby College was an opportunity to turn her whole life around. Canada saw things a little differently. If Baby College helped Shauntel herself, that was good news. But Baby College wasn't really *for* Shauntel; it was for her unborn daughter. The point of the course—the point of the $1.2 million Canada was spending each year on Baby College—was simply to improve Treasure Lee's unfortunate odds, and the odds of other kids like her. Canada believed that he could get Treasure Lee to college no matter what, but he knew that it would be a lot easier if she stayed out of foster care; and it would be even easier if Shauntel sang with her and told her stories and praised her. Shauntel might never be able to read novels to her daughter, and she would probably never be a big help with her math homework, but she could give her other things: love, warmth, order, the kind of confidence that comes from a close bond with a parent. Given where Shauntel was starting from, that alone would count as a fairly miraculous gift. And it would put Treasure Lee that much further ahead on the day that she entered the Harlem Children's Zone's prekindergarten program and Geoffrey Canada could begin to share with Shauntel the responsibility for Treasure Lee's future success.

VICTOR AND CHERYL HAD already named their unborn baby, just as Shauntel had; she was going to be called Takiyah Forever Boria. During the second brain-development class, when all the parents were making books for their children out of luggage tags, Cheryl wrote "Takiyah" on every page, using different-colored crayons. She and Victor didn't know for sure that they were having a girl, but they both felt certain; a girl was what they wanted. And then on Halloween they went to the clinic and got an ultrasound, and it turned out they were having a boy. They cried a bit when they found out, but by the time the next Saturday rolled around, they were getting used to the idea. "We're going to have to be more stern," Cheryl told me. "If we don't tell him what to do in life, he's going to be out on the street, and we're trying to avoid that early."

Cheryl was a bit tired that morning, and she said she hadn't slept well. The night before, she and Victor had watched a bootleg DVD of *Saw III,* which Victor had bought from a sidewalk vendor on 125th Street for five dollars. It was bloody and scary, but they both loved it. (Victor's capsule review: "*Saw* is the best, *Saw II* is the extremely best, and *Saw III* is just magnificent.") Cheryl had a nightmare after the movie, but it wasn't about mutilation. "I dreamed that a girl tried to take Victor," she said. "I was crying in my sleep, and then I woke up and he was still there, and I said, 'Oh, good, he's mine! He's mine!'"

That class, the sixth week of Baby College, was a happy one for them both. After breakfast, they watched an educational film for parents, starring Jamie Lee Curtis, called *Ready to Learn,* and while it played, the lights low, Cheryl put her arm around Victor. He nestled into her shoulder, and they pressed their foreheads together as they watched the actress talk about the importance of reading, talking, playing, and singing with your child. After the movie, Marilyn Joseph called up a couple dozen parents who had had perfect attendance for the first three classes. Cheryl was one of them, and she got a twenty-five-dollar check—"a small token from the Harlem Children's Zone to you, to say thank you," Marilyn said. It was a good day.

The next week, though, on the way to Baby College, trouble found Victor and Cheryl again. They slept at Cheryl's house in Englewood the night before, and in the morning, they took the bus over the George Washington Bridge and then got on the subway to come down to PS 197. On the platform, Victor turned on his portable radio, and the two of them sat there listening to it quietly, still sleepy. A police officer approached them and told Victor to turn it down.

"Why?" Victor asked. Later, looking back, he regretted saying anything. He wasn't rude about it, he said, but maybe his voice was a little too defiant. The officer arrested him and charged him with disturbing the peace and resisting arrest and took him to Central Booking, down on Center Street. He had to stay there all night, sitting in a smelly cell on a hard bench between two men who exchanged threats with each other, right past Victor, for hours. The same thought kept going through his mind all night: "But I was on my way to Baby College!" When he'd been in trouble before, he had usually deserved it. This time, here he was trying to become a good father, and yet that didn't seem to make a difference.

In the morning, Victor was sent up to the courtroom to be arraigned. He had a bad feeling. He had two active warrants and a sketchy arrest record, and he figured the judge would throw the book at him. When his name was called and he got up to approach the bench, he was too depressed to act tough. He looked contrite because he felt contrite, and, incredibly, that stirred something in the judge. She told him he was on thin ice, but she dismissed his case—after all, he had only been playing a radio—and she cleared his record, and the next thing Victor knew, the court officers were taking off his handcuffs.

"She said, 'Stay out of trouble,'" Victor recounted the next weekend, still a little stunned at his good fortune, "and I was like, 'Yes, all right, I will.' And it's true, I will. As soon as the officer says, 'Turn your radio down,' I'm turning it *off*. He says, 'Come here,' and I'm going to go. I'm going to live life correctly."

He'd been given a second chance—or maybe this was his third, or fourth; he'd lost count. He was determined not to blow it.

A week later, the parents of cycle 21 assembled in the gymnasium at the Harlem Children's Zone headquarters on 125th Street for their graduation. It was Cheryl's eighteenth birthday, and halfway through the ceremony, Victor was called up onstage with the other fathers. He was feeling something special. There were a dozen fathers graduating, and each of them was invited to say a few words. Victor turned to Francisca, his outreach worker, who was up onstage with him, and asked if he could go last.

When his turn came, he strode to the lectern, looking sharp in a white button-down shirt and dark jeans. There were about 300 people in the gym at this point, all sitting on folding chairs facing the stage—103 graduating parents, plus family and friends, the entire Baby College staff, and some of the top managers of the Harlem Children's Zone. Geoffrey Canada sat in the front row, with George Khaldun, his deputy, on one side of him and on the other, his wife, Yvonne, and his son Geoffrey Jr.

Victor looked out at the crowd and swallowed.

"OK, hello," he said into the microphone. "How is everybody doing?" His voice, high and nervous, filled the gym. "Um, my name is Victor, and I had a great, great time at Baby College. It was one of my best times ever." There was a little applause. The graduates were in the center section, sitting by class, everyone decked out in white and looking clean-cut.

"I would like to call up Cheryl Waite," Victor said. "Could everybody give her a round of applause? Today is her birthday."

Cheryl looked surprised and a little embarrassed, and she slid out of her row and walked down the aisle to where Victor stood watching her.

When she got up onstage, Victor turned back to the microphone. "And the surprise part of this," he said, "and I'm so nervous, is because I would like to propose."

The gym erupted in shouts and hoots. Cheryl started laughing and crying at the same time. Someone in the back yelled at Victor to get down on one knee. So he did. He held the microphone in one hand, and with the other, he took Cheryl's hand. "Cheryl Waite," he said, "I love you, and you're my world—the only one in this world. So I just want to know, will you marry me?"

Pandemonium, applause, more shouting, grandmothers crying. Geoffrey Canada, in the front row, got to his feet and clapped. Somewhere in there, Cheryl said yes, and she and Victor embraced in front of everyone.

Victor wasn't quite ready to give up the mike. "I'm extremely excited," he said, looking out at the crowd. "A lot is about to happen. We've just begun. So thank you."

George Khaldun turned to Canada. "Well," he said, "that was a first."

VICTOR MANAGED TO make graduation day particularly memorable, but for the parents who had made it through all nine weeks of Baby College, it was already special. The gym was decorated with balloons and streamers, and at the beginning of the ceremony, the graduates all came in together, walking in formation, doing a little stutter-step and clapping along with "Enjoy," a breathy ballad by Janet Jackson, which was playing over the public-address system. After Victor's dramatic flourish, each class took a turn onstage for a brief performance, usually a children's song. They all went over well, especially "The Itsy-Bitsy Spider," which Shauntel and Darryl and the other expecting parents delivered in full voice, waving cardboard cutouts of rain and suns and waterspouts. The mothers in the French class stole the show, though: they wore colorful African dresses and headscarves, and for their performance they did a raucous, hip-shaking traditional dance—punctuated by the mild-mannered Khaldun jumping onstage and shimmying along with them. ("We went back to the motherland, didn't we?" Marilyn Joseph said from the lectern afterward, laughing. "Our chief operating officer took us back to the motherland.")

After the dance, Canada took to the stage, offered his own congratulations to the parents of cycle 21, and explained that he hoped that Baby College would be just the beginning for them and their children. "We created the Harlem Children's Zone for you," he said. "We are trying to create a future here in Harlem for your children that will be unlike anything you will find anyplace else in America." And then, just as he had done at the Promise Academy lottery, he laid out the deal: "We're going to do what we can do for your child, and you are going to have to do for your child what you have been taught. If you do that, I will guarantee we can get your child into college. We won't just get them *in* college; we will see that they graduate from college." He told the parents that if he didn't keep up his end of the bargain, they could track him down and call him a liar. "I've been with this organization for twenty-three years," he said—referring to both Rheedlen and the Harlem Children's Zone. "I've been here longer than some of you have been alive. So you know where to find me."

Three days earlier, Damita had given birth to a healthy baby boy, and after the ceremony, Darryl walked from one knot of people to the next, showing off a color photocopy of a few photos from the hospital: Darryl in green scrubs in the delivery room; Damita beaming; Darryl Jr. holding his new baby brother. Angelique was in a good mood, too. An apartment had come through, and in another month, at the end of December, she and her daughter Bria were supposed to be moving out of the shelter and into their new home. Victor and Cheryl had their own housing plans—that Monday, they were going to try to move into Covenant House, the shelter for homeless teenagers on the west side of Midtown. Cheryl said that if they stayed there for thirty days, they'd be eligible for a city apartment. Victor still wanted to move down south, but the Covenant House idea seemed to him like a good interim plan, until he could get things worked out in North Carolina. Shauntel brought her sister-in-law to the graduation, and introduced her proudly to the rest of the expecting class. Treasure Lee was due in two more months.

▪

BABY COLLEGE ISN'T the only program of its kind in the country. But nationwide, organized efforts to improve the parenting skills of low-income parents have a record that is uneven at best. A study published in 1999 that compared several home-visiting programs from around the country discovered that most of the programs had a hard time recruiting and retaining families. When graduates of a variety of programs were compared to control groups, it usually turned out that only a few families had benefited from the visits, and even then, the benefits were modest. As for Baby College, there isn't much hard evidence to prove how much of a difference the program makes; the sparse data that the Harlem Children's Zone has collected so far doesn't yet show conclusively that the children of Baby College graduates have a significant advantage over other Harlem children. For now, the evidence of its success is mostly anecdotal (though the anecdotes can be quite persuasive).

There are a handful of other programs that seem to produce real and lasting effects. In her forthcoming book, *Changing the Odds*, Susan B. Neuman, a professor at the University of Michigan School of Education, identifies three initiatives with superior results: Early Head Start, a federally funded program that offers low-income families with young children services that can include home visits from professional social workers, parenting classes, and assistance with government and medical bureaucracies; Avance, a nine-month program for Spanish-speaking parents, mostly immigrants from Mexico, that was founded in San Antonio in 1973 and now operates in 10 cities and rural areas in Texas, with a separate chapter in Los Angeles; and the Nurse-Family Partnership, which sends trained nurses to visit and counsel poor mothers during and after their pregnancies. A fourth program, which Neuman doesn't mention but which also has a long history and respectable results, is the Parent-Child Home Program, a home-visiting initiative for low-income parents of two- and three-year-old children that operates in more than 150 sites around the country.

The $1.2 million a year that the Harlem Children's Zone spends on Baby College works out to be about $3,000 per graduating parent. There is no government support for the program, so the entire amount comes out of the organization's operating budget. Although the overall price tag may seem high, the cost is comparable to other successful programs; the Nurse-Family Partnership spends about $4,500 a year, per family, and the Parent-Child Home Program costs about $2,500 per child per year. And in fact, the Baby College budget is quite lean. Outreach workers and administrators generally make between $18,000 and $32,000 a year. The instructors are paid about $20 an hour, and the childcare workers are paid about half that. About $100,000 each cycle goes in some way to the parents themselves, which includes lunch and breakfast each Saturday, the $10 and $25 gift certificates that are raffled off after every class, and the $100 check that each parent receives upon completing the course. Some of that money goes for the lavish gift baskets that are given to every expecting parent at graduation, packed with baby clothes and blankets; some goes for the safety equipment that is given out to every parent after the safety class, including socket plugs, cabinet locks, a baby gate, and an infant thermometer. There are extra expenditures on an as-needed basis: halfway through the course, Victor took Francisca, his outreach worker, aside and told her that he and Cheryl couldn't afford a crib, so Baby College bought one for them.

The generous budget is an important part of Baby College's success. But another critical factor is its unique culture. In 2002, Richard Weissbourd, a lecturer at the Harvard Graduate School of Education, helped create a program for poor parents in Cambridge, Massachusetts, called the "Let's Talk" Campaign. The program is based on the research of Betty Hart and Todd R. Risley into language development, and it encourages parents to talk more to their children in everyday settings. Weissbourd's outreach workers visit new mothers from local housing projects while they are still on the hospital maternity ward, instruct them about the importance of talking to their children, and give them bibs and wash-cloths printed with the program's "Let's Talk" logo. They follow up with "reading parties" and seminars. It all sounds good on paper, but so far, Weissbourd says, it's not really working with African American parents. "To some of these parents, I think, this is straight-out cultural imperialism," he says. "It's mainstream afflu-ent white folks telling parents of color how to parent." Christopher Jencks and Meredith Phillips, in 1998, warned of the same prob-lem: "As a practical matter," they wrote, "whites cannot tell black parents to change their practices without provoking charges of ethnocentrism, racism, and much else."

In contrast, everyone at Baby College — every administrator, every instructor, every childcare worker — is black or Hispanic, with African Americans making up a solid majority. (The parents are almost all black or Hispanic, too, although there was one young woman from Japan in cycle 21; she had moved to the United States, and Harlem, because she liked and admired African American cul-ture, and she was now raising a baby with her black boyfriend.) The feel of Baby College was intimate and accepting: laughter and jokes were everywhere; when music played, it was always hip-hop or R & B; the language used was casual and familiar.

White America didn't come up very often at Baby College, but when it did, it was regarded with a certain distance. The idea wasn't to adopt middle-class white culture, or even to imitate it — it was more like poaching an idea or two, borrowing some tricks and cus-toms, like adapting a recipe from a foreign cuisine. One day over lunch in the cafeteria, as Russell, the instructor, called out raffle numbers in his booming bass voice, Francisca, Victor's outreach worker, talked with me about going to the children's section of the Barnes & Noble bookstore on the Upper West Side with her daugh-ter and seeing white parents sitting on the floor with their kids, reading, books strewn everywhere. "Our parents don't think you can do that," she said. Another day, an instructor named Wanda Osorio told her class that she sometimes heard parents in Harlem dismiss the time-out method as a white thing: "Ah, come on with the time-out," she said, imitating the complaint. "Time-out's for white people. Get out of here with that." But that was the wrong way to look at it, she responded. Time-outs *worked*, no matter who you were.

Often when a parenting program fails or falls short, the blame is placed on the parents themselves—they won't show up, or they're resistant to change, or they're too defensive in the face of criticism. The parents of cycle 21, though, seemed eager to learn. They were not the best-prepared parents in Harlem—far from it. The intensive recruiting that Marilyn Joseph's outreach workers did meant that there was little of the self-selection that happens in some voluntary programs, where the parents who sign up are already the most-engaged parents, who need help the least. The parents in Baby College had *more* problems than parents in other programs, even than other programs in the Harlem Children's Zone. There were more teenage parents, more parents on welfare, more homeless parents, more parents with prison records and parents with histories of substance abuse. And yet the atmosphere of Baby College somehow made them feel open and confident, as eager for new child-raising information as the parents at the Canadas' playground in suburban Valley Stream. The staff members never acted as though they were doing the parents a favor, and parents weren't made to feel as though they should be grateful for the program. Quite the reverse, in fact: the parents were made to feel appreciated, like *they* were the ones doing a good civic deed.

One of the rhetorical devices used by Baby College staff—both outreach workers and instructors—was to describe the program as a conversation. When recruiters went knocking on doors, part of their opening rap was to say, "We want you to come and share your expertise." And that approach extended into the classroom, where instructors solicited ideas and opinions from parents, offering plenty of praise and sparing amounts of criticism. In the end, the real goal of Baby College was not to impart information. It was to change the parents' whole vision of themselves as parents, to encourage them to accept the idea that their child's education and intellectual development began at birth, if not before, and that they, as parents, had a crucial role to play in that development. If they got that—and by the end of cycle 21, it seemed that most of the parents did—the details would be more likely to work themselves out.

4 Contamination

THE RELATIONSHIP between race and poverty in the United States has long been a complicated and contentious one. There are more poor white Americans than poor black Americans, a fact that some observers cite to argue that the common perception of poverty as a black problem is wrong and misleading. But it is also true that the official poverty rate among blacks, at more than 24 percent, is three times higher than the poverty rate among whites, which is about 8 percent. And black poverty has different characteristics than white poverty. Black Americans are more likely than white Americans to be consistently poor for a long period; when whites experience poverty, it is more likely to be for a limited time. Downward mobility is more common among blacks than whites: a 2007 study found that 45 percent of children born into "solidly middle class" black families slipped into poverty as adults; only 16 percent of white children followed the same unhappy path. The numbers go on: Poor black Americans are much more likely to live in high-poverty neighborhoods than poor white Americans. African Americans make up about a quarter of the total population living below the poverty line, but if you look only at children who grow up in long-term poverty—meaning kids who were poor for at least nine years during their childhoods—that group is 80 percent black.

The formal mission statement of the Harlem Children's Zone never mentions race. Officially, the organization is dedicated to improving the lives of all poor American children, whatever the color of their skin. But at the same time, it's clearly no accident that Geoffrey Canada has chosen to work in a neighborhood that is almost all black, or that he is running an organization whose ranks, including senior management, are mostly populated by African Americans. The mission that Canada has taken on is not just about Harlem; it's also about black America. In a very real way, he is trying to deliver his race as much as he is trying to save a neighborhood.

That fact has something to do with Canada's understanding of those national statistics, but it has more to do with his own life story—a story that is inextricable from the history of race in America. His ancestors were slaves and sharecroppers in the South, and on both his mother's and his father's side, his family came north as part of the great migration of black Americans. He is a product of the black church and of the black postwar ghettos, and his political awakening, when it came, was entirely racialized. From his teenage years, he saw the world as irredeemably divided by race, us versus them—and it was painfully obvious to him that *them* was winning. Canada's view of the racial divide has tempered with age, but what gets him up in the morning is still the connection he has with black children, and the responsibility he feels for their fate. To a startling degree for a man who has risen so far, his motivations and passions are not very different from those of the boy he was.

Canada was born in the South Bronx, in the winter of 1952, into a family that was already starting to fall apart. His mother, Mary Williams, had married McCalister Canada, his father, at the age of twenty-one, in a rash moment, a fleeting act of rebellion against her family and its suffocating rules. Mary's parents, Leonard and

Lydia Williams, were people of God, fierce Baptists who migrated from North Carolina to Harlem in the 1920s and then, after ten years of Leonard blocking hats and peddling vegetables and Lydia baking pies to sell to their neighbors for extra cash, moved on to the Bronx, which they thought would be a safer and cleaner place to raise their children. Mary, the oldest, was a bright, opinionated girl, and when she turned seventeen her parents sent her away to school, a four-year college in North Carolina. She was the first person in her immediate family to go to college—her father had dropped out of the fifth grade—and for a moment, her future seemed full of promise and possibility. But after two years, Leonard and Lydia had to tell their daughter that her college money had run out, and in 1947 Mary came back to the Bronx, looking for work. Instead she found Mac Canada, a smoker and a drinker and a gambler and the most exciting man she had ever met.

Mac's family were southern Pentecostals, wild and tough and a little mysterious. The whole clan had fled to Pennsylvania and New York a generation earlier from the small Appalachian town of Vicar's Switch, West Virginia, after a white man in a store called two of the Canada brothers niggers and they responded with their fists—a bold, perilous move in the Jim Crow South. When Mary met Mac, there were a lot of rumors flying around about his family in the Bronx, none of them good. Leonard and Lydia didn't need to know the details. One look at Mac and they knew he was trouble. They sat Mary down and told her not to marry him, told her he'd break her heart and ruin her life, but of course she married him anyway, and of course they were right. She had four sons in quick succession, first Dan, then John, then Geoffrey, then Reuben, and then Mac was gone, vanished into drink and dissolution. He never sent a dollar to help raise his boys. He never even sent a birthday card.

With Mac gone and her parents unsympathetic, Mary slipped out of struggling-working-class life and into poverty. The city wouldn't let her into a housing project—she was a single mother, and the projects were for married couples only—so for a few years she moved her young children from one cramped apartment to another, trying to stay ahead of the rent and the bills. She went on public assistance, and though it was against the rules, she took in sewing and did other jobs here and there to supplement welfare's meager living. She was able to survive, barely, as a seamstress and an occasional secretary, picking up what she could when she could, until 1959, when her youngest boy, Reuben, answered the door to the knock of a welfare inspector. The woman asked where his mother was, and Reuben, only four years old and not knowing any better than to tell the truth, said his mother was at work. That meant the welfare checks quit coming, and that meant the family was down to twenty-five dollars a week. And that meant they had to move to Union Avenue.

Everyone was poor on Union Avenue, a litter-strewn street of low-rise walkup tenements cutting through the heart of the South Bronx, but even on Union Avenue, Mary's family was poorer than most. A single mother, four sons, never enough money, feeding her boys with rice and beans and powdered milk and government-surplus cheese and government-surplus peanut butter. Meat maybe twice a week. A soda for each boy on Friday as a treat. No babysitter, no family around, which meant that the boys stayed alone after school from the age of eight or nine, fixing their own lunch and letting themselves in and out of the apartment.

But in one important way, Mary Canada was different from most of the mothers on Union Avenue. She was educated, still pining for her lost college years, and she bombarded her sons with books and educational experiences before they could even walk. She would read Tom Swift adventure stories to young Geoff and his brothers every night and by day take them to the library and the Bronx Zoo and the Museum of Natural History. ("My mother was famous for finding out when things were free," Canada recalled.) She had grown up immersed in the strict values of the striving black working class. She rebelled against some of those values, and in many ways she and her family suffered for it. But she also did something that very few welfare mothers in the Bronx were doing in the 1950s and 1960s: she passed on her parents' aspirational values to her own children.

IN RECENT YEARS, African American scholars have disagreed strongly over whether investigating the potential contributions of black home life to the racial achievement gap is a good idea. Glenn Loury, an accomplished black economist who teaches at Brown University, has been outspoken in arguing that the political price of publicly examining black parenting outweighs the potential benefits. At a 2006 conference at Harvard on the achievement gap, Loury gave a cautionary speech warning the conferees that they were "engaged in the construction of a narrative"—and if they chose to make it a narrative about problems in black homes, rather than inequities in the economic structure of the country, they would in effect be giving comfort to the enemy and ignoring the true problem. "What's really going on," Loury said, "is that society as a whole has failed to commit itself to the development of the human resources of all of its people."

But there were other scholars at the conference who were determined to look at cultural explanations for the gap. Over the two days of meetings, Ronald Ferguson, the Harvard economist who organized the conference and leads the school's cross-disciplinary Achievement Gap Initiative, raised a number of politically awkward observations and hypotheses about racial differences: Children of African American college graduates, he reported, do no better on standardized tests than children of white high school dropouts. Between 1988 and 1992, he went on, the number of black seventeen-year-olds who said they read every day for pleasure dropped sharply, from 35 percent to 15 percent, and in the same period, test scores among black youth, which had been rising rapidly since World War II, reached a plateau and, by some measures, began to decline. This plateau began just when sales of hip-hop music took off; Ferguson, who is black, mused that maybe there was a connection. Ferguson's list of disconcerting statistics continued: Black children from well-off families are twice as likely to have a TV in their bedroom as white kids from comparable families. White kindergarten students with a college-educated mother have, on average, twice as many children's books in their home as black kindergarten students with a college-educated mother.

Loury's response was that there was no point lingering over leisure-time statistics while there are so many straightforward structural ways in which blacks and poor people are discriminated against in public education. He pointed to the fact that under current work rules, the most experienced teachers are allowed to choose where they teach, and since most state and city contracts offer teachers no bonus or incentive for teaching in a school with a high population of disadvantaged children, the best teachers tend to go where they are needed the least. Unlike TV watching and hip-hop listening, Loury argues, these are problems that are in the political arena, and they have political solutions. So before analyzing (and publicly criticizing) the fine points of African American parenting styles, Loury said, let's pass laws that fix those structural inequities—enforce national achievement standards, amend teacher contracts to offer financial incentives that encourage the best teachers to teach the students who need their help the most, rectify the imbalances in federal financing for poor students, which right now varies greatly from state to state. Not only are cultural issues a less effective place to put society's reforming energies, Loury argued, but engaging in the kind of analysis Ferguson does lets the government, and white Americans in general, off the hook.

Ferguson is very much conscious of this tension. Since 1999, he has been surveying young black and white Americans about their experiences in the classroom, at home, and with friends, and looking through the data for new racial patterns. He says he knows that discussing his research in public, in front of a mixed audience, may well create political problems. "It will add to racial stigmas," he admitted when I met with him in his office a few weeks after the Harvard conference, "and it may give whites more excuses not to support black communities: 'Look, they shot themselves in the foot. *We* didn't do this. They aren't reading to their kids! It's not my problem. Don't ask me to pay more taxes to support that.'"

But even if the project he had embarked on turned out to be politically perilous, Ferguson said, he felt it was essential to start talking to black parents about issues of racial disparities in parenting. "There really is a dilemma here," he said. "I don't see a way to get the attention of the black community, to the degree that I think we need their attention, without having some discourse that is racially conscious." He allowed himself a half smile. "I just wish I could do it in a way that the white community couldn't listen in."

GEOFFREY CANADA, for his part, understands why many social scientists and black activists are reluctant to identify parenting as a cause of the racial achievement gap. But in Harlem, he believes, the simple reality is that most of the neighborhood's poor, black parents are not adequately preparing their infants and children to be educated. And to him, the practical advantages of addressing that fact overshadow the political costs. If there are, in fact, specific mechanisms by which poverty in parents produces bad outcomes in children—mechanisms like speech, or cultural messages, or certain parenting practices—then there's a chance that he and his staff, in Baby College and elsewhere, can target the very behaviors and ideas and tendencies in poor families that are having an outsized negative effect on the life chances of their children.

Canada knows that the struggles of parents in Harlem are in part an issue of resources. Few of the parents he works with can afford the kind of toys and books and educational games that he buys for Geoffrey Jr., and so one thing Baby College does is simply provide parents with those items. But the bigger problem, to Canada's mind, is that poor parents in Harlem generally don't see life as a constant series of educational opportunities, and middle-class and upper-middle-class parents in the rest of the city do. "In homes where people are conscious about this, it happens every day," Canada told me. "Every minute, a parent is saying, 'How can I say more to help this kid understand his environment?'"

We were talking in his office on 125th Street on a warm afternoon in late June. The previous day, Stan Druckenmiller, the chairman of the Harlem Children's Zone board, had offered Canada a pair of field-level seats to the Yankees game, and Canada had taken his son to watch the Yankees defeat the Atlanta Braves. "It was very hot," Canada recalled, "and Geoffrey was trying to figure out whether to take his hat off or leave his hat on. When he took the hat off, he felt cooler. But that didn't make sense to him, because the hat was shielding him from the sun. I explained that it felt cool because he was sweating on the top of his head, and the water was evaporating when the wind blew, and that was how air conditioning worked. Now, that's not a science class, that's just having a conversation with your father. Do I believe Geoffrey will remember that for the rest of his life? Absolutely, I do. He heard it in a way that he understood it."

To Canada, it was just one example of the kind of interaction that a certain group of parents in the city and the country have with their children all the time, and that "our parents," as he calls them, the parents in Harlem he is targeting with his programs, do not.

It was partly a question of knowledge—his parents might not know the physics of evaporation well enough to explain it to a child. But it was something more than that too. "For lots of children, in particular black children, their parents believe the children are being fresh when they talk back and when they question," Canada explained. "They think they're being disrespectful. You're not supposed to ask why. And even when we try, in Baby College, to give parents some larger, broader thinking about this issue of opening up the conversation to children, they often think that we're trying to get them to act in a way that they're not going to be respected."

Many Harlem parents, Canada said, start from the belief that education is something that takes place in school, when you're sitting down at a desk with a pen and a notebook. But the new and growing class of very involved, very focused parents want to cram education into almost every moment. These parents tend to view life as a race, and just as the sociologist Annette Lareau described, they do everything they can to give their children a leg up in that race, even if they often don't realize, or won't admit, that that's what they're doing. Every day, Canada works with kids who are being brought up by the first group of parents. And then each night he goes home to a product of the second group—a member of America's new class of miniature superachievers.

In the fall of 2005, when Geoffrey Jr. was seven, Canada started reading *Harry Potter and the Order of the Phoenix* to him every night before putting him to bed. "I have been stunned by the evolution of Geoffrey's ability to sit still and pay attention," he told me. "When we got to the second book, I noticed he started reading along with me, and it's already clear to me that he is going to be a different kind of reader because of this experience; having to do with nothing else than every night when I'm home on time we go upstairs and I read him four or five pages of Harry Potter.

"I think that there are a bunch of children getting that experience—and what a deep, rich intellectual experience that is. But if you added up sales to black families . . ." Canada's voice trailed off for a moment. "Put it this way: There are 10 million people reading Harry Potter in this country. I will tell you maybe 9.85 million of them are white kids. So now there's a whole group of Americans who have an ability to either read or listen to 800 pages of information as part of a story. And then there's this whole other group of kids"—the kids he sees every day, whose main source of entertainment is television—"who have to be stimulated every fifteen or twenty seconds or they lose their focus."

There's nothing natural about the process of preparing your child to be competitive in this new world, Canada says. It might feel natural to upper-middle-class white parents, because they've been culturally saturated by a certain set of values and priorities: prenatal vitamins, Baby Einstein videos, competitive preschools, piano lessons, early admission to college, summer internships. But many black Americans, he says, have been outside of that club for years—forever, in fact. "They don't even know how the club operates. They don't know any of the subtle or nonsubtle ways that you prepare a kid to enter into the club." What seems simple and obvious to people on the Upper West Side or in Park Slope is not always obvious in Harlem. "People think you should just be able to go into one of these families, sit down and talk to the mother and say, 'Listen, these are the six things you have to do with your kid'"—read to your child every day, don't feed them junk food, turn off the TV, take them to the museum once in a while, and so on—"but it's not like that at all."

Canada reached for an analogy from a series of front-page newspaper articles on diabetes that had been published earlier that month in the *New York Times*. The series described diabetes as an epidemic in the city's poor neighborhoods. One article, which hit especially close to home for Canada, was set in East Harlem, and it followed several poor diabetes patients through their days as they flouted the advice of their doctors to eat less and exercise more, despite the very real danger of amputation or even death. "Listen, if I want to eat a piece of cake, I'm going to eat it," one diabetic was quoted as saying. "No doctor can tell me what to eat. I'm going to eat it, because I'm hungry. We got too much to worry about. We got to worry about tomorrow. We got to worry about the rent. We got to worry about our jobs. I'm not going to worry about a piece of cake."

Canada knew what most of the *Times*'s readers thought when they read that article. "People say, 'What's *wrong* with these people?'" he said. "But the story actually explained the day-to-day issues that people face that make it almost impossible for them to make the sane, rational decision that you or I might make in this same situation. And it's the same thing with this issue of culture. It seems like rationally you should be able to sit down and say, 'Don't you understand that this is your kids' future, and you need to act differently?' But these folks are so beaten down that they're not able to just sit down and understand this in a couple of hours or weeks."

WHEN CANADA LOOKS at his own family history, and his wife, Yvonne's, it becomes clear to him that the transformation, when it happens, can take generations. Canada's mother saw childhood as a process of constant education, and all of her children went to college. In Yvonne's family, things didn't progress in the same way. Her grandparents were poor and uneducated and rural, and her parents were poor and uneducated and urban. Her mother, an alcoholic, never read to Yvonne and her brothers and sisters when they were growing up, and none of them went to college as young adults. (Yvonne did go, but later in life.) Now Yvonne's siblings are all dead before their time, one from AIDS, one from drugs, a third whose body was dragged out of the Harlem River, all gone except for Yvonne. And Geoff and Yvonne are hovering over her nieces and nephews, who are mostly teenagers, and trying to pass on to them the middle-class cultural values that they were never exposed to as children: stay in school; stay away from drink and drugs; work hard; don't get pregnant; get married if you do. Canada is under no illusions that this is going to be an easy process—just like it isn't easy to redirect the kids in his programs in Harlem. "It's not something you can give somebody in a week or a month," he said. "It takes years and years of beating kids up with this set of values for it to become part of their understanding."

Only about a third of the parents of the children in his programs, Canada estimates, have what he calls "that middle-class set of aspirations." The rest, whether they're working class or on some sort of public assistance, have not adopted the Harry Potter values, the values that say that your children's education is your own responsibility, that you should use all the resources of the community to improve them. It is not that they are not good parents, Canada says. "They just don't know. No one told them that your kid is slipping behind because you're not doing this sort of thing. And it's hard to just think up a new set of values by yourself."

Social commentators from Charles Murray to Bill Cosby have in recent years defined the problems of American ghettos as a matter, primarily, of misplaced values. In the *Wall Street Journal* in 2005, Murray wrote, "Unemployment in the underclass is not caused by lack of jobs or of job skills, but by the inability to get up every morning and go to work." Canada talks about values, too, but he sees the bad decisions that many Harlem parents make as a natural consequence of their environment and their history, rather than as a moral failure—a problem, like their children's lousy reading scores, that has a distinct cause and a clear (if difficult) solution.

Public critiques of ghetto values have a way of veering toward a criticism of urban black culture. When Cosby delivered his much-discussed speech on inner-city dysfunction to an audience of black leaders in 2004, he blamed high crime and unemployment rates not only on widespread illegitimacy and lax parenting, but also on black slang, baggy pants, "people with their hat on backwards," and "names like Shaniqua, Shaligua, Mohammed, and all that crap."

Canada's own upbringing, which was steeped in the values and traditions of African American street culture, has put him in a different position on this issue. "It's easy to see black children as purely having problems and issues," he says. "But what you miss is all the richness of the culture." While he wants Harlem's children to embrace a certain set of middle-class values, he doesn't want them to reject completely the values and habits of Harlem. In contrast to most social critics, there is plenty in the culture of the ghetto that Canada likes and admires.

WHEN CANADA WAS growing up in the South Bronx in the 1950s and early 1960s, the neighborhood was almost entirely African American, and Union Avenue was almost entirely populated by mothers and children. Some mothers had boyfriends, and some boyfriends stuck around for a few months or a few years, but actual fathers were a rare species. In their absence, the block was ruled by teenagers, fifteen- and sixteen-year-old boys who called themselves the Young Disciples. They taught the younger boys to fight—*made* them fight, in fact, pitting them against one another as a rite of passage, forcing them to learn the code of the street so they would be prepared to defend Union Avenue, if it should ever come to that. When Canada's family first moved to the block, he had never been in a fight before, and he couldn't believe that at the age of seven he was supposed to know how to defend himself. But after the big kids pushed him into his first fight, with another seven-year-old named David, he decided it wasn't so bad. And it was worth it for the privilege of hanging out on the block, where it seemed like there was always something wild and exciting going on.

He soon came to love Union Avenue. He loved watching the action and hated when his mother called him inside for dinner or bed. Under the tutelage of the Young Disciples, Canada learned how to fight for real—how to size up his opponent, how to lean into a punch, how to move his feet—and he learned the code of the block, and soon that code came to make more sense to him than anything else did. Your friends were what mattered. You had their back no matter what. You'd fight to defend them, literally to the death if that was what it took. Outsiders weren't to be trusted. Never show weakness. Never back down. The block could be cruel and the block could be violent, but Canada felt like there was no place and no idea more important. Union Avenue was the whole world.

The only other thing that counted, a little, was school. The young kids all went to PS 99 on Intervale Avenue, a couple of blocks away. Students there were tracked, split up into ability levels, as they were in every school in New York at the time, and Canada was placed in 4–1, the highest class in fourth grade, and then 5–1 and then 6–1. At first he liked the way this felt, like he was special, smarter than his brothers, smarter than just about everybody. But in truth, he didn't really feel like he belonged in 4–1 and 5–1 and 6–1. The kids in his advanced classes, the smart kids, the well-behaved kids, he couldn't figure them out. They didn't know how to throw a punch. Sometimes Canada had to fight some loud-mouth or other to defend the honor of the top class, just so they wouldn't get picked on all the time. His friends from the block were all in the lower-scoring classes, 4–3s and 5–4s, and things looked even worse for them; they were barely ten years old and they had already been quietly written off by the school system. Canada saw it happen to his brothers, and he saw it happen to his friends: the teachers stopped trying to teach them anything, and they soon gave up trying to learn.

When it came time for junior high, his friends from the block all went to the local junior high school, JHS 136. But JHS 136 didn't offer an advanced seventh-grade class, and Canada needed one: on his sixth-grade reading test, he scored a 2.5, meaning that he was reading on the level of an average child in twelfth grade. JHS 133, six blocks away, had a "special progress" class for the top students, and so Canada's mother sent him there, and for the first time since he had moved to the block, he found himself with no allies; there wasn't a single kid from Union Avenue in the school.

Every day he walked the six blocks back and forth between his two worlds. At school, the kids in his special-progress class were joining academic clubs and studying hard and talking about college. On the block, Canada and his friends hung out on the stoop like they always had. At twelve or thirteen they started smoking marijuana and drinking wine, screw-top swill like Gypsy Rose or Thunderbird or Swiss Up. They went to parties and tried to find girls and got into brawls. Canada carried a knife, a popular brand of switchblade called a K55.

Canada liked his classes well enough, and he did care about his grades, but not as much as he cared about the streets. "My body was at JHS 133, but my heart was on Union Avenue," he told me. "If I failed a test in school, I was hurt about that, but not nearly as hurt as if I failed a test on Union Avenue. The set of values and standards that I learned there became so important to me that I would do anything to keep from being pulled out of touch with them." As he made his way through junior high, the block became still more compelling and the classroom less so. By ninth grade, he was barely paying attention in school.

In the winter of 1967, after three years at JHS 133, Canada started applying to high schools. There were only a very few New York City public high schools with good academic reputations and competitive admissions exams: Bronx Science, Stuyvesant, Brooklyn Tech. Canada took the tests, halfheartedly, and he failed them all. That meant his options were down to two, both in his zone in the Bronx: Clinton High and Morris High. He knew from the older kids on the block that they were violent and brutal places. Morris was one of the worst schools in the city. The first time someone Canada knew personally was shot, it happened at Morris. And Clinton, an all-boys school, was even harsher, his friends told him. He was convinced that if he went to one of those schools, he wouldn't get out alive. Maybe not literally: he thought he would probably survive physically. But he also knew that surviving would take all his time and attention. Posturing and fighting and threatening and not backing down would be a full-time job. If he graduated, it would be into a life like those of the young men he saw around him: crime or unemployment or full-time drinking or all three. And for all his love of the block, Canada knew he wanted more than that.

He saw just one way out. His two older brothers, Dan and John, had recently moved out to Wyandanch, an hour's drive east of New York City, to live with their grandparents, Leonard and Lydia. Could Geoff take refuge there, too? The house was crowded, Canada knew, and he didn't always get along with his grandparents—they were still strict Baptists, and they wouldn't like his smoking and swearing and drinking and fighting. But he also knew that if he stayed in New York, his chances of ever making anything of his life were slim. So Canada mustered his courage and made the call, and his grandfather, a little warily, said yes.

WYANDANCH SEEMED A million miles from the Bronx. Everyone was black; that was the same—Wyandanch was where real-estate agents sent you in the 1960s if you were an aspiring black family trying to escape New York City—but everything else was foreign. Back in the Bronx, Canada and his friends had a uniform for going out: Converse sneakers, Wrangler blue jeans, and gaudy multicolored Italian knit shirts. In Wyandanch, the kids just wore regular, boring clothes. No one knew how to fight, and no one particularly cared what you could do with your fists. They cared about who was in which club and who was friends with whom and which girls weren't speaking to each other—all of the social anxieties of a typical American high school. Canada didn't know what to make of it. He would go back to the Bronx every weekend and get high and put on his Italian knit shirt and his Wrangler jeans and try to explain to his friends just how strange it was—how *country*—out where he was living now.

Wyandanch, at that point, was relatively comfortable and calm. But in the rest of the country, the black race was in great turmoil. Malcolm X was assassinated in 1965, when Canada was in seventh grade at JHS 133. In the summer of 1967, as Canada was moving to Wyandanch, race riots engulfed Newark and Detroit, and the following spring, Martin Luther King was killed. Apart from teachers and cops, Canada had little contact with white people, and he liked it that way. He knew some of them were well meaning, but for the most part, he considered them the enemy. Young black men like him were being beaten in the South, were being sent off in great numbers to die in Vietnam, were being harassed or even killed by the police in New York. Canada didn't believe in coexistence or nonviolence; like most everyone he knew, he thought Martin Lu-

ther King was an Uncle Tom. If any political movement made sense
to him, it was the Black Panthers. Getting some guns and taking
on the police and the racists—that was a program he could get
behind.

In his junior year of high school, Canada was invited as part of
a delegation of Wyandanch youth to take a brief trip to the nearby
town of Dix Hills. It was a miniature cultural exchange. White liberals in Dix Hills were worried about the riots and racial anger
in America, and they thought the answer might be as simple as
a good conversation. Many of them had never really talked with
a black person—though Dix Hills was only five miles north of
Wyandanch, just across the Long Island Expressway, it was all
white—and so they invited groups from Wyandanch to visit Dix
Hills and chat. Canada wasn't much interested in the chatting part.
He figured the smiling liberals of Dix Hills were probably racists,
just the same as the snarling monsters of Birmingham, Alabama.
But he went along. He wanted to find out what things were like on
the other side of the LIE. And what he saw at the high school in
Dix Hills troubled him. Away from the Bronx, Canada had been
giving more time to his studies, and he was quickly becoming one
of the top students at Wyandanch High. But as he talked to the Dix
Hills kids and looked around at their facilities, he came to realize
that Wyandanch High was actually a pretty lousy school. The average student in Dix Hills, he reckoned, was better prepared than he
and the other kids at the top of the class in Wyandanch were. No
one in Wyandanch, not a single student, was getting a real first-rate
education, and without that, how could they ever keep up with the
kids in Dix Hills? And the friends he had left behind in the Bronx,
trapped by broken families and violent streets and plentiful nar-
cotics—what chance did *they* have?

When he got back to Wyandanch, he felt for the first time a sense
of mission. There was a struggle going on in America—he had
known that for a while—and now he thought he saw a role for
himself. He would become a teacher, maybe even a principal, and

he would devote himself to teaching poor black youth. Of course, this revelation didn't change the main priorities in Canada's seventeen-year-old life, which were smoking pot and drinking wine and going to parties and having a good time. He had figured out how to negotiate the rules and codes of Wyandanch, just as he had mastered the rules and codes of the South Bronx, and by the time he was in his senior year, Canada was the biggest big man on campus: he was athletic, tall, and confident, the captain of the football team, the president of the senior class, and a member of the drama club.

College, though, was a big question mark—his family still didn't have any money for tuition. But he got a lucky break. A local African American chapter of the fraternal order of Masons was offering scholarships to state school to a handful of the top black students in the area, and Canada was one of the young men they chose. He didn't even have to ask—they just reached out and picked him. He applied to the Stony Brook campus of the State University of New York, not far from Wyandanch on Long Island, because he'd heard it was the best party school around. He got in. As an afterthought, he applied to one other school: Bowdoin, a small elite college in Maine. He didn't have any particular interest in going to Maine—to tell the truth, he wasn't exactly sure where it was—but there was a secretary at school, a white woman, who liked Canada and was convinced he belonged there. She told him that if he wrote a personal statement, she'd type it up and fill in the application and send it in. He figured it was easier to say yes than no, so he scribbled down a few sentences and gave it to her and didn't give it another thought. A letter came a little later, and he put it in the bottom drawer of his dresser and made plans for Stony Brook.

He spent the summer after he graduated from high school working in the mailroom of a big textile company in Manhattan by day and at night hanging out with his friends and with Joyce, his future wife. It was a good summer, and time passed quickly, and it wasn't until July that he realized he hadn't heard anything

from Stony Brook recently. He called the school's admissions office
and asked what was going on. The woman who answered the
phone checked the files and came back with some disturbing news:
there was no record of his admission to the school. He was not, in
fact, an incoming freshman, as he had thought. No Masonic scholarship. Nothing.

This was a problem for two reasons. The first, of course, was that
Stony Brook was the school he had his heart set on. The second
problem was more serious: Vietnam. This was 1970, and if you
were an eighteen-year-old African American male without plans
to go to college, you'd get your draft letter and find yourself in Da
Nang before you knew it. And Canada had no interest in going to
Vietnam: the war had already killed and wounded boys he knew,
from Union Avenue and from Wyandanch. So it was Vietnam that
sent Canada off to root around in the bottom drawer of his dresser,
and Vietnam that got him to open the letter from Bowdoin and see
that he'd been accepted, and Vietnam that made him call up the
registrar's office and smooth talk them into finding a place for him
in the class of 1974—despite the fact that it was July and the letter
said he was supposed to declare his intention to attend Bowdoin
before May 1. As Labor Day 1970 approached, Canada was as surprised as anyone to find himself heading not to Long Island's best
party school but to Bowdoin College, which had been solemnly
educating the privileged sons of the white northeastern establishment for more than 150 years.

Canada didn't do a lot of research about Bowdoin before getting
on the plane in New York, and when he arrived on campus, the
surprises kept coming. He hadn't understood, for instance, that
Bowdoin was a men's college, and he wasn't happy when he heard
the news. He hadn't understood that the African American population of the entire state of Maine could be measured in the thousands, and that the total black population of Brunswick, the sleepy
town where Bowdoin was located, was about sixty, almost all of
whom were at Bowdoin, including two professors and a few cafete-

ria workers. Canada had never gone to school with white people, never lived on a block with white people; he'd never had a white friend. And suddenly, in the fall of 1970, Canada found himself in just about the whitest place he could imagine.

THERE WAS ONE other important fact Canada didn't know when he arrived at Bowdoin, and that was that it was no coincidence the admissions office had let him in—and given him a full scholarship—despite the fact that he hadn't sent in his acceptance letter on time. As it turned out, Canada was a hot commodity at Bowdoin in 1970: an underprivileged black incoming freshman.

Like most elite white institutions, Bowdoin had a long and troubled history with African Americans, beginning in 1826, when a Bowdoin student named John Brown Russwurm became the third black American ever to graduate from an American college. The college did not enroll another African American until 1907, and by 1963 had managed to graduate just twenty-eight black men in its 169-year history. That year, inspired by the civil rights movement, a group of Bowdoin undergraduates created an initiative called Project 65 to increase the number of blacks on campus. The students raised money themselves and on their spring break visited high schools in black neighborhoods around the country to encourage the best students to apply to Bowdoin. They found some highly qualified young men, and the Rockefeller Foundation supplied Bowdoin with some money to pay for scholarships, and the number of incoming African American freshmen crept up for the next few years, gradually, from three to five to eight, out of a student body of about a thousand students.

The assimilation process did not go smoothly, though. Each year, the same pattern repeated—a few more black students would be admitted, they would find Bowdoin alienating and white and oppressive, and they would demand that the administration admit more African American students. After the death of Martin Luther King in April 1968, Bowdoin's black student leaders formed an

Afro-American Society and lobbied the administration to increase the number of African American students at the college to at least eighty-five by the fall of 1970, with more aggressive recruitment of poor students from the inner cities. By the summer of 1968, the college was up to a grand total of just "twenty-three Negroes," as a Bowdoin press release announced, but the acting president of the school, Athern P. Daggett, agreed that the proposal for eighty-five black students by 1970 "seemed not unreasonable." He established the Committee on Bowdoin's Responsibilities to the Disadvantaged to help locate new black students.

The class of 1973, admitted in the fall of 1969, included about twenty-five black men, which brought the school's total to about forty-five—a big jump. The incoming black students were labeled the "pizzazz class," and they were more militant than the classes that had come before. They used the campus's newly opened Afro-American Center to hold events to educate their white brothers about the reality of racism in America. At the Black Symposium on the Contemporary Psychology of Black Aesthetics, the black painter Dana Chandler, dressed in a dashiki, gave a talk that the campus newspaper described, admiringly, as "basically anti-white," in which he "pointed out," the paper reported, "that most contemporary art by whites is bullshit."

In February 1970, just as Geoffrey Canada was making plans to go to Stony Brook that fall, Robert Johnson, the student president of the Afro-American Society, suspicious of the administration's dedication to the goal of increasing black admissions, led thirty-three black students into Hawthorne-Longfellow Hall, where the president's office was located. Wearing black berets and menacing expressions, they delivered a statement demanding that the college "meet its commitment of a minimum of eighty-five black students by this fall." A faculty meeting was called, and negotiations were held with the leaders of the Afro-Am (as the society was called), but the black students remained unconvinced that the administration was taking their demands seriously. They decided to enact what they called a silent protest. The black students simply stopped talking in public—not just to white people, to everyone. When called upon in class, they would stare back at the professor and not say a word. If a student greeted them on the quad, they wouldn't answer. At the student union, they ate their meals in complete silence.

The campus freaked out. Rumors went around that the black students were plotting something big. Were they going to kidnap the president of the school? Blow up the administration building? If you asked them what they were protesting, they would just stare at you. If you asked them for a list of demands, they would just stare at you. Finally the president sent word through one of the school's two black professors that he wanted a meeting, and he promised that he would try to increase black enrollment if the students would just start talking again.

By the beginning of the summer, though, only about thirty black high school seniors had accepted offers of admission, bringing Bowdoin's projected black population for the next fall to less than seventy-five, still more than ten short of the target. So when Geoff Canada placed his call to the admissions office in July, visions of the Vietnamese jungle dancing in his head, he seemed like a gift from the heavens. He and Bowdoin needed each other—even if it was, on both sides, something of a marriage of convenience.

AT THE START, at least, the union wasn't a happy one. Canada's first few weeks at Bowdoin seemed to him only marginally better than being in Vietnam. He was quickly able to confirm what he had feared to be true after his visit to Dix Hills—the education he had received before coming to Bowdoin had been completely inadequate. In every class he felt like he was several laps behind the white students. Plus he was lonely, his family and friends and culture were far away, and even though it was only September, the Maine air had turned cold and it seemed to be threatening to snow: more whiteness. He had always been convinced that white America was conspiring against him and his black brothers, but back in New York, that had been an abstract notion; he had never really had the opportunity to get a good look at the conspirators. Now they were everywhere he turned: well-off white kids who joined frats and owned cars and went around in blazers.

Canada's refuge became the Afro-American Center. He started going to weekly meetings, where the upperclassmen, angry young intellectuals with Afros and leather jackets, would debate philosophy and psychology and politics and black unity. "I thought that these guys dropped in from outer space," Canada told me. "They were the most highly educated black people I had ever seen in my life. They would talk and I wouldn't know what the hell they were saying. I was in awe of these guys." Canada started to feel that old intensity that he used to feel on Union Avenue—like he was in the middle of something exciting and dangerous and important. The more time he spent at the Afro-Am, the more it felt like home.

The African Americans in the class of 1973 and the class of 1974 (Canada's class) stood out on campus, and not only because of their numbers. The black students who came before them, as well as those who came after, were generally from middle- or upper-middle-class families—many had attended prep schools—but the black men in those two classes were almost all from poor, urban families, and many of them arrived on campus already well versed in radical politics. One student, George Alston, a year older than Canada, was a member of the Nation of Islam and a student of Mao and Marx. He had renamed himself George X. His classmate Gerald Lewis was active with the Congress of African People, a militant black political group based in Newark, New Jersey; he adopted the name Rasuli. Canada soon became part of a hard core of maybe twenty-five students, about a third of the black student body, who were dedicated to a struggle against racism and oppression. To them, every protest was part of the same fight—against Nixon, against the war, against racist white students on campus, and against the administration, which they accused of trying to

Geoffrey Canada in front of a map of the Harlem Children's Zone, which by 2007 stretched across ninety-seven blocks in central Harlem. Canada's plan—his mission—is to flood the zone with educational, social, and medical services, to create a safety net woven so tightly that children in the neighborhood just can't slip through.

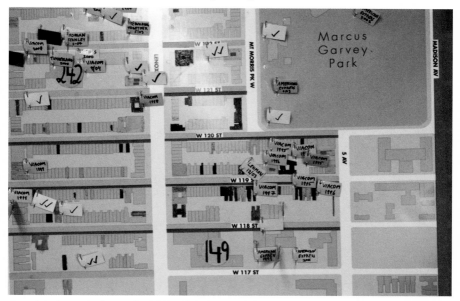

Canada's theory is that each child will do better if all the children around him are doing better. So instead of waiting for residents to find out on their own about the services his organization provides, recruiters seek out participants by going door-to-door in housing projects and low-rent high-rises. On a map of Harlem, Canada and his staff plot their course.

Photographs by ALEX TEHRANI

George Khaldun (left) and Geoffrey Canada met in the fall of 1970, when they were under-graduates at Bowdoin College in Maine, both part of a small, militant group of black students on campus who fought the administration at every turn. Khaldun, then known as George X, was a follower of Mao and Marx and a member of the Nation of Islam; Canada had grown up poor in the South Bronx and was a semireformed street fighter. Thirty-five years later, the two men manage a nonprofit with an annual budget of $58 million, with close allies on Wall Street and in the nation's corporate boardrooms.

Two expecting mothers attending Baby College, the Harlem Children's Zone's parenting-skills program, where parents and parents-to-be learn strategies for discipline, safety, and brain development.

Wanda Osorio told her students in Baby College that she sometimes hears parents in Harlem dismiss the time-out method of discipline as a white thing: "Ah, come on with the time-out. Time-out's for white people. Get out of here with that." But that was the wrong way to look at it, she told her class. Time-outs *worked,* no matter who you were.

When Cheryl Waite first heard about Baby College, she was seventeen, three months pregnant, and confused. Things were rocky between her and her boyfriend, Victor. Twice, they had been to what she called "the mean-danger-zone place"—an abortion clinic—but each time they weren't quite able to go through with it.

Shauntel Jones was thirty-two when she came to Baby College. Her other children had been taken away from her by the Administration for Children's Services, New York City's child-welfare agency, and her new pregnancy didn't seem to be built on a very strong foundation.

Victor Boria Jr. and his young father represented two separate generations of Harlem youth. Geoffrey Canada's staff had one program that would help Victor Jr. complete all his immunizations and another to help Victor Sr. complete high school. But while the Harlem Children's Zone was prepared to work with both Borias, the prospects of the infant and those of the young man seemed very different.

Monica Lucente and the other teachers in Harlem Gems, the organization's intensive pre-kindergarten program, did their best to squeeze language enrichment into every spare minute of the day.

Ryan Sparzak was one of the youngest teachers at Promise Academy, and one of the only white people on the school's staff. He didn't grow up in a particularly urban environment, or around many minorities, but when he became a teacher, he felt drawn to work in a low-income, inner-city community like Harlem.

At Promise Academy elementary school, students started preparing a year in advance for the third-grade state reading and math tests. Some parents and teachers thought exposing young kids to work beyond their grasp might frustrate them. But the principal, Dennis McKesey, thought a little frustration could be a positive thing. "I *want* the children to be frustrated at this point," he said. "I don't want them to be comfortable with where they are."

McKesey with a Promise Academy student. "With all these resources, there's no reason why these children can't make it," he said. "There's none."

Efiom Ukoidemabia, or Mr. U, was the math coach at Promise Academy middle school. When he taught, it was at top volume, and he sometimes got himself so worked up that he looked like he was about to have a heart attack.

Terri Grey, the first principal of Promise Academy middle school, saw two competing paradigms at work at the school: hers, which was about raising achievement over the long term by gradually molding students into learners, and Geoffrey Canada's, which was all about cramming, preparing, testing, and raising scores.

Glen Pinder, the second principal of the middle school, thought the main problem at Promise Academy was what he called "ticky-tack, annoying kind of behaviors": disrespecting teachers, chewing gum in class, snickering, eye rolling. But he believed that kind of bush-league misbehavior was no less disruptive than the serious stuff.

Geoffrey Canada in Marcus Garvey Park, addressing the Harlem Children's Zone's annual Peace March, a public rally that brings together the organization's entire staff.

shut down the Afro-American studies program and marginalize the African American student population.

Canada and his allies considered the Afro-Am Center to be the equivalent of an embassy in a foreign country. It was sovereign territory, and the black students believed it to be under constant threat of attack. In October, a few weeks after Canada arrived on campus, the society issued a proclamation, printed in the college newspaper, that the Afro-American Center was hereafter closed to uninvited guests—to white people, in other words—after 5:00 P.M. each day. "The society will no longer permit our ideals to be stifled," the statement read. "Necessary action will be taken if it is needed."

The confrontations that were roiling the nation and the black race in the early 1970s were played out, in miniature, within the Afro-American Society. There were the down brothers, Canada and his friends who were committed to a separatist political struggle, and they had strong and often harsh opinions about every other black student on campus. If you didn't come to the weekly meetings at the Afro-Am, if you didn't take part in the protests and sign the petitions, it meant you were either an Uncle Tom or a sellout. The Uncle Toms were the students who were seen to be intentionally currying favor with the white power structure, including those who criticized the Afro-American Society as too radical. The sellouts were the ones who just didn't care about politics, who seemed to want to use the opportunities they had at Bowdoin only to get into positions of respectable power and make money.

In many ways, Bowdoin's experiment in racial integration was a disaster. At least part of the administration's goal had been an idealistic one, even a noble one: to show these black students, most of whom felt cut off from opportunity, that there was a path to middle-class success open to them—that the American dream applied to all. Instead, when Canada and his fellow African American freshmen arrived at Bowdoin, they encountered a system that they saw as rigged and racist. It made them feel further cut off from white America, not closer to it: they could see all these white boys being taught the codes of oppression, making the social connections that would ensure that once they graduated, they would get more and the underprivileged would get less. The school's administration had hoped that the Afro-American Center would help integrate the black students into college life. Instead, it helped keep them separate. The black students all ate together at the student union, around one big table; white students were not welcome. If a black student was dating a white woman, his brothers would often pressure him to find a more suitable partner. (Bowdoin had begun to admit women in the fall of 1971.) The black students clustered together on one floor of one dorm, which they called the Ghetto. They adopted "The Ghetto," by Donny Hathaway, as their theme song.

After two years of relatively vigorous recruitment of underprivileged black students, the admissions office retreated, and the class of 1974 was the high-water mark at Bowdoin, with a higher percentage of black students than any class before or since.

NOW, MORE THAN three decades later, Canada has become in many ways a full-fledged member of the vast American middle class, earning a six-figure salary, commuting from the suburbs every morning in his SUV, playing golf on weekends, reading Harry Potter to his son. But unlike many people who escape poverty, he has not abandoned his connections to his background; on the contrary, he sometimes seems never to have left Union Avenue. And his brothers from the Afro-American Center—well, he literally hasn't left them. After Canada was hired by Rheedlen in 1983, he reconnected with several of his old Bowdoin friends, often by accident. Canada ran into George X—who was now going by George Khaldun—on the street near Columbia University, and hired him to be Rheedlen's educational coordinator, later promoting him to chief operating officer. Another day, Rasuli Lewis called out to him from the window of a city bus, and Canada recruited him to run a new program at Rheedlen that taught conflict resolution to teen-agers. The two men are now part of Canada's inner circle — a slice of the Afro-American Society's hard core, reconstituted thirty years later on 125th Street.

On a personal level, the people Canada connects with most in-tensely all came up from poverty and the streets. Geoff dated mid-dle-class women after his divorce, but nothing ever quite clicked. And then he met Yvonne, whose family had been even poorer than Geoff's, who dropped out of high school and had a child at fifteen, and who was determined to make something of her life anyway, and he fell in love. "We were the missing pieces in one another's life," he told me. "The motivation for my work is all based on a personal understanding of what these kids go through and what the rest of the world doesn't see. There was nobody better to un-derstand that than Yvonne. She knew it firsthand."

Canada looks at himself, his son Jerry, and his son Geoffrey Jr. as representatives of three different generational attitudes toward inner-city African American values. (The three Canadas were born, respectively, in 1952, 1972, and 1997.) "Me, I love walking around Harlem, where I am no different than anybody else," Canada said. "I don't feel like anybody's looking at me; I can just be out there and it's fine." When he is hanging out with George Khaldun or Ra-suli Lewis — or almost any black man who grew up in urban pov-erty — he can relax and be himself in a way that he can't with white men, even white men he counts as good friends, like Stan Druck-enmiller or Ken Langone. "There is not a closer group of people than African Americans," Canada explained, "in particular, men who want to show love to one another and want to acknowledge that you're part of a group. I have found that to be comforting beyond belief, being able to share and understand that. It's hard for any other group to communicate in the way that African Amer-icans do when they get around one another and they're loose, they're not uptight. It's just you. You can say what you want. You can express yourself."

But when he walks around Valley Stream, where the population is less than 10 percent African American, or when he finds himself, as he often does while raising funds and meeting with government officials, to be the only black man in a room full of white folks, Canada says he is unable to feel entirely at ease—even if his social skills (and years of practice) enable him to *seem* perfectly at home. His son Jerry, by contrast, "is 100 percent comfortable being in the majority culture," Canada said. Jerry grew up effortlessly traveling between racial groups and classes, attending a high school evenly divided between black, white, and Hispanic kids, and as an adult, he is able to feel welcome anywhere. Race is rarely a consideration for him.

And now, Geoffrey Jr. is having a third experience, growing up in Valley Stream, deep inside that majority culture and far from the ghetto. Canada is not convinced that it's necessarily a better experience. "I worry that Geoffrey is not going to be able to relate to black kids from the inner city," Canada said. "My wife says, 'Who gives a damn?' She says, 'So what, he's not going to want to be a thug!' But I really care about this. It would really bother me if he grew up feeling uncomfortable around the average black kid, if he felt somehow that he couldn't relate to them, he didn't understand them."

This feeling influences Canada's approach to the issue of the effect of home life on a child's development. Many programs that try to help poor children, including charter schools, charities, and social service agencies, take as their premise that the best way to help children in a bad environment is to separate them as much as possible from that environment, to insulate them from the problems and values of the ghetto or even to extract promising kids from their homes and drop them into elite boarding schools. Canada, by contrast, wants to leave Harlem's poor children exactly where they are, so that they change the neighborhood and the neighborhood changes them.

The word that Canada tends to use when talking about this

process is "contamination." He often uses it the way it's usually used—he talks about how negative values from the media or the streets can contaminate a housing project or a neighborhood or an individual child. But he also uses it positively, to describe the change he wants to bring to Harlem. He does want Harlem's parents to adopt what he calls middle-class values, but to him, those are not the values of Valley Stream, exactly, or the values of Stan Druckenmiller's children. They are the values, more or less, that he grew up with, race-conscious and proud, devoted to the block and the neighborhood but also focused on success, learning, working hard, getting to college. If he can borrow some of these new ideas from the manic superparents downtown and combine them with the hanging-out-on-the-stoop beliefs that he grew up with, he thinks that he can carve out a unique set of Harlem values that will make instinctive sense to both parents and kids.

"This is what I'm betting," he explained. "When you've got most of the kids in a neighborhood involved in high-quality programs, you begin to change the cultural context of that neighborhood. If you are surrounded by people who are always talking about going to college, you're going to end up thinking, 'Hey, maybe this is something I could do, too.' You can't help but get contaminated by that idea. It just seeps into your pores, and you don't even know that you've caught the virus.

"And that kind of contamination can be spread. If we touch enough kids at the same time with the same message, then it won't seem unusual to think, 'I should do well in school, I should speak proper English, I should do my homework.' These things won't seem like you're not being from the hood or you're not keeping it real. And the same way that this went bad, that it went from kids being respectful and decent to kids being disrespectful and indecent, I think it can go good."

5   Battle Mode

Iᴛ ᴡᴀs ᴛʜᴇ ꜰɪʀsᴛ ᴅᴀʏ of school, September 7, 2004, and at 8:30 ᴀ.ᴍ, Promise Academy's first-ever sixth-grade class was looking a little scared. Five months had passed since their names were pulled out of the gold drum in the school's admission lottery, and now here they were, back in the same auditorium, at PS 242 on West 122nd Street. This building would be their makeshift home for the next four months; their real school, which would take up three floors of the new Harlem Children's Zone headquarters on 125th Street, was still under construction. The students sat tucked into the auditorium's first few rows, ten and eleven and twelve years old, their haircuts sharp, their uniforms crisp, their book bags still wearing price tags. Those lucky enough to have located a friend from the neighborhood clustered together, and the rest sat alone, or next to strangers, looking tough or vulnerable or both. The first day of school—that on its own was enough to leave the mouth a little dry, the stomach a little unsettled, but this was the first day of a brand-new school and, everyone kept telling them, a brand-new *kind* of school, like nothing Harlem had seen before.

That was the message that Doreen Land, the superintendent of

Promise Academy, was trying to get across. She stood onstage, behind a lectern, a sturdy, serious black woman in her early forties, wearing a sober black dress with white piping and looking tired but confident. "Yesterday was a holiday," she said to the sixth grade. "But we were all here working. Your teachers wanted to make sure everything was ready for you to learn." Land acknowledged that the school might not yet feel like something special to the students, especially since they were sitting in a public school auditorium just like the ones most of them had sat in the previous year and the year before that. But this was just a temporary arrangement, she reminded them. The new building would be clean, the textbooks and computer programs would be up-to-date, the teachers would be well prepared. "Everything we do at the Promise Academy is going to be different," she said. "Even the food we serve you will be better than the food that the students eat in other schools. Our motto is that anything that a private school can pay for, we are going to provide for free. We have thought of every detail. Every detail."

Land introduced Geoffrey Canada, and after a few words of encouragement, Canada introduced the woman who would have direct responsibility for the success of the sixth grade: Terri Grey, the principal of Promise Academy middle school. Grey, an African American woman in her early thirties, was gracious and softspoken. She looked down as she crossed the stage to the lectern, watching her step. Her dark hair hung down her back in long tight braids. "I feel so honored to be able to be here today," she said to her young charges. "I have been working for this my entire life, and I know that you have been working your entire life to get to the sixth grade." She smiled. "It took a lot of hard work to get to the sixth grade, didn't it?"

When Grey asked if the students had any questions, there was no response. And then a girl in the front row in a spotless regulation plaid jumper timidly raised her hand. Grey pointed a finger at her. "Yes?"

"Some of us might want to go to college," the girl said, a little tentatively. It wasn't quite clear if it was a question or a statement.

"I'm glad to hear that," Grey replied. "How many of you want to go to college?"

Every student raised a hand.

"Well, that's good news," Grey said. "Because that's what we want. We want every single one of you to go to college." The students stared back at her, some of them a little skeptical. "How many of you believe we can do this?" Grey asked.

This time, only half the hands went up, and some of them only partway.

"You *should* believe it," Grey said. "We can do this. Together we're going to do this."

And then someone brought a length of yellow ribbon on the stage, and Terri Grey held one end and Geoffrey Canada held the other, and they both smiled for a waiting camera as a woman on the school's board of trustees cut the ribbon with a pair of scissors. It might not have been the most lavish ceremony ever, but it was now official: Promise Academy middle school was open for business.

The students had a lot to worry about during those first few weeks of school—finding classrooms, making friends, keeping all the new rules straight—without contemplating their role in the national debate over schooling. But the fact was, in the previous couple of years, a perennial battle in the politics of education had flared up hotter than ever, and students like the ones in the sixth grade at Promise Academy were at its center. New broadsides had been published, angry letters were being exchanged in the pages of newspapers and journals, congressional hearings were being held, all over the same simple question: How much can a school do? More precisely, how much can a school do for kids like these, black kids from homes that were poor or troubled or both, from neighborhoods with high crime rates and low employment rates?

The debate was in some ways a legacy of the Coleman Report,

the federal study by the sociologist James Coleman that was intended to demonstrate how minority students were shortchanged by funding inequities but concluded instead that students' home environments and peer groups mattered more than their schools. Ever since the report's publication in 1966, scholars had been arguing over what it really meant. Could good schools overcome bad environments, or not?

When the sixth-grade class arrived at Promise Academy in 2004, the "not" case had just been made in a particularly adamant fashion by Richard Rothstein, a research associate at the liberal Economic Policy Institute who had recently left his position as the education columnist for the *New York Times* to become a visiting professor at Columbia University's Teachers College. In a new book titled *Class and Schools,* Rothstein argued that it was unfair and misguided to put all the blame for the anemic academic performance of poor and minority students on schools and teachers. The "influence of social class characteristics is probably so powerful that schools cannot overcome it," Rothstein wrote, "no matter how well trained are their teachers and no matter how well designed are their instructional programs and climates." The disadvantages that stood in the way of children like those in Promise Academy were simply too many and too large; trying to fix their schools was hopeless without fixing their other problems as well. "Lower-class children, on average, have poorer vision than middle-class children," Rothstein wrote. "They have poorer oral hygiene, more lead poisoning, more asthma, poorer nutrition, less adequate pediatric care, more exposure to smoke. . . . Each of these well-documented social class differences is likely to have a palpable effect on academic achievement, and, combined, the influence of all of these differences is probably huge."

The opposing argument to Rothstein's had just been given new voice by Abigail and Stephan Thernstrom, well-known conservative writers about race, in their book *No Excuses: Closing the Racial Gap in Learning.* "Sure, some kids are easier to teach than others," the couple wrote. "But dysfunctional families and poverty are no excuse for widespread, chronic educational failure." They acknowledged that the unfortunate circumstances of students in neighborhoods like Harlem made educating them more of a challenge. But the real problem, they argued, was not socioeconomic disadvantage; it was a school system that didn't educate poor children.

For the Thernstroms, the power of schools to overcome the disadvantages of poverty had been demonstrated most clearly by a small group of schools and teachers who, they said, had met with great success teaching poor minority students. Their exhibit A was the KIPP family of charter schools. The first KIPP school was founded in 1994 in Houston by David Levin and Michael Feinberg, two young inner-city public school teachers who met while working for Teach for America. Over the next decade, KIPP had expanded into a network of thirty-eight schools, mostly middle schools, all aimed at low-income and minority students and almost all chalking up consistently impressive scores on standardized state tests. Levin and Feinberg offered an extended day and an extended year that provided KIPP students with about 60 percent more classroom time than most public school students. They set clear and strict rules of conduct: their two principles of behavior were "work hard" and "be nice," and all the other rules flowed out of those. At the beginning of each year, parents and students signed a pledge—unenforceable but generally taken seriously—committing to certain standards of hard work and behavior.

The KIPP schools were clearly the Thernstroms' favorites, but the authors also held up as models a few other high-scoring charter schools, including Amistad Academy in New Haven, Connecticut, and North Star Academy in Newark, New Jersey, whose founders had to a considerable extent modeled their methods on KIPP's. The success of all these schools, the Thernstroms wrote, proved that poor minority students could succeed if they were immersed in an educational environment that was demanding, disciplined, and well run.

Rothstein argued, in reply, that KIPP's elevated test scores in fact proved little or nothing about what schools could accomplish with poor children. Though it was true that the kids who attended KIPP schools were from low-income families, he wrote, they were "not typical lower-class students." The fact that their parents were willing to sign a contract like the one KIPP used—as well as the fact that their parents had bothered to enroll them in the admission lottery in the first place—set them apart from other inner-city children. There was "no evidence," Rothstein concluded, that KIPP's strategy "would be as successful for students whose parents are not motivated to choose such a school."

The two sides sniped at each other in web postings and in the pages of the *New York Review of Books,* with Rothstein accusing the Thernstroms of proposing a "simplistic remedy" and calling their arguments "wildly implausible," and Stephan Thernstrom replying that Rothstein was the "chief excuser" of the failure of the education system and accusing him of demonstrating, through his work, "the bankruptcy of current progressive thinking about America's public schools."

And where did Canada stand? He agreed with Rothstein that the public school system needed more money, not less. But on the other basic principles of the education debate, Canada found himself with the Thernstroms, on the right. "I'm for vouchers, I'm for charter schools—I'm for anything that blows up the status quo," he told me. Canada felt that liberals' hearts were in the right place on poverty and education, but something—maybe it was their dependence on teachers' unions, maybe it was an overly idealistic view of how public education worked—had led them astray on this issue. "It is my fundamental belief that the folk who care about public education the most, who really want to see it work, are destroying it," he said. Anyone who looked at the urban public school system not as an abstract idea but up close, every day, the way Canada had for the past twenty years, would want to blow it up, too.

Canada knew that schools couldn't do everything on their own, but he thought they could do a whole lot more than they were doing—or at least than public schools in Harlem were doing. As he saw it, the incoming sixth-grade students were the victims of years of educational neglect. They had been written off too early by a system that used as an excuse the idea that it was impossible to educate poor children. Canada was convinced that it wasn't too late for the sixth grade, and over the next few years he planned to prove it.

THE PREVIOUS SPRING, in the weeks leading up to the Promise Academy admission lottery, recruiters from the Harlem Children's Zone had canvassed Harlem in order to get the kind of applicant pool they wanted: not the best and the brightest, the students whose parents normally went out of their way to find educational opportunities for their children, but a true cross-section of the neighborhood, students who reflected the degree to which, by the sixth grade, most Harlem students had fallen behind. The effort seemed to have succeeded. The middle school's student body was 90 percent black, 10 percent Hispanic, and 0 percent white, and more than 90 percent of them were eligible for free or reduced-price lunch, the Department of Education's determiner for a low-income household. Their scores on the citywide tests in fifth grade, the year before, were on par with the dismal results from the rest of Harlem—only 27 percent had scored on or above grade level in English, and 14 percent in math.

At the beginning of the school year, the school's administrators gave each incoming sixth-grade student two detailed standardized tests to measure their academic abilities: the Iowa Test of Basic Skills in math and the TerraNova achievement test in English. When the results came back, in late January, the most basic numbers—how many students were on grade level and how many were behind—weren't too surprising. They were pretty awful, but they weren't too surprising. Thirteen percent of students were at or above grade level in math, and 16 percent of students were at or above grade level in English—numbers that more or less reflected what the school's administrators already knew from the students' fifth-grade test results. But what the Iowa and TerraNova tests allowed the administrators to do for the first time was to see how *far* their students had fallen behind. And that was where the unpleasant surprises began to emerge.

Canada and the other administrators had assumed that the kids who were behind were behind by only a year or two. The test results, though, told a grimmer story. Forty percent of the incoming sixth-grade students had math skills on a second- or third-grade level, and another 26 percent were on a fourth-grade level, meaning that two-thirds of them were at least two years behind their peers. In English, the results were even worse: 57 percent of the sixth-grade students were at least three years behind, reading at a third-grade level or below.

The scores set out in stark relief the task that the school's teachers and administrators had ahead of them. Geoffrey Canada had guaranteed that every student entering sixth grade would graduate from high school with a successful academic record, meaning that they would be ready for college, and that they would be, at the very least, on grade level in math and English. But here were sixth-grade students reading on a second-grade level—eleven-year-olds reading like seven-year-olds. Twenty years earlier, when Canada was a teacher himself, his rule of thumb had been that using the best tools he had at his disposal, he could move a child two years forward in a single year. In other words, if a student was reading at a fifth-grade level at the beginning of sixth grade, Canada believed that he could have that child reading at a seventh-grade level at the beginning of seventh grade. But this was a new puzzle. If a student in sixth grade is reading at a second-grade level, how do you make up that kind of deficit? And what does it mean for his educational future?

At Promise Academy, these were not idle questions. There was a very real deadline looming: the 2005 citywide math and reading tests, which every New York City public school student in grades three, five, six, and seven would take on April 12 and April 19. The tests were a big deal not only for the city's students but for their teachers and administrators, too. Each school's results were posted on the Department of Education's website and published in the newspapers for everyone to see. For charter schools, consistent substandard results meant that the charter could be revoked and the school shut down. For a new school, the results were critical — especially for a new school, like Promise Academy, that had been born in a blaze of publicity. (When the new school building finally opened, that January, Bill Clinton came by to say a few words.)

Canada believed there was only one way to accelerate kids who were as far behind as the Promise Academy students were: expose them to a whole lot more instruction. He had already extended the school day and the school year for exactly this reason. Now he was wondering where else he could find time for the kind of remedial catch-up drills he thought his students needed: Early mornings? Saturday? How about Sunday? "It is going to be a monumental effort to get these kids from where they are right now to grade level," Canada told me that winter. And he didn't have long, he knew. The school's funders and its board of trustees were expecting results quickly, and they were all going to have their eye on the citywide test. "The clock is ticking," he said.

TERRI GREY, the principal of the middle school, was hoping for good scores, too, but she thought Canada and the board were getting too worked up over the tests. Grey and Canada were both alumni of the Harvard Graduate School of Education, but they held to very different theories of schooling. When Canada was at Harvard, in the 1970s, he had specialized in the study of behavioralism, and ever since, he had seen education as something of a mathematical process, in which teachers could tinker with students' progress by adjusting their methods and increasing or decreasing the intensity of instruction, as if they were changing variables in an equation. Grey, who had received her master's degree in

2002, came away with a more holistic model. For her, educating a student was a delicate process, as much about making emotional connections as it was about drilling a kid with information.

Canada's thinking about Promise Academy was also heavily influenced by Stanley Druckenmiller, and not just because Druckenmiller was providing so much of its funding. Canada had come to agree with Druckenmiller that a business model was exactly the right approach for Promise Academy, and for his entire organization. The overall goal of the Zone might be liberal and idealistic—to educate and otherwise improve the lives of poor black children—but Canada believed the best way to achieve that goal was to act not like a bighearted altruist but like a ruthless capitalist, devoted to the bottom line. He didn't think it was right to hold himself or his employees to a looser standard of achievement simply because they happened to be making the world a better place.

But Canada wasn't always sure that message was getting through, especially to the administrators and the staff of Promise Academy. He worried that they didn't quite understand how seriously he and the board of trustees took the situation at the schools. While Grey was organizing the middle school's move from its temporary home inside PS 242 to the new building on 125th Street, the principal of the elementary school, Jesse Rawls Jr., was overseeing the progress of the first kindergarten class, which occupied a corner of PS 175, on West 134th Street. And at a meeting of the board in January 2005, Rawls casually let slip that some of his students had already missed twenty days of school. Druckenmiller and Kenneth Langone, the wealthy investor who was the chair of the school board, hit the ceiling. Were they spending all of this money so that kids could stay home and watch TV?

Canada wasn't happy. After the board meeting, he called Land and Grey and Rawls up to his corner office on the sixth floor of the new headquarters, overlooking 125th Street. "If a kid is missing twenty days of school, this organization should treat that like a crisis," Canada said. "That should be automatic. It's incomprehensible to me that this would happen without anyone thinking that we needed to come up with a massive response. This is a big problem, and everyone in this organization should think of this as *their* problem."

Canada was in general an amiable, supportive boss, telling amusing stories in meetings and offering encouragement to his employees. But when things weren't going well, he could cloud over, his speech turning quiet and deliberate, his displeasure palpable. Now, sitting in his office, he brought up what seemed to the school administrators like a strange subject: Wal-Mart. Earlier that month, he said, he'd read an article in the business section of the *New York Times* that described the way the giant retailer had reacted to lackluster sales on Black Friday, the day after Thanksgiving, which traditionally marks the beginning of the Christmas shopping season. According to the article, sales numbers from across the country came in weak that morning, and within hours the entire Wal-Mart corporation was in crisis mode. Employees from the top of the hierarchy to the bottom offered suggestions to the company's executives. Slow-selling flat-screen TVs were moved to a better location in each store. Hanes fleece separates were marked down from $5.84 to $4.64. And in just a few weeks, the effort paid off. Wal-Mart's Christmas shopping season was saved.

There's our model, Canada said. It doesn't matter that they're selling flat-screen TVs and we're educating children. We have to be every bit as focused on results as they are. If we want this thing to work, he told them, we've got to act more like Wal-Mart.

And so at the next board meeting, in the middle of February, when Betina Jean-Louis, the director of evaluation, presented the troubling Iowa and TerraNova results, nobody was nonchalant. Jean-Louis handed out a series of multicolored bar graphs showing how the sixth-grade students were scoring at second- and third-grade levels in math and reading, and Druckenmiller asked Doreen Land, the school superintendent, what she was doing to fix things.

Land had an answer prepared. Her staff had already divided the students into different achievement levels, based on their test scores. The students who were furthest behind grade level had been assigned to remedial classes three mornings a week, from 7:00 to 7:45 A.M. Then, for more advanced students, children who had scored below grade level but who might, with a small push, be able to get up to the standard, there was a separate class on Saturday mornings, from 9:00 to 11:00 A.M. In addition, there would be special test-prep tutoring in the afterschool program, and on Mondays and Tuesdays teachers would do test prep in class, drilling students on math fundamentals and vocabulary words and instructing them on test-taking strategies. For the next two months, Land said, until the citywide tests in April, the whole school was going to be concentrating on one thing: raising the test scores.

The day after the board meeting, reflecting in his office, Canada said he was mostly satisfied with the new plan. But he was still worried that his staff hadn't fully bought into the intensive approach he favored. He feared that there was a disconnect developing between the middle school's administrators, on the second floor of the new headquarters, and the Zone's, on the sixth floor. "We may not all be on the same page on this," he said. Terri Grey and Doreen Land were saying the right things, but he wasn't sure that deep down they were really willing to push hard enough to raise the scores. The attitude Canada feared he was seeing in the school administrators was one that asked, "How much can we *afford* to do? How many hours of test prep can we fit in without exhausting our teachers or our students?" Canada wanted them to flip the question around, to ask, "How much do we *need* to do?" He wanted them to think like he did: start from the result you want to achieve, however improbable, and then work backward, figuring out every single thing you have to do in order to get there.

IT WAS TEN MINUTES after seven on a chilly March morning, the sun barely out of the East River, but in room 208 of Promise

Academy, the shouting had already begun. Efiom Ukoidemabia, the school's math coach, had written a long number on the black-board — 333,444,395,421 — and he wanted one of the four students sitting in front of him to read it aloud.

"Hit it!" he yelled. Mr. Ukoidemabia yelled a lot. He had broken the number into chunks, to make it easier to swallow, and now he wanted someone to take it piece by piece. "All right, look at the 395," he said. "What period is it in?" Silence.

In the sixth grade, they'd been over this a dozen times in the last couple of weeks. Mr. U, as the students called him, was talking about a way to avoid getting lost in the middle of a long num-ber. You split the number into three-digit "periods," divided at the commas. So 333 is in the billions period, and 444 is in the millions period, and so on. Mr. U wanted someone to tell him that 395 was in the *thousands* period.

"What period, Mr. Percy?"

Jean Percy squinted at the number. A small voice: "Units?"

Mr. U removed his reading glasses and turned to examine the board. "So that's 395 units?" he asked.

No answer.

"You *might* be right," Mr. U said, in a voice that made it clear that in fact Jean was wrong. "Mr. Smith?"

Jamel Smith ventured a guess. "Billions?"

"So that's 395 billion, correct?"

"Yes."

Mr. U gave a look like he'd smelled something bad. "Ah, no."

Jean spoke up again: "No, it's thousands, 'cause—"

"*Thousands?*" thundered Mr. U, sounding outraged. This was one of his favorite tricks: when someone finally got an answer right, he would act shocked, like the answer was so far-fetched he couldn't believe anyone could be foolish enough to suggest it.

Jean stood his ground: "Thousands."

"So that's 395 thousand?" Mr. U said, still incredulous, pointing at the board.

"Yes."

"You're right," Mr. U said, dropping the act. "It is."

Jasmin Bonner, in the back row, giggled. Even at seven o'clock in the morning, being in Mr. U's class was a little like watching stand-up comedy—or maybe stand-up comedy crossed with boot camp, with a bit of tent revival meeting thrown in. Mr. U was a native of Harlem, a big man in his midforties with a shaved head and a handlebar mustache, and today he was wearing a striped tie and a perfectly pressed purple shirt. He spoke quickly, a blur of words, and he had an oddly formal manner, using lots of dependent clauses and circuitous phrases. He liked to address every child as Mr. This or Miss That. When he taught, it was at top volume, and on mornings like this, when Mr. U was trying to prepare his struggling students for the big citywide math test, he sometimes got himself so worked up that he looked like he was about to have a heart attack.

"So if that is thousands," Mr. U said, pointing at the 395, "and this is the units, or ones"—he indicated the 421—"then this period is what, in here?"

"Millions," the class said aloud, more or less together.

"And this?"

"Billions."

"So Mr. Gregg will say that number for us," Mr. U went on.

Dashaan Gregg began. "Three hundred and thirty-three—"

Mr. U interrupted him: "Do not say 'and.'" This was a particular obsession of Mr. U's: he hated it when students put the word "and" in the middle of a number. "Say it again."

Dashaan tried again, but it was a hard rule to remember. "Three hundred and thirty-three billion—"

Mr. U interrupted him again, a little testier this time. "Say it again without the 'and.'"

"Three hundred thirty-three billion, four hundred and forty-four million—"

"Do not say 'and'! I need Smith."

Jamel Smith looked up. "Three hundred thirty-three billion, four hundred and forty-four million—"

Mr. U boosted the volume again. "There's no 'and'! There's no 'and'! Start again."

"Three hundred thirty-three billion."

"Louder! Prouder!"

Jamel raised his voice over the morning traffic on 125th Street, out the open window two floors down. "Three hundred thirty-three billion, four hundred forty-four million, three hundred ninety-five thousand, four hundred twenty-one."

"Excellent. Bonner, you're next."

"Three hundred thirty-three billion, four hundred forty-four. . . ." Jasmin Bonner's voice trailed off. She looked at the board, searching for a clue to what came next.

"You don't *guess!* Look at what you see, and tell me where it is. Come on!"

"Three hundred thirty-three billion, four—"

"Louder!"

Jasmin's reedy voice turned into something close to a shout. "Three hundred thirty-three—"

"I didn't say start all over again; I just said louder."

Jasmin was getting flustered. "Four hundred forty-four billion."

"That's not billion. Start all over."

"Three hundred thirty-three billion," Jasmin began, and then the door to the classroom opened, and Jasmin stopped. Four more students walked in, twenty minutes late. They made their way to their seats in silence, as Mr. U stared at them over his glasses.

"You stop the whole class when you come in late," Mr. U said, his voice thick with disappointment. "You stop the whole class."

"It wasn't our fault," Devante Garcia said, forcing a plaintive note into his voice. It didn't work.

"This is your *job,*" said Mr. U. "Come on. The custodians come in late, we're in trouble. The cooks come in late, we don't eat. Let's be here on time. It's 7:20. Class starts at 7:00. You're responsible." He turned and nodded at Jasmin. "I'm back with Bonner," he said.

"Three hundred thirty-three billion—" Jasmin said. Then the

door opened again. A guilty silence fell over the classroom as four more students filed in.

"Please don't come in *late*," Mr. U said as the new arrivals took off their coats and dropped into their seats. "We just lost two or three minutes. We don't *have* two or three minutes." He looked stern. "This test is coming on the nineteenth whether we're ready or not. Fail enough of these tests, and bye-bye Promise Academy." He stared at his students, and they stared at their desks. There were twelve of them now, out of the twenty who were supposed to be there. They were all sleepy, all hungry—breakfast wasn't until 7:45—and all dressed in the school uniform: white shirts, black pants and ties for the boys, plaid jumpers for the girls. On some of them, the outfit still looked crisp and clean and perfectly pulled together, but on a few boys, after almost seven months of school, the uniform was barely a uniform anymore: their shirts were stained or dirty; their shirttails were untucked. There was silence in the classroom. The students shifted uneasily in their seats. Finally, Mr. U turned to Devante and said, "Garcia, read that number."

"Three hundred thirty-three billion, four hundred forty-four million, three hundred ninety-five thousand, four hundred twenty-one."

"Thank you. Mr. Hall, hit it."

"Three hundred thirty-three billion, four hundred forty-four million, three hundred ninety-five thousand"—Keith Hall was doing great, almost home, but then he stumbled—"four hundred and twenty-one."

Mr. U exploded. "Do! Not! Say! And! I've only said it thirty *times*. We have to *go*, folks. April 19 is upon us. We can't get stuck on reading this number. This test is coming. *Life* is coming. Each minute we waste is gone. We never get it back." He pointed out the window, across 125th Street and south, away from Harlem, down where the competition lived. "Kids downtown are studying," he said. "Kids in California are studying. We better be studying, too."

■

EACH MORNING, WHEN the students walked into their brand-new school building, they passed a handmade sign on brown butcher paper that someone had taped up in the lobby, over the elevators. "HCZ Promise Academy Countdown to CITYWIDE TEST," it read. And then there was a separate square of paper underneath that changed every day: 30, 20, 15, 10.

The early-morning test-prep students—the ones with the lowest scores—alternated, each day, between Mr. U's math class and Sarah Snyder's English class. As March turned into April, Mr. U moved beyond periods, into rounding and estimating and exponents. In Ms. Snyder's class, students were learning new vocabulary words—"voyage," "threaten," "imaginative," "critical"—but their progress seemed frustratingly slow.

On one cold, gray morning at the beginning of April, the students in the English class took a few minutes to work in silence on a page in their textbooks that asked them to select words from their new vocabulary list to fill in blanks in short sentences. One presented a particular challenge for the students:

The hurricane _____ every village along the shore.

The correct answer was "threatens," but when students read their answers aloud, only a few had it right. Patrice Brown chose "critical," as in, "The hurricane critical every village along the shore." Keith Hall opted for "splendor." Jean Percy chose "blends." Someone else picked "suspends." Ms. Snyder, always upbeat and encouraging, explained slowly and clearly why each one was wrong, going over the difference between a verb and an adjective and a noun, explaining how "threatens"—which most of the students rejected as the answer because they associated it with a person making verbal threats—could also be used with a more abstract subject, like a hurricane.

For many students, who had spent six years essentially killing time in one Harlem public school or another, with few demands or expectations from teachers, Promise Academy was hard to get used to. The new building itself was different: The walls were freshly painted, the stairwells were open and airy, and next to the elevator, a bank of south-facing windows let the sunlight stream in. The library was carpeted and quiet and full of new books. The bathrooms smelled clean. Even the floors gleamed. But it wasn't just the architecture that was new; the school's teachers and administrators were focused on the students like no one had ever focused on them before, not only drilling them and testing them and disciplining them for every misstep they made, but also hugging them and congratulating them and encouraging them. Most of the students had never had so many people around them who seemed to believe that they were going to succeed in life. It was gratifying, but it could be overwhelming too, especially as the tests drew nearer, and with them, the possibility of failure. Over breakfast one morning in the cafeteria, Rudy Forbes, the sixth-grade math teacher, told me that students were starting to show signs of strain. In class the day before, he said, he was hounding one boy for an answer—nothing unusual, just regular classroom theatrics—and the boy burst into tears. Just that morning another girl told him, sadly, that she couldn't go to 7:00 A.M. test prep anymore. She was just too tired, she said.

But from above, from the offices on the sixth floor, Doreen Land and Terri Grey were getting pressure to do still more. One afternoon they received an unexpected visit from a woman they both admired: Lorraine Monroe, the founder of the Frederick Douglass Academy, one of the first high-performing schools in Harlem. Grey and Land had both read Monroe's inspirational book about her school, and they had borrowed many of her techniques of classroom organization and teacher training for Promise Academy; it was Monroe, in fact, who had recommended Land for the superintendent's job in the first place.

On the day of her visit, Monroe dropped in on Canada first, and Canada brought her down from the sixth floor to the second floor, to Land's office. There, along with Terri Grey, they sat and talked about the progress the school was making. Canada told Monroe about the Iowa and TerraNova scores, and about how far behind the students were.

"You've got the test coming up?" Monroe asked.

"Yeah," said Canada. "It's soon."

"So how does it look?"

"We're going to get creamed," Canada said.

"Well, what are you doing about it?" Monroe asked.

Grey explained the program: afterschool sessions, two hours on Saturday morning for the most advanced kids, and early-morning classes three days a week for the students furthest behind.

"Oh, you've got to expand that to every *day*," Monroe said matter-of-factly. "It's got to be *five* days. You've got to drop everything and cram."

This was music to Canada's ears—his mantra, always, was more, more, more—but it wasn't the message Grey wanted to hear. Given all the extra test prep the children were doing in class and in the afterschool, she felt that they were cramming enough already.

After the meeting, Canada spoke to Land and asked her to consider increasing the test-prep regimen. Land consulted with Grey, and a few days later she came back to talk to Canada. "We're going to five days," she said. "But not for the kids in the 7:00 A.M. class. We want to give the extra time to the students who are doing the best."

Canada didn't object at the time, but looking back on the conversation later on, he said Land's decision was bothering him. "I think that we may have thrown in the towel on the kids at the bottom," he told me. "And strategically, that might be exactly right, because we want our kids to get 3s and 4s. That's all we get scored on."

He explained what he meant: Reading scores in New York City public schools are reported in four categories, the higher the better. A 4 means the student is reading above grade level; a 3 means the student is reading at grade level; a 2 means below grade level; and a 1 means significantly below grade level. The situation Canada was describing—that the school was scored only on its 3s and 4s—was the result of a particular quirk of the system. Scores do come in four levels, but only three numbers are publicized: how many children score above grade level (4s), how many are on grade level (3s), and how many are behind (1s and 2s combined). A low-scoring 1 and a high-scoring 2, in other words, are treated as part of a single mass of failing students. This means that if you are a New York City principal, there is a big incentive to get your high-scoring 2s to level 3, and no incentive at all to get your 1s to a 2.

"Let's say we've got 50 percent of our kids on level 1," Canada explained. "And we get them all to level 2." That would be an amazing achievement for Promise Academy, and one that would mark a significant first step for dozens of kids. But in the public eye, it wouldn't matter, Canada said. "We'd get no credit for that. Our numbers in the paper would still say they're all below grade level."

Canada knew that what many principals in New York City do, as a result, is go for the low-hanging fruit: they tend to ignore their level 1s and concentrate instead on their high-scoring 2s. He worried that Land was following that path now, motivated at least in part by a desire to raise the numbers that end up in the paper. But Canada's mission had always been to change the lives of the 1s, the students at the bottom, where his friends had been stuck growing up in the Bronx.

"I understand how it makes strategic sense to focus on our 2s," Canada said. "But that's not the war. The war is those 1s, those kids we don't think we're going to move. We can't surrender that ground. I know the tests are a few days away, and we need higher scores, and we don't get credit for moving those 1s. But there's something in me that says, 'Don't put this off. Go into battle mode now and stay there. Fight the war now.'"

"TRAINED OR UNTRAINED?" shouted Mr. U.

"Trained," his students replied.

"Trained or untrained?" he asked again, a little louder.

"Trained!" they shouted back.

For the last few weeks of test prep, Mr. U had heightened the boot-camp atmosphere of his morning classes by borrowing a line from the Denzel Washington movie *Man on Fire*, an action thriller that had just come out on DVD. "There's no such thing as tough," the actor, playing a bodyguard, says at one point to the nine-year-old girl he is assigned to protect. "You're either trained or untrained." The sign in the lobby said Mr. U's students had nine more days to get trained.

The kids in Mr. U's class were mostly level 1s, the students who were furthest behind. This morning in room 208, their subject was order of operations. Mr. U had given them a mnemonic device to help them remember what to do first when faced with a complex equation: Please Excuse My Dear Aunt Sally. What it meant was: you do operations in Parentheses first, then Exponents, then Multiplication, Division, Addition and Subtraction.

He wrote an equation on the board:

$$12 \times (5 + 4) =$$

In the front row, Chastity Williams raised her hand. Back in September, Chastity was obsessed with math, always going to Mr. U for extra problems and special math games. For the past few weeks, though, she and Mr. U had been feuding—she acted up in class one day, he called her mother to report her misbehavior and Chastity decided she couldn't stand him. ("We're both Geminis," Mr. U said by way of explanation.) Today, for the first time in a while, she had decided to participate in his class instead of sitting in the back, sulking, and so far this morning, she had been getting every question right.

"I'm going to let Chastity have this one because she's hot today," Mr. U said. "Everyone listen, please."

"Twelve times five equals sixty," Chastity said, "plus four is sixty-four."

"Okay, this one is simple enough," Mr. U said, turning to the board. "Twelve times five is sixty, plus four is sixty-four. Correct?"

From his seat in the middle of the second row, Thomas Porter spoke up: "No."

Chastity turned around to stare at him. "Yes!" she said.

"What do you mean, no?" asked Mr. U.

"I said no because you've got to do five plus four first."

"Why would you do five plus four first?" Mr. U was back to his incredulous act.

"Because of the parentheses," said Thomas.

Mr. U walked slowly over to Thomas's desk and slapped him five. "Mr. *Porter,*" he said admiringly. He turned back to the class. "Trained or untrained?" he asked.

"Trained," they said.

Chastity didn't say anything. She couldn't believe she'd messed up My Dear Aunt Sally.

Each week, the students in the sixth grade took a practice test, and afterward, Grey and her staff would sit down and analyze the scores. As the citywide tests drew closer, Grey began to notice something a little disturbing: after climbing steadily for the first couple of months of test prep, the numbers had hit a plateau. Many students seemed to be scoring below their potential, missing questions that she knew they knew. There were some, like Chastity Williams, who were motivated by the competition and the scores, eager to raise themselves from a 2 to a 3 or a 3 to a 4. But then there was another group, the students who were already the hardest to engage, who seemed to be losing interest. Attendance in the morning test-prep classes was down to about 50 percent, despite a system of cash incentives to encourage students to show up.

Grey was well aware that Geoffrey Canada and Lorraine Monroe thought the correct approach to these tests was simply to do more and more and more. But she wasn't so sure. She saw two paradigms emerging at the school: the sixth-floor paradigm, which was all about cramming, preparing, testing, and scores; and the second-floor paradigm, her paradigm, which was about raising achievement over the long term by gradually molding students into learners. Test prep had started eating into classes like music and gym, which Grey thought were essential to creating well-rounded students who could succeed not just at multiple-choice tests, but in life. She worried that this obsessive focus on tests was burning the kids out. They were still absorbing the culture shock of moving from schools where no one really cared how they did to a school where everyone seemed to care very intensely. To put all this additional pressure on them—especially on the lowest-performing students—felt counterproductive.

In room 208, Mr. U wrote a new question on the board:

$$5^3 =$$

"You have one minute," he said.

Ten seconds later, Chastity, in the front row, had her hand up as high as it could go. "Ooooooh!" she said. She looked like Arnold Horshack from *Welcome Back, Kotter,* if Arnold Horshack had been black, twelve years old, and a girl. But at the end of the sixty seconds, Mr. U called not on Chastity but on Bianca Renteria, a small girl with a high voice in the back row.

"Hands down, please," Mr. U said. "Pencils down. Thank you. We are trained. We are trained. Renteria, take us to breakfast, please. Read the question."

"Three to the fifth power . . ."

"Flip that," said Mr. U.

"Five to the third power?"

"Five to the third power. Richardson, what does that mean?"

Roshauna Richardson looked up.

"But I thought *I* was doing the problem," said Bianca, her voice trailing off to a whine. "That's not fair."

Chastity interrupted: "Can I do the problem, please?"

Mr. U ignored her. "Calm down, Renteria," he said. "I was going to go back to you. Richardson, five to the third power means we use the number *blank* how many times?"

"We use the number five three times."

"All right. Miss Renteria, solve the problem, please."

Bianca looked at the board. "Five times five . . ." she said.

"Which is?" said Mr. U.

"Ten."

"And then?"

"And then another five times five. And then it equals twenty-five." Silence. Bianca corrected herself: "No, no, twenty!"

Roshauna Richardson spoke up. "I disagree."

"Prove it," said Mr. U.

"I disagree because five times five times five—"

"Oh!" yelled Bianca. "It's fifteen! It's fifteen!"

Roshauna concurred. "It's five times five times five. Three times. Five times three equals fifteen."

"So the answer's fifteen? We all agree, the answer is fifteen?"

Heads started nodding until, from the front, Chastity shouted "No!" Chaos erupted. Everyone started calling out answers at once, with Bianca's piercing voice cutting through the noise: "Fifteen! Fifteen!" Things were suddenly looking pretty untrained.

Chastity couldn't stand it anymore. She stood up in the front row with her arm raised, glaring at Mr. U. "*Me!*" she shouted.

Finally Mr. U nodded in her direction. He raised his hand to quiet the room.

"The answer is 125," Chastity said, still standing. "Five times five is twenty-five. And then five times twenty-five equals 125."

There was a stunned silence.

"What?!" a voice cried from the back of the class.

But Chastity was right. "The answer is 125," Mr. U explained, multiplying the 5s on the board. "Very nice."

"I thought I was *right!*" said Roshauna.

"That's okay," said Mr. U. "You can be wrong today. Just make sure you're right on April 19."

It was twenty minutes to eight. Nine days to go. Mr. U gathered his papers together and looked out at the class. "All right, it's almost time for breakfast," he said. "Do you have this down?"

"Yes," they said together.

"You've got this?"

"Yes!"

"You've *got* this?"

"Yes!"

He stared at them over his reading glasses.

"We shall see," he said, almost to himself. "We shall see."

THE DROP-EVERYTHING-AND-CRAM campaign had gone far enough, Grey decided. She ended test-prep classes early, a few days before the English test, in order to take some of the pressure off the students. The sixth-grade basketball team, the Promise Academy Panthers, had a big game on Friday night against Harlem Village Academy. The Panthers had an undefeated record in the Charter School Athletic Association, and Grey planned a schoolwide pep rally before the game, where everyone could blow off a little steam. It turned out to be a big success: the cheerleaders swished their pompons and danced and stepped, the coaches drew up plays and yelled and pointed downcourt, and the Panthers crushed Harlem Village, 40 to 24, which meant they would play in the championship game in a few weeks' time.

But the tests were still on everyone's mind. The day before the math test, Tiffany Vargas and Diamond Quilles went over to Taylor Brown's place to study. They knew they still needed to work on their math skills, so they invented a jump-rope game as a way to get in some last-minute cramming. The two girls turning the rope would fire math questions at the one who was jumping, and she could keep going as long as she was getting them right. As soon as she got one wrong, the girl who stumped her would get a turn in the middle. The three of them played until the sun went down, calling out times tables and division and exponents, jumping and turning.

On the morning of the first test, a Tuesday, the students gathered in the cafeteria at 7:45 for a hot breakfast and a final pep talk. Mr. U took the handheld wireless mike and reminded everyone to eat something nutritious. Michelle Brown, the school's director of instruction, said a few encouraging words and told the students that when she woke up that morning, she had butterflies in her stomach, as if she were the one taking the test. Then Terri Grey took the microphone, and everyone was quiet. She walked slowly between the tables as she spoke. There had been an altercation in school the day before, she said, a small scuffle, and as punishment, the children who took part had been given detention and had lost the right to attend the school dance scheduled for the end of April. But Grey announced that as of this morning, she was rescinding some of the punishment. Because of the test, she said, today was a "do-over day." Everyone was going to start clean, which meant that everyone was allowed to go to the dance.

"Sometimes you do get second chances," she said as she walked between the tables. "Like we're going to have a do-over day for behavior. But today is our test day, and that is *not* a time when you're going to get a second chance, because there are going to be no second chances for this assessment." She was wearing loose brown suit-pants and a black knit shawl, and as she walked, she drew the shawl tighter around her shoulders. "All of the scores are going to be published in the newspaper," she said into the microphone. "Everyone will know how our school is doing. So we need you to understand that this is a very important event for our school." She pointed at a girl in the corner. "Sharlynn, spit out your gum," she said. Sharlynn Vasquez walked over to the garbage can, opened wide, and let a pink wad drop from her mouth.

Grey kept moving, still talking. "A couple of students came up to me this morning and said, 'I'm ready for this test,'" she said. "I said, 'That's great.' They said, 'I think today is going to be easy.'" She shook her head. "That's wrong. I want you guys to understand that today is not going to be easy. These assessments are challenging. They're going to take some thought. You're not going to understand everything that they're asking." She had made it back to the front of the cafeteria. She looked out at the students. "All we're expecting is for you to do your best," she said.

Each test lasted sixty-five minutes. There were ten passages in the reading test—poems, mock advertisements, little stories—and a handful of multiple-choice questions about each one: What would a good title for this passage be? What is the main idea of this story? In math, the trickiest questions involved adding fractions, long division, and probabilities. When it was all over, there was cake and ice cream at lunch, and then a long wait for the results.

The scores finally arrived on a Monday at the beginning of June, and as soon as Geoffrey Canada saw them, he knew they were bad news. On the English test, twenty-one students out of one hundred scored at or above grade level—eighteen on level 3 and three on level 4. Fifty-nine were on level 2, and twenty were on level 1. Math was worse: nine students on grade level—level 3—and then forty-nine on level 2 and forty-one on level 1. Chastity Williams, who had nailed 5^3 in Mr. U's test-prep class, got a 2 in math. Thomas Porter, who outsmarted her on the parentheses, got a 1. Bianca got a 1 as well. The jump-rope trio did better than most: Taylor and Diamond both got 3s in math; Tiffany fell below grade level, but she did get a 2. Only five children managed to score on grade level in both math and English; the other ninety-five fell short in at least one subject.

Meanwhile, the headlines in the newspapers were about how well students had done all across the city. Sixth-grade English scores in New York were up sharply, from 33 percent of students scoring on grade level citywide to 48 percent; math scores rose for sixth-grade students, too, though only slightly, from 40 percent on grade level to 41 percent on grade level. There were even more impressive numbers in other grades: fifth-grade students scoring on grade level on the math test rose from 39 percent to 54 percent; in English, that number jumped from 49 percent to 69 percent. Mayor Bloomberg was thrilled. "Our reforms are working," he said in a press conference at the Education Department headquarters the day the scores were announced. "We have made more headway in improving students' classroom performance than at any time in the city's recent history."

The city's charter schools had done especially well. The Harlem Village Academy, whose basketball team had been trounced by Promise Academy's team just before the tests, trounced Promise on the tests themselves: 71 percent scored on grade level in reading, and 74 percent scored on grade level in math. (Like the students at Promise Academy, Harlem Village students were all black or Hispanic, almost all poor, and all chosen by lottery.) Other charter schools achieved similar success: A story in the *New York Post* reported that "charter-school students in the city are more proficient in reading and math than their peers in traditional public schools, according to an analysis of recently released scores on citywide standardized tests." Charter school students were ahead by seven percentage points in reading and eleven in math, the *Post* said. It was exactly the kind of article Canada had been hoping to read after the tests—except for the final line: "But overall gains were hindered by low scores among sixth- and seventh-graders in both subjects at Promise Academy and the Opportunity Charter School, two new and large charter schools in Harlem." Canada was used to glowing coverage in the press: he had been interviewed by Matt Lauer on the *Today* show and appeared on the cover of the *New York Times Magazine;* his full-page portrait by Richard Avedon had been part of a special portfolio in the *New Yorker.* He wasn't used to being singled out as a failure in the *New York Post.*

The Promise Academy scores may have been unimpressive when compared to other charter schools in the neighborhood—even when compared to many public schools in the neighborhood—but perhaps the most troubling comparison was between the sixth-grade scores and the scores the same students had received on their fifth-grade citywide tests, a year earlier. Twelve students had gone up a level in English, and eleven had improved in math. But thirteen students had gone *down* a level in English, and twenty-one had dropped a level or more in math. Admittedly, the school's administrators had been openly skeptical of those fifth-grade scores all year—mediocre though they were, they seemed inflated, because they exceeded the students' incoming Iowa and TerraNova results. But even if the comparisons with the fifth-grade scores were unfair, they were still being made, and it wasn't an attractive picture: after a year of the finest standards-based charter school education money can buy, Promise Academy had succeeded in lowering more scores than it raised.

6   Bad Apples

IN SEPTEMBER 2005, Promise Academy's first middle school class returned to school after a summer vacation that seemed ridiculously short. The students were in seventh grade now—most of them, anyway; a handful had been held back and were making a second attempt at the sixth grade—and they were joined in the school's hallways by almost a hundred new sixth-graders and a new crop of teachers. The student body had doubled in size overnight, and the school had expanded upward; the middle school now occupied both the second and third floors of the Harlem Children's Zone headquarters. Meanwhile, a few blocks uptown, the elementary school had grown, too, adding a new kindergarten class. And a second elementary school—Promise Academy II—had opened inside an existing public school on 121st Street, with both a kindergarten and a first-grade class.

It was a new year, but it didn't feel that way to Terri Grey. She and her staff, like most schoolteachers, were used to two months off in the summer. But at Promise Academy middle school, where the academic year lasted until early August, summer vacation was pretty much a mirage, and Labor Day didn't bring with it the usual excitement of back-to-school; to Grey, the first day of school felt like being startled awake from a too-short nap. It meant the beginning of another round of test prep, discipline problems, critiques from the school's board of directors, and demands from Geoffrey Canada. Up on the sixth floor, the Harlem Children's Zone veterans were still grumbling about the citywide test scores. They had heard the official response from Grey and from Doreen Land—that the scores were exactly what everyone should have expected, that it was impossible to accelerate kids from a second-grade reading level to a sixth-grade reading level in a year—but many of them still felt resentful, even angry. In its first year, it seemed to them, the middle school had managed to swallow all of Canada's attention and a sizable portion of the institution's resources, and yet the people on the second floor had wound up embarrassing them all.

Canada had resisted calls from his staff in June to fire Grey or Land or both, but he was determined to improve the situation, and the test scores, at the middle school. "I feel like I underreacted back when we were getting ready for the test," Canada said in his office before the new school year began. "There were times I intuitively felt, like, I don't know about this—but I didn't want to overrule Doreen and Terri. There were some things I thought we should push on, and in deference to the experts I didn't push. I should have. Now it's full steam ahead, guns blazing. We're going to get this done."

Stanley Druckenmiller was feeling the pressure, too. As well as committing a fair-sized chunk of his personal fortune, Druckenmiller had raised millions of dollars for the Harlem Children's Zone from financiers and CEOs, his friends and colleagues and competitors and golf partners, and although nobody was yet asking for a refund, Druckenmiller knew that they all expected results, and that they were all disappointed by the 2005 test scores. "If we don't show serious movement by the end of next year, and success by the ninth grade, then I think things could become very challenging," Druckenmiller told me that summer. "If a few years go by and we're not producing what we said we could produce, then the donors have every right to ask questions and, frankly, maybe to divert their funds elsewhere."

Druckenmiller and Kenneth Langone, his fellow billionaire on the school's board of trustees, were anxious to hear from the school's administrators that there was a plan in place to fix things, but so far they hadn't been getting the kind of response they wanted. At board meetings, they kept pushing for answers. If they were going to be losing sleep over what was going on at the school—and they were—they wanted to make sure everyone else was losing sleep, too. The bottom line, Druckenmiller told Land and her principals, was quite simple: "We can't fail."

Druckenmiller's aggravation was heightened by the fact that other charter schools in the city and around the country seemed to be achieving the kind of results that had so far eluded Promise Academy, and they were getting a lot of attention from the news media and from Joel Klein, the city's schools chancellor, for doing it. There were a handful of these standout charter schools scattered across the Northeast, including many of the schools that Abigail and Stephan Thernstrom had celebrated in their book *No Excuses,* like KIPP Academy in the Bronx, Amistad Academy in New Haven, North Star Academy in Newark, and Roxbury Prep in Boston. Most of them were founded in the late 1990s by young, well-educated idealists—education entrepreneurs, they were sometimes called—and designed with the express purpose of closing the achievement gap.

Druckenmiller decided to do some research on his own, to ask around and find out why Promise Academy wasn't enjoying the same kind of success as these hot schools. The first person he consulted was an old friend named Paul Tudor Jones II. Druckenmiller and Jones had a lot in common: they were both hedge-fund managers in their early fifties who occupied a slot on *Forbes*'s list of the four hundred richest Americans; they were both philanthropists; and each of them had in the fall of 2004 put several million dollars into his own brand-new charter school targeted at poor African American children. Druckenmiller's was Promise Academy; Jones's, located in the Bedford-Stuyvesant neighborhood of Brooklyn, was called Excellence Charter School, and it was New York City's first charter school for boys only. Jones invited Druckenmiller to visit with the principal of Excellence, and when they met, Druckenmiller liked what he heard, especially the school's emphasis on discipline, what Druckenmiller later described, approvingly, as the "intense monitoring and shaping of behavioral patterns."

That fall, Druckenmiller asked two of the school's cofounders, both members of the charter school world's emerging elite, to take a tour of Promise Academy and then give him and Canada their assessment of the school's progress and prospects. The two young men toured the school, dropped in on a few classes, observed discipline and instruction and organization, and then they sat down with Canada and Druckenmiller in a conference room on the sixth floor to debrief. Their verdict wasn't very positive.

"Their impressions were that the school had some issues," Canada told me later. In fact, the two visitors delivered what sounded to Canada like a sweeping critique of his entire model. "The end result of their conversation was, basically, Harlem Children's Zone can't run schools," he said. "That was their analysis. They didn't say it like that, but that's really what the statement was, that you needed to give Promise Academy over to one of the institutions that run schools, like KIPP or Amistad." The case the men made, Canada said, was that the leaders of those school networks had experience and know-how, and, what's more, they weren't trying to run a school and a social service organization simultaneously, the way Canada was. As long as Canada kept trying to do both jobs at once, they said, it was going to be hard for him to compete with specialists who did nothing but operate charter schools.

Canada was taken aback. What the two men were describing would mean an enormous tactical change—giving an outside organization control over one of the key elements of the Harlem

Children's Zone strategy. But Canada seemed to be the only one who thought it was such a radical suggestion. When he spoke later with Druckenmiller and Langone, they said they thought the idea made a lot of sense. At the very least, they told Canada, it was worth considering.

THE CHARTER SCHOOL movement was in a period of transition. A decade earlier, when only a few states were granting charters, every charter school was an island, trying out its own mad or brilliant educational theory. But as charter school proponents studied the successes and learned from the mistakes of their predecessors, patterns, even a consensus, began to emerge. There were certain practices that seemed to deliver consistently positive results, and those became increasingly popular—especially within the growing contingent of charter schools that were dedicated specifically to educating poor and minority students.

"More time on task" was the most basic principle—an extended school day and an extended school year—but there were other common threads. The schools all devoted an abundance of resources to teacher and principal recruitment and training. They considered classroom instruction and lesson planning as much a science as an art. Explicit goals were set for each year, month, and day of each class, and principals had considerable authority to redirect and even remove teachers who weren't meeting those goals. The schools tested their students frequently, and they used the test results to make adjustments to the curriculum and to personalize instruction for each student.

The most striking thing about these schools, though, especially to a casual visitor, was their intense focus on discipline and the careful molding of what the leaders of these schools called character. The walls of KIPP schools were festooned with slogans and mottoes ("Team Always Beats Individual," "All of Us Will Learn"), and there was a conscious effort to guide the behavior, and even the values, of their students. Using chants, motivational posters, incentives, encouragements, and punishments, the school leaders directed students in everything from the principles of teamwork and the importance of an optimistic outlook to the rudiments of how to sit in class, where to direct their eyes when a teacher was talking, and even how to nod appropriately. Many of the schools followed a system for classroom behavior invented by KIPP's founders, David Levin and Michael Feinberg, called SLANT, which instructed them to Sit up, Listen, Ask questions, Nod, and Track with their eyes whoever was speaking. On one visit to KIPP Academy, I was standing with Levin at the front of a music class of about sixty students, listening to him talk, when he suddenly interrupted himself and pointed at me. "Do you notice what he's doing right now?" he asked the class. They all called out at once, "Nodding!" Levin's contention was that Americans of a certain background learned these methods for taking in information early on and employed them instinctively. KIPP students, he said, needed to be taught the methods explicitly.

The strategies these educators were employing seemed to be working: students at their schools consistently scored well on statewide and citywide standardized tests. At North Star in 2005, 94 percent of eighth-grade students were proficient in language arts, compared with 57 percent of students in Newark and 83 percent of students in New Jersey as a whole; in math, 81 percent were proficient, compared with 37 percent of students in Newark and 72 percent of students in the state as a whole. At Amistad, 87 percent of the eighth-grade class was proficient in math, compared with 76 percent of students in Connecticut as a whole, and 85 percent of the class was proficient in reading, compared with 75 percent of students in the state.

The scores that were most impressive (and distressing) to Druckenmiller came from KIPP's schools in New York City. In 2005, 79 percent of sixth-grade students at the Bronx academy scored at or above grade level on the citywide reading test; only 21 percent of Promise Academy's sixth-grade students had hit that mark. The math scores were even more disparate: 97 percent of KIPP's sixth-grade students scored at or above grade level, compared to 9 percent of Promise students. And it wasn't only the Bronx school, which had been around for close to a decade, that was putting up solid numbers; just a few blocks west of Promise Academy, another KIPP school, in only its second year of operation, managed to get 84 percent of its sixth-grade students to grade level in math in 2005, and 72 percent of them to grade level in reading.

The ability to contemplate data was what had made Druckenmiller wealthy, and to him, this data seemed crystal clear. The KIPP model—what Druckenmiller described as "more of a military-style, real rote-learning, rote-behavior discipline thing"—delivered results. He spoke with David Levin to find out more about KIPP's methods, and he encouraged Canada to look more closely at the KIPP way. To Druckenmiller, the issue seemed straightforward: KIPP and Promise Academy were trying to achieve the same goal, and KIPP was doing a better job. But to Canada, things weren't so simple. Though he admired KIPP, he thought what Levin was doing in the Bronx was something very different from what he was trying to achieve in Harlem.

Like all charter schools, KIPP Academy officially had a nonselective admissions policy—incoming classes were chosen by lottery, and any family in the city was welcome to enter the lottery. But many outside observers had charged that KIPP was able nonetheless to attract a disproportionate number of high achievers, and KIPP's internal statistics bore out that claim to some extent: students at the Bronx academy arrived scoring better on average on tests than typical children in their neighborhoods. If you looked back at the fourth-grade citywide math-test results for students entering KIPP in fifth grade, their scores were well above the average for the South Bronx. And on their fourth-grade reading tests they often scored above the average for the entire city—well above the dismal level of incoming Promise Academy students.

In addition, the motivational strategies used by schools like

KIPP's, Canada knew, often had the effect of establishing a separation between the KIPP kids and the other kids in the low-income neighborhoods where they lived. Teachers and administrators at KIPP made a point of contrasting KIPP's well-behaved, attentive students with kids in "normal school" who didn't pay attention in class, and they often reminded students that the extra hours they were putting in would elevate them above the average inner-city student. Most KIPP schools in New York were tucked away on one floor of an existing public school, and when visitors came by, KIPP administrators liked to show off the contrast between the orderly, sedate way that the KIPP children behaved in the hallway or the cafeteria with the shoving and pushing and yelling of the public school kids. As a motivational technique for their students, it worked: if you are made to feel special and elite, you tend to work harder. The effect, though, was that KIPP students often became isolated from their community; some of the kids at the Bronx academy said they had drifted away from their elementary school friends, either because their friends resented their newfound academic success, or because the KIPP students were simply working too hard to have time to hang out like they used to.

And this situation—a blighted neighborhood producing a select group of high-achieving kids who manage to accomplish great things and succeed beyond their peers—was exactly the one Canada was trying to avoid when he set up the Harlem Children's Zone. If Canada's model was one of contamination, in which positive ideas and practices spread within a family and throughout a neighborhood, the KIPP model sometimes seemed by contrast to be one of quarantine, walling off the most promising kids from a sick neighborhood's contagion. As Canada often said, he was tired of programs that helped a few kids "beat the odds" and make it out of the ghetto; his goal was to *change* the odds, and to do it for all of Harlem's kids. The idea that Promise Academy might stand as an island of success in the middle of Harlem's ocean of failure—that felt entirely wrong to him.

So Canada told Druckenmiller that he thought it would be a mistake to give up control of the schools to an organization like KIPP. The Harlem Children's Zone and KIPP, Canada explained, were operating on "dueling models," and only one of those models could win. Either Levin was right, and the best approach was to take the inner-city ten-year-olds who really wanted to learn and give them a concentrated, life-changing dose of high-quality education in middle school, or Canada was right, and the only way to save large numbers of poor children in a neighborhood like Harlem was to give them *all* a high-quality education, even the least motivated and least prepared, beginning at a very young age, and to do it in the context of a broader transformation of the entire community. If he gave up the schools, Canada said, it would close off the conversation about whether his approach was the right one. And that, he said, would be devastating not only to him personally, but also to the future of his organization.

Still, Canada's short-term problem was one that was quite familiar to Levin: a middle school full of poorly prepared inner-city kids and a staff that seemed unable to catch them up as quickly as Canada needed them to. Levin had a model and a system that had proven to be very good at solving that problem. So why not copy it? Why not bring SLANT and slogans and orderly lines in the hallways to Promise Academy? In other parts of his organization, Canada hadn't hesitated to look around for what management gurus like to call "best practices"; when he wanted to set up Baby College, he found the person he thought was best at educating parents — T. Berry Brazelton — and hired him as a consultant and based the entire program on his ideas. Why not do the same thing now, but with David Levin instead of Dr. Brazelton?

When I asked Canada to explain his reasons, he turned, as he often did, to the example of his son Geoffrey Jr. In his son's public school in Valley Stream, there were no uniforms, no special rules, no extraordinary methods; the walls weren't filled with motivational posters, and no one was teaching the kids where to direct their eyes and how to nod. And yet the school worked just fine, and the students' scores were ahead of grade level.

Now, Canada knew full well *why* the scores in Valley Stream were so much better than in your average Harlem public school—it was mostly due to the fact that Geoffrey Jr. and his classmates had parents, like Canada and his wife, who were well-educated, nurturing, and obsessed with their children's development, and the kids in Harlem didn't. But still, the idea that children in Harlem and the Bronx needed an entirely different kind of schooling than children in the suburbs—that made Canada more than a little uncomfortable. He felt it sent the wrong message to the rest of the country. "To the extent that we present this population of students as so different from the rest of America in terms of who they are and what they require, I think that's a problem," he said. If white, middle-class Americans are told that children in Harlem need their own special category of educational practices, he said, they will get the message that those Harlem kids "are not like us. They're not the same as us. There's something wrong with them."

Druckenmiller was sympathetic to Canada's desire not to isolate Promise Academy from the larger community of Harlem. But he and Langone were also adamant that things at the school had to change—and it was hard for them to accept that KIPP's highly successful model was somehow wrong for Promise students if it was working so well a couple of miles away in the South Bronx.

So in the winter of 2006, Langone, Druckenmiller, and Canada agreed that they would continue to try things Canada's way—but they also agreed that time was running out. If Canada wasn't able to make real progress with the school in another year or eighteen months, then it would be time to look at handing the schools over to an institution like KIPP.

Canada agreed to the terms. "If we can't work it, I'll bring someone in to run the school," he told me later. "I'm not going to argue with Ken and Stan over a decision like this. I'll hold my nose and do it."

■

AS CANADA SAW IT, the only thing that needed to be fixed at Promise Academy was what he called "blocking and tackling," the basic nuts and bolts of school management that Terri Grey sometimes seemed to him unable to master: solving discipline problems, collecting useful data on students' progress, developing curriculum, managing teachers.

Grey, not surprisingly, didn't think the problem was that simple.

The previous year, Grey's impression had been that she and Canada were working from two competing paradigms—hers a progressive model concerned with educating the whole child and avoiding burnout in both students and teachers, his a results-oriented model in which every available resource was devoted to improving test scores quickly. But this year, she told me, she felt like the competition between the two paradigms was over, and Canada had won. "It was just kind of a swallowing of 'OK, this is the way it's going to be, so I'm just going to make the best of this situation even though it may not be what I philosophically believe is best for students,'" Grey explained. Unlike the previous year, when it wasn't until February that there was a plan in place to prepare students for the standardized tests they would be taking, this year test prep was under way by the third week in September. There were morning test-prep sessions, a test-prep block during the school day, test prep in the afterschool program, and test prep on Saturdays. Students went over the basics again and again: grammar, spelling, punctuation, how to write a coherent essay, as well as multiplication, fractions, and geometry. Grey tried to safeguard the elements of the curriculum that she cared about more than test prep: project-based learning; art and music; "advisories," the regular small-group discussions between teachers and students about real-life problems and concerns that were becoming popular at many middle and high schools. But as the year went on, the time dedicated to test prep only grew, and the time dedicated to everything else was forced to shrink further.

Grey didn't much like the test-prep regime, but it wasn't her biggest headache; her biggest headache was the behavior of her students. There was no dean of students or vice principal at Promise Academy to enforce discipline, so Grey was the one who had to deal with the frequent disruptions in class, as well as the occasional fight in the hallways or the cafeteria. And the more she learned about the home life of her students, the more their outbursts and breakdowns made sense to her. "Somewhere between 60 and 80 percent of our students have serious emotional needs or behavioral challenges," she told me. She could rattle off a list of the issues they were dealing with at home: "substance abuse, domestic violence, foster care, involvement with ACS"—the city's child-welfare agency—"as well as mental illness or emotional disturbances within their family." Her students needed help, and lots of it, and she didn't always know how to give it to them.

To Grey, that was the crucial difference between Promise Academy and KIPP Academy: the relative circumstances and abilities of their incoming students. KIPP's tendency toward self-selection was reinforced by the demands that KIPP placed on their parents, she believed, and specifically by the contract every parent was asked to sign. For Grey, that was the most important element of the equation. "At most charter schools," she said, "if the school is not a good fit for their child, the school finds a way to counsel parents out"—to firmly suggest, in other words, that their child might be happier elsewhere. "Whereas Promise Academy is taking the most disengaged families and students and saying, 'No, we want you, and we're trying to keep you here, and we *don't* want to counsel you out.'" The result, she said, was that Promise Academy had plenty of students and parents who just wouldn't survive at a KIPP school. Grey estimated that a third of the students at Promise Academy were "very disengaged"—but they were precisely the population that the school's charter was written for; they were the kids, she knew, that Canada cared about the most.

Grey didn't disagree with Canada's philosophy of inclusion, but it made running the school difficult. When she told parents they had to come in to pick up their children's report cards and meet with their child's teachers, many parents simply didn't show up. Their understanding of the "promise" in Promise Academy, as Grey saw it, was that the Harlem Children's Zone had promised to educate their child, which meant that they as parents didn't need to play much of a role. So when Grey or another administrator at the school asked parents to take more responsibility for making sure a student completed homework or paid attention in class, Grey explained, "They say, 'I thought Harlem Children's Zone was going to help me. I thought Promise Academy was going to take care of my student.' They want Harlem Children's Zone and Promise to take care of everything for them."

And when that didn't happen, Grey said, parents often reacted badly: "They're quick to blame and come in and speak rudely or loudly to staff, rather than come in and be calm and sit and listen."

Grey felt that Canada was demanding KIPP-like results without giving her the tools that KIPP principals had to select students and make demands on parents. And although she never said it to Canada directly, Grey believed that it was just wrong to say, as Canada did, that every student in Promise Academy middle school was going to make it to college.

"I *know* that some are not going to make it," she said as the school's second year progressed.

She explained her calculations. "About 20 percent of our population is special-needs students," she said. "These students are receiving a lot of attention. They get special tutoring in their classrooms to help them, they're receiving counseling, they're receiving pullouts"—where students are pulled out of their regular class for one-on-one instruction with a specialist. "But these students are never going to be ready to go into a college environment, because they do not have the basic skills. They're making improvements—maybe they entered earning a 30 on their test, and now they're earning a 65—but they're not going to get to twelfth grade ready to enter college."

Behind closed doors, Grey had talked about this issue with a few of her teachers, a rebel band she called, with tongue in cheek, "a small group of radical educators at Promise"—and they had concluded that "some sort of vocational or technical school is needed for these kids, or just a real serious acknowledgment of the fact that these children are not going to be able to do this." It wasn't just the 20 percent who had been evaluated and designated as special-needs students, Grey said. There was another 10 percent who had serious learning issues but hadn't been given any kind of official diagnosis. So that meant that about 30 percent of the students, by her estimate, were not likely ever to be college material.

This 30 percent were, generally, the same kids with the disengaged parents, the same kids who made trouble in the classroom, the same kids who took up all Grey's time so that she couldn't evaluate teachers or rethink curriculum or do all the other things she knew she should be doing. And Grey wasn't alone in thinking that Promise Academy might do better without them. Druckenmiller and Langone talked frequently with Canada about the subject of the students Druckenmiller called "bad apples," and whether they were holding the school back.

In fact, it often seemed that there was only one person in favor of keeping the bad apples exactly where they were, and that was Canada. "It's reassuring to me that we've got kids with these really deep emotional problems," he told me. "These kids need a lot of help and a lot of support, but that just suggests to me we're working with exactly who we need to be working with." That was what set Promise Academy apart from other public schools, and even other charter schools, Canada believed: because it was surrounded by all the other programs of the Harlem Children's Zone, the school could offer additional supports to those 10 or 20 or 30 percent of kids who had the most serious problems.

When Canada sat down with me to reflect on this, he was in his office on the sixth floor of the Harlem Children's Zone building. On his office walls, there were two ad hoc photo galleries. The one on the west wall held the official photos—Canada with Mayor Bloomberg, Canada with President Clinton—and the one on the north wall was more personal: photos of his family and friends and, most prominently, his karate students, the ones he worked with in the 1980s, when he first arrived at Rheedlen. He thought about these kids all the time, especially when conversations about "bad apples" came up. They had come to him unstable and angry and eager to fight. He had taught them martial arts and mentored them through one crisis after another; he drove them in a rented van to tournaments all over the Northeast. He had lost some of them, to gun violence and prison and drugs, and those losses still haunted him. But twenty years later, most of them were now thriving—college graduates holding down decent jobs.

"There are some kids up on that wall that there was no way they should have gotten through college," Canada said. "But you can get them through." He leaned back in his chair and looked up at the faces in the photos. "Now, if you've never done it yourself, then, absolutely, you can look at certain kids when they're eleven and think, 'This kid can't make it.' You *do* think that—until you've actually taken some of those kids that everybody else has said can't make it, and you help that kid make it. And once you've personally made it happen, you never lose that. You see that kid as a grownup, going on with his life, and you think, 'How many kids like this one have we thrown away?'"

Canada wasn't thinking only about his karate students; he was also thinking about himself, his brothers, the kids on Union Avenue. He turned for an example to two of his colleagues: Ron Carlos, a senior manager of Harlem Children's Zone, and the chief operating officer, his old college friend George Khaldun. Like Canada, Carlos and Khaldun had survived difficult, violent, impoverished childhoods. "When Ron and George and I get together," Canada said, "we talk about what the odds were of us ending up in this place that we're in. The odds were all against us. So that kid who is eleven, and someone is saying he can't make it—that could be me! That could be Ron. That could be George. It could be any of us." That perspective was what underlay everything that Canada was working toward, and it was the motivating force behind his approach to Promise Academy.

"The fact is," he said, "we're in the saving-kid business. That's not what schools traditionally do, but that's what we do."

SINCE EARLY ON IN the fall, Canada had been talking with Druckenmiller and Langone about whether he should fire Grey or keep her on for a third year. As the statewide tests approached, Canada grew convinced that replacing her was the right thing to do, no matter how the scores turned out. Some days, he wondered whether he should let Doreen Land, the superintendent, go, too—maybe the problem went higher than Grey. He didn't make any definitive announcements, but he started quietly looking around for a new principal. He asked David Levin and Joel Klein for recommendations, and they gave him some names of possible candidates.

The man he finally found to take Grey's place was Glen Pinder, the principal of a successful elementary school in Red Bank, New Jersey. Pinder was a burly African American in his late thirties with a reputation as a disciplinarian. He had been through KIPP's principal-training program, and he liked the KIPP model, especially when it came to guiding and controlling student behavior. At his job interview, Pinder asked Canada what kind of job security he'd have as principal of the middle school, and Canada told him he'd have none. No contract, no grace period, nothing. If he didn't deliver results, he'd be fired. Pinder took the job anyway.

In May, Canada called Grey and Land into his office, and he told Grey that her tenure at Promise Academy was over. He knew that he was taking a risk, trying someone new, but he felt that it was a bigger risk to start the third year with a leader in place with whom he didn't see eye to eye. "In the end, she didn't believe it could be done," Canada said a few days later. "In the end, she felt the teachers were overwhelmed, that, you know, it's a long school year, it's a long school day, people are feeling burned out. And, well, yeah, so you've got to go in and rally the troops. That's why you're a leader. We're in a war." He described the qualities he thought a successful principal needed. "You have to walk in the door with a take-no-prisoners, I'm-in-charge, move-over-a-new-sheriff's-in-town, let-me-at-them attitude," he said. "You almost need to be someone who looks in the face of reality and laughs and simply says, 'That's not for me. I don't believe that. I don't care what the evidence is, I believe there's a way of getting this done.'"

Pinder made his first appearance at Promise Academy on June 22, 2006, on a night when the parents of the next year's incoming sixth-grade class, chosen by lottery in April, were invited to gather in the cafeteria to get acquainted and oriented. He wore a tan suit, perfectly tailored to his substantial frame, and a purple-and-orange-striped tie. It was a hot day, but he kept his suit jacket buttoned, and he was perspiring heavily. Every minute or so he removed his glasses, took a thick blue handkerchief from his pocket, and used it to mop the beads of sweat that had formed on his brow.

His appointed task for the evening was simply to say a few words of welcome to the parents, and when his turn came, he walked slowly and purposefully to the lectern, his handkerchief in his left hand and his notes in his right.

"Good evening," he began. "I want to start by congratulating the incoming parents at Promise Academy." This was the first the sixth-grade parents had seen of the school, and so they didn't have any reason to think Pinder's speech was at all unusual. But the teachers and administrators in the audience who had been at the school for the last two years noticed a difference right away. Pinder didn't talk much about the promises that Promise Academy was making. Instead, he made demands, one after another. "I want to give you a brief overview of what I expect from you as parents and what I expect of students, and what you should expect of us as a school," he said. "Promise Academy will provide a vigorous academic program. We will prepare our students for college, to excel in college, and to graduate from college. For the parents, I expect you to have your child here, on time, on a regular basis, every day. A child cannot learn if they're at home. We want you to support the activities and the programs that we have here at the Promise Academy. This means checking homework, following up with teachers, and supporting the rules and regulations of the Promise Academy. Expectations will be set very high for your children. If we try to reach the stars, we will land on the moon."

Pinder explained that he had two fundamental rules that he would use to govern the school, and to anyone familiar with the KIPP schools, they were immediately recognizable: "work hard" and "be nice," the two rules that David Levin and Michael Feinberg developed twelve years earlier for the first KIPP school back in Houston. "By working hard I mean you have to make every effort at all times to succeed," Pinder said, reading from his notes. "Failure is not an option. Excuses will not be accepted. By being nice I mean your child always has to behave. We expect your child to be responsible for his or her behavior, and failure to adhere to these commitments will result in a loss of privilege. We have a lot of fun activities planned for the school year, and if you're not working hard and you're not being nice, you will not participate. No exceptions."

The new sheriff had apparently arrived.

A month later, Doreen Land told Canada that she was leaving, too, and more than a dozen teachers followed Grey and Land out the door. It wasn't until September that the results came back for the state reading test that the students had taken way back in January. Canada had predicted that 50 percent of the kids would pass, but that turned out to be wildly optimistic. Just 25 percent of sixth-grade students and 24 percent of seventh-grade students scored on or above grade level. Canada felt physically ill when he saw the numbers, not sure whether he should be enraged or depressed or both.

The math results, which arrived in October, were a little better—40 percent of the sixth grade and 34 percent of the seventh were on grade level. The numbers were a significant improvement over the 9 percent the school's first sixth-grade class had recorded the previous year, but they were still a long way from acceptable. Promise Academy had just wasted a year, Canada realized, and he didn't have a year to waste.

He called Druckenmiller. "I want to fire somebody," he said. "But everyone's already been fired."

7   Last Chance

GLEN PINDER TOOK possession of room 212, the principal's office, on July 5, 2006. In most of the city's public schools, the classrooms were empty, but there was still a long, hot month to go until Promise Academy's middle school students were released for summer vacation. Geoffrey Canada had let Pinder know that there was no time for a leisurely transition: the school needed to make an immediate turnaround, and that meant improved test scores right away. For the first week or two of his tenure, Pinder merely observed, a large, dark storm cloud gliding ominously through the hallways, slipping into the back of one classroom or another during a teacher's lesson, filing away mental notes and judgments. He soon concluded, as Terri Grey had before him, that the school's biggest problem was behavior. There were a handful of troublemakers in each class, repeat offenders who were frequently called to the office for one infraction or another. These weren't seriously bad kids, he told me. He'd dealt with actual bad kids when he was a teacher in Atlanta and a principal in Trenton, New Jersey, kids with "real live issues and real live criminal records." The problem at Promise was what Pinder called "ticky-tack, annoying kind of behaviors": disrespecting teachers, chewing gum in class, snickering, eye rolling. But that kind of bush-league misbehavior was no less disruptive than the serious stuff, Pinder believed. It interrupted the learning process and slowed down classroom instruction, and that meant lower test scores, and that meant it had to stop.

As Pinder looked ahead to September, he contemplated how best to get the message across to the teachers and the students that things were going to be different. With the staff, he figured, it wouldn't be too difficult. Twenty of the twenty-seven teachers at the school would be brand-new—some hired to replace the ones who had left with Grey and Land, and others brought on to accommodate the school's expansion from two grades to three, as Promise Academy's inaugural class moved on to the eighth grade. And even the veteran teachers were ready for a change. But the students were another story. They were obstinate and truculent and academically lazy, Pinder thought, comfortable with the relative chaos of the previous two years and convinced they knew better than he did how the school should be run.

Pinder concluded that he needed what Grey had only dreamed of: a dean of students, an individual whose sole responsibility was maintaining order in the school. He promoted Chris Finn, a well-regarded science and social studies teacher who had been with the school since its founding, and in July and August, Finn took a crash course in student discipline. He went to see Lorraine Monroe, the founder of the Frederick Douglass Academy, and she put him in touch with Victor Lopez, the principal of PS 96 on East 120th Street, who had a good reputation for keeping student behavior in check. Finn had already visited Amistad Academy in New Haven, North Star Academy in Newark, and one of the KIPP schools in Harlem, where he took careful notes on how those schools ran their elaborate systems of punishments and rewards. Finally, on the Friday before Labor Day, Pinder and Finn conducted an all-day discipline seminar for every teacher in the school, sharing the tips and strategies that Finn had gathered. This year, Finn told the staff, the school was going to suspend fewer students. Staying home for a few days to watch TV — that wasn't much of a disincentive for a middle school student, and if the kids weren't in class, their test scores weren't going to improve. Instead, he said, he and the staff were going to solve problems on the spot, as soon as they occurred.

"Mr. Finn is the new sheriff," Pinder explained, "and you are all deputies."

But Finn corrected him, adjusting the metaphor a bit. "There are no deputies," he told the teachers. "Everyone in this room is a sheriff. Criminals look at the deputy like, big deal. A deputy is like mall security with no gun. So as of" — he checked his watch — "10:02 A.M. on September 1, 2006, you have all been turned into sheriffs."

The following Tuesday, at 7:00 A.M., Pinder was standing on the northwest corner of Madison Avenue and 125th Street, outside the main entrance to Promise Academy, wearing a fresh light-blue shirt and dark-blue suit pants and a dark-blue striped tie, ready to greet the new and returning students and their parents as they arrived. It was a beautiful morning, sunny and cool, but Pinder's forehead was already beading with sweat. He hadn't slept at all the night before, lying in bed in the new apartment he'd found just a couple of blocks away, thinking about the first day of school, planning what he was going to say to the students, playing and replaying different scenarios in his head.

The goal for day one was to make the students understand how completely things had changed at Promise Academy. Pinder and Finn had decided to start with the eighth grade. Those students were the biggest problem, as Pinder saw it, the ones who had had the most time to get infected with what he saw as the lackadaisical approach of the past two years. So at 9:00 A.M., the eighth grade was called to the cafeteria to hear the new rules.

The kids sat five to a table, looking unimpressed. The eighth-grade teachers, most of them new, stood silently against one wall, and Pinder and Finn stood against another, conferring in low voices. From a distance, the two men looked similar — both imposing African American men in their thirties, both round-shouldered and a little overweight around the middle. Finn had hair on top of his head, and Pinder didn't; this imbalance was reversed when it came to facial hair: Finn had just a dusting of scrub on his chin and another one on his upper lip, while Pinder's beard was a work of art. It started with a neatly trimmed pencil-thin line of sideburn in front of each ear, and as it made its way down his cheek, it gradually expanded until it became a two-inch-wide stripe of thick, dark bristle that concealed his chin completely. Their manner was different, too. Pinder, who grew up in poverty, raised by a single mother, was stern and serious, and he seemed at times as though he belonged in another era; he didn't have children, and he told me once that he couldn't imagine trying to raise kids amid the vulgarities of contemporary American life. Finn, a few years younger than Pinder, was by contrast in love with black urban culture. He had grown up deeply immersed in hip-hop music, and he co-owned a company called End of the Weak Productions that hosted an open-mike night every Sunday at a club in the East Village. He had grown up in the middle-class suburb of Teaneck, New Jersey, but he walked with a decidedly urban limp, a kind of a bop and a roll, and that wasn't his only hip-hop mannerism: when other teachers used the handheld microphone in the cafeteria, they gripped it at the base, but when Finn wanted to address the students, he wrapped his whole hand around the very top of the mike and pulled it right up to his lips, like a rapper getting ready to rhyme.

Finn's love of hip-hop gave him a common point of reference with the kids in school, and over the last two years he had become a student favorite at Promise Academy. Part of his agenda for the first day of school was to convince the students that this year, Mr. Finn was going to be no fun at all.

Pinder went first. "We're not going to spend the whole year fussing and fighting back and forth," he told the eighth grade. "This year, it's going to be our way. We tried your way for two years, and what did we get? Less than 50 percent of our students are reading and writing on grade level. Eighteen of our sixth-graders were retained in the same grade. When I look at your academic records, I see no straight-A students. We have to do better. The sole purpose for everybody being here—teachers, instructional assistants, everybody—is to prepare you to go to college. Every decision that I make, every choice that we make as educators is going to be made so that you can be—" He stopped himself abruptly and turned on a girl at a nearby table who was slumping in her seat. "Please sit up." She unslumped slightly. "Please sit up!" She sat a little straighter. "Please sit up!" Pinder's voice was rising rapidly and his forehead was creased into a scowl. "If you're not interested in what I'm saying, you better *act* like you're interested," he shouted. "Act like it. Fake it!"

He turned back to the rest of the students. He was perspiring more heavily than ever, and he had replaced his usual handkerchief with a small white terry-cloth towel that he had draped over his left shoulder. He reached for it now and wiped his brow dry. "If you find by the end of this week that you're not prepared to do what we're asking you to do," he went on, "it's very important that you let someone know so we can make other arrangements for you, because we have a very long waiting list of students who would love to be here at the Promise Academy. We have not lowered our standards this year; we have raised our standards. What you did last year to get a C or a B won't get you a C or a B this year. And if you are found to be one of those people who continues to disturb the learning process, your days here will be very, very short."

Pinder handed the mike to Finn.

"If you would rather go to public school, that is really your option," Finn told the students. "You go home tonight, you speak to your mother, you tell her to come in tomorrow morning and speak to Mr. Pinder, and you can be out of here as early as tomorrow. But if you decide to stay, you better recognize: This is not the place you once thought it was. This is not the place it was in June and July of this year. This is a new day." He let those words hang in the air for a few seconds as he took a few slow steps toward the students, staring them down. "Some people already are not taking me seriously," he said. He frowned. "I can look in your eyes and see it. What that means is you're going to be a victim. I can guarantee it. Because we are going to the top this year, with or without you." His voice had taken on a sharp edge. "There is *nothing* stopping me from doing my job this year. Nothing."

AT TWO FORTY-FIVE that afternoon, in each classroom of Promise Academy, the public-address system crackled to life. The students were surprised; they hadn't even known the school had a public-address system. Mr. Finn's voice came through the speakers: "The following students must report to the blue room immediately." And then, in a deliberate tone, he read a list of twenty-nine names, all students from the seventh and eighth grades. A hush fell over the entire school, and everyone listened carefully. No one knew what the list meant, exactly, but when you heard your name, you knew one thing: it wasn't good news.

This was the last act in the bad cop/bad cop routine that Pinder and Finn had worked up for the first day of school: the gathering of the bad apples. The two men had selected the twenty-nine hardest cases, the troublemakers, the class clowns, the unrepentant back-talkers, the habitual offenders, the students who had found their way into the principal's office most often last year. The idea was to bring them together and scare them straight on the very first day, in the hope that they might be persuaded to choose the right path before drifting too much farther down the wrong one.

The blue room was right off the cafeteria on the first floor, a windowless cube used for meetings and as an overflow classroom. The students filed in one by one. Black chairs were arranged in narrow rows, all facing the front, where Pinder and Finn stood, looking dour. Along the side of the room were arrayed the school social worker, the school psychologist, the special-education coordinator, and another discipline specialist. Fluorescent lights glowed overhead. Each student took a seat and followed Finn's curt orders: No talking. Nothing in your hands. Sit up. Look straight ahead. The room was silent.

When the final student had arrived, Pinder stepped forward and said just one sentence: "This is your absolute last chance to get yourself together."

Then it was Finn's turn. "The students who have been called to this room are the people who were repeatedly sent to the office last year, who were repeatedly sent out of their classes, repeatedly spoken to about negative behavior and horrible attitudes," he said. "I decided that if I were to start this year without giving you this warning, I would feel bad. I would feel like, Mr. Finn, you didn't give those particular people a heads up. You didn't give them a chance." He cleared his throat. "This morning I wanted to start with a clean slate for everyone. I would love to show up for the first day of school and say everybody gets to start over. That's what my heart wants me to do. But then I go to my office and I see that about nine of the people who are sitting in this room right now have already been sent to my office, some of them *two times* already. And it's not even three o'clock on the first day of school."

Ymani Jones, a bright, energetic eighth-grade girl with above-average grades, was sitting in the second row, looking miserable. She was having a very bad day, in trouble first thing for arguing, then in trouble for talking back to Mr. Pinder, then in trouble for wearing earrings and the wrong color socks, all of which culminated in a bit of a breakdown in the first-floor hallway. "Every single time you are sent to my office there will be a form explaining your behavioral issue, and it will go in your permanent folder," Finn said to the students. "Ymani Jones already has two forms in there. If it ever comes down to the point where we have to call Ymani's mother to come in for a discipline hearing with Mr. Canada, I'm going to open up her folder, and one of the things that Mr. Canada is going to see is a form that says this girl got in trouble on the *first day of school*—at 9:15 in the morning! That's disgusting. That is unacceptable." Finn shook his head. "I will be contacting the parents of all of the students who are sitting in this room right now to explain to them the new procedure at this school."

In the front row, Julien Coutourier let out a sigh.

Pinder turned toward him, eyes blazing, finger pointed. "Do you have a problem with what's being said in here?"

Julien, in the eighth grade, was a big kid, heavy and tall for his age, quick to make a joke and quick to take offense. Last year, he'd been suspended for fighting more than once. "No," he answered.

"Are you sure?" Pinder asked.

"Yes."

"Sit up in that chair, young man," Pinder ordered. "Sit up and adjust your attitude."

Julien sighed again, a little more quietly.

"You're breathing heavy," Pinder said sarcastically. "You OK? You need to see the nurse?"

"No."

Finn took over again. "That little jolt that you got in your heart when you heard your name get called over the loudspeaker, that little oh-my-God-am-I-in-trouble, that was on purpose. You need to feel that. You need to feel like I am almost going to be kicked out of here if I mess up one more time. You need to really swallow that, get that in your brain. All of that extra talking back, breathing heavy"—he stared at Julien—"sucking your teeth, falling apart in the hallway"—he shot a glance at Ymani—"that is unacceptable. Unacceptable. Some people act like they came back this year just to play around—back to school, back to playing around again. For those people, I'm going to pray for you. That's not even a joke. I'm going to say a silent prayer when I go home tonight that you can turn this around. Remember, Mr. Pinder said it: this is your last chance. This is the rope that we are trying to use to pull you back out of the darkness. If you want to attend college, if you want to graduate from this school, if you want to *be* in this school, you will take heed to what I'm saying."

He looked at them, a few faces still defiant, most just downcast. "You know what's the other part?" he said. "I don't want this to be all so grim and dark." He turned toward Marceline Diop, a tall, striking eighth-grade girl with regal features and a reputation for trying to egg the other girls on to trouble. "Marceline, you are a leader among your peers," Finn said. "I don't know if you recognize it or not. You can use that energy for something good. Julien, the same goes for you. All of that energy you spend beefing, being pent up, arguing with people, you can spend that energy on something else. You can be leading your group of friends to something else. All of this huffing and puffing—you're not that dude. You are a kind kid. Your mother raised you so well. All of this extra tough-guy business, that's not even you, son."

Finn turned to a boy in the third row. "Merrick. You want to be funny, class clown all the time. You want attention that way. Let's get attention in a positive way. Antoine, same thing. Dasheer, same thing. Making beats, making songs, your whole team be with you, like, 'Oh, g'head, Dasheer, spit that!' Yo, use that same energy to do something good.

"You, too, Ymani. I just told the drama teacher I have the best supporting actress in the school play already. I don't even have to see what the play is. Too much good stuff with you to be falling apart, acting like that. Use your energy for the right reasons. All of you. And trust me, we will all be watching all of you. I'm looking for the best from you. That's all I have to say."

Mr. Pinder stepped forward again. "Does everybody understand what's been said?"

"Yes," the students said.

"Any questions?"

"No."

"Any comments?"

"No."

"Any concerns?"

"No."

"Does anyone think they've been falsely accused and shouldn't be sitting here?" The principal looked around the room, from face to face. "Be honest." A long silence. "I didn't think so."

And with that, the bad apples were dismissed.

THREE WEEKS LATER, one member of the Gang of Twenty-nine, a girl in the seventh grade, got into an argument with a classmate and took off after her with a pair of scissors. She had had a rough September already, cursing at teachers, disrupting class, spending a lot of time in Mr. Finn's office, and after the scissors incident, even Geoffrey Canada agreed that she needed to be expelled. But for the remaining twenty-eight, things seemed to be improving. Most of them had made at least a few small steps toward conforming to the school's rules, and some of them, it seemed, had turned over a new leaf and were flourishing. The eighth grade was still the most difficult class—"they're just irritating," Pinder told me that fall, "irritating and hardheaded beyond belief"—but even those students were coming along. The halls felt calmer than the year before, and inside the classrooms, there was clearly learning going on.

The statewide tests were scheduled to take place early in 2007—January 16 for the English language arts test and March 13 for math. So whatever time and energy wasn't dedicated to discipline that fall was dedicated to test preparation, and that meant extra pressure not only for the teachers at Promise Academy, but also for the tutors in the afterschool program. In the fall of 2005, the academic component of the afterschool program had been stepped up a few notches, thanks to Stanley Druckenmiller's largesse, and forty new part-time reading and math specialists had been hired for the school's second year. But even with that additional manpower, the administrators had struggled to coordinate the one-on-one tutoring provided in the afterschool program with the curriculum being taught in the school. Canada's plan for this year was to gather so much data on each student and to crunch and sort and cross-reference it so carefully and completely that every adult who came into contact with a child would know exactly his or her academic strengths and weaknesses: comfortable with quadratic equations; weak on negative numbers; needs help with inferences. If the teachers and tutors were all on the same page, Canada reasoned, they would be able to pinpoint exactly those skills that a high-scoring 2, say, might need to become a solid 3 on this year's tests.

In September, Canada named a new director for the afterschool academic program: Kate Shoemaker, who like Canada was a graduate of Bowdoin College, though from a considerably later era. She was in her early thirties, and hers was one of the rare white faces in the upper reaches of the Harlem Children's Zone hierarchy. Her official title was director of policy and special projects, which usually meant that she took on tasks that didn't fit into anyone else's job description. She had been the agency's point person on the design and construction of the new headquarters, for instance, and for two years she had spent a lot of time wearing a hardhat and talking to architects and engineers about water pressure and construction permits. Now her job was to manage forty tutors and about two hundred kids from 4:00 to 7:00 P.M. every day and from 9:00 A.M. to 1:00 P.M. on Saturday.

Shoemaker was comfortable with numbers, and for the most part she was able to gather and arrange the student data in a way that appealed to Canada. Every student took a practice test in each subject in October, another in November, and another in December, and after each test, Shoemaker and her education coordinator, Sophie Ricard, created an elaborate spreadsheet that showed exactly which questions each student had answered correctly and incorrectly, as well as how each student's performance was changing over time. In December, Canada presided over a long summit meeting at which senior staff from both the school and the agency sat around the main conference table on the sixth floor and pored over the spreadsheets, looking for patterns, targeting students for extra help, identifying specific areas that tutors should focus on.

But as the tests drew closer, Shoemaker began to get the feeling that for at least some of the students in the afterschool program, the most relevant contributing factor to their score was going to be something deeper and harder to identify than simply their ability to "use context clues" or "identify literary devices," as the spreadsheets put it. This was the first assignment that Shoemaker had had at the Harlem Children's Zone where she was working so closely with the children themselves, and what struck her most that autumn and winter was how many of the students had problems that seemed more emotional or psychological than they were academic or intellectual. There were academic problems, too, of course—the students simply didn't know as much as they needed to know—but on top of those there were the students who were in foster care, whose parents had just split up and were fighting over custody, who had a brother in prison, who didn't have a quiet place to sleep at night, who were angry or depressed or just plain sad. Shoemaker's tutors were hired for their abilities in English and math instruction, but as the relationships between the tutors and the students developed—they sat together, one-on-one, for at least two hours a week, week after week—the tutors often found themselves drawing on a very different set of skills.

One afternoon, Shoemaker told me, a student asked her tutor to read a journal entry she had written. It was one long cry for help: I don't want to live, I want to die, I hate my mom, my mom's a slut. "How can you focus on a reading-comprehension test if those are the feelings that are going through your head?" Shoemaker asked. But at the same time, she realized, the fact that the child had chosen her tutor to express such painful feelings to, that clearly meant something. The tutor informed the school's social worker about the journal entry, and the social worker agreed to speak to the student. Then the tutor let the student know that she had let the school know what the girl had written. She didn't want her young charge to think that she had ratted her out. "She said, 'I'm very worried about you, and it's my job to let the social worker know about this,'" Shoemaker explained. "'I did this because I love you and I care about you, and I need to make sure that you're OK.'"

The emotional and psychological issues the children were struggling with had a clear effect on their test scores, Shoemaker believed. She told me about one girl in the eighth grade who got an 85 on the October test, the second-highest score in the entire grade—and then on the November test she got a 15. "It's almost like a big, pardon my French, but, 'Screw you, I'm not trying. I'm not in the mood, I don't feel like it,'" Shoemaker said. "This student has major, major, major anger-management issues. But she is a smart kid. She could easily get a 4."

Sophie Ricard was working with one struggling child on test-taking strategy, and as she was offering him some encouraging words one afternoon, he suddenly interrupted her. "Why should I care about this test?" he demanded. "No one cares how I do on this test. I don't care, either."

"But *I* care how you do," Ricard replied.

And with those words, tears sprang to the boy's eyes and started running down his face. "Why do *you* care?" he asked.

"Because this is your future, and I care very deeply about you."

It was the X factor, the magic ingredient that could outweigh all the careful calculations behind Promise Academy's strategy for success: on top of the hours and hours of cognitive training, what made the difference in many students' lives was a personal connection that was impossible to measure and difficult to replicate. If the kids didn't get that, all the tutoring in the world might not help them. And in the countdown to the test, Shoemaker found herself going through her list of students again and again, lingering over the names of those whom no one had yet been able to reach, who had fought with or shut out one tutor after another.

There were moments that fall when middle school seemed simply too difficult to pull off. It was Promise Academy's third year, and the school had been through two principals, dozens of teachers, millions of dollars, and a half-dozen different strategies by

Canada to get things back on track. It had been more than a year since the charter school experts Druckenmiller had brought in had suggested that it might be impossible for the Harlem Children's Zone to run schools, almost a year since Canada and Druckenmiller and Langone had agreed the clock was ticking, and some days, even Canada found himself questioning the whole project.

"It was my decision to do the middle school," he said in his office in January, a few days before the statewide reading test. "It wasn't the board's. This was pure Geoff. Everyone said we should just start with kindergarten. But I wanted to do middle school. It reminds me how critical all of this work is."

The Promise Academy elementary schools were, after a bit of a rocky start, beginning to thrive, but to Canada, that was no surprise. "In the primary school, there is no sense of crisis," he said. "There, it feels like we've got a nice solid strategy, good data, plenty of time. Well, that's not the way it feels in the middle school. The middle school feels like we better do something *today* to save these kids." He tilted back in his chair and ran a long hand over his scalp. "Would I change my mind now, knowing how hard it's been to get that school where I want it?" He meant it as a rhetorical question, though for a tiny moment it looked like he wasn't sure of the answer. "No. I wouldn't," he said. "Crisis is good. As worried as everybody is about the reputation of the organization and the school and all of that, I think it's well worth it to be in the heart of this battle and to struggle with it. It's been a long time since we as an agency have really had to put ourselves on the line."

It was a Monday afternoon at the beginning of January, a cool day after a freakishly warm winter weekend. Behind Canada, out the window, a flock of pigeons was circling over 125th Street, breaking apart and reforming, dipping and rising with the drafts and crosswinds. "Having said all that," he concluded, a little more quietly, "it's clear to me that if we don't get good scores this year, things will have to change. We'll bring in somebody like KIPP or Amistad to run the Promise Academy. Our days of running schools will be over."

8 The Conveyor Belt

For the teachers and administrators at the middle school, it was often hard to reconcile Geoffrey Canada's deeply held ideals about the inherent potential of each child with the frustrating reality they confronted every day in the classroom. Maybe it was true that the school's problems were simply a case of growing pains, a clash of pedagogic styles that Glen Pinder would soon resolve. But there were those at the school and in the leadership of the Harlem Children's Zone who had begun to wonder whether there weren't deeper and more intractable factors at work. Was there really a system out there that could turn poorly educated ten-year-olds into successful scholars, en masse, in a predictable and repeatable way? Or for some of them, was sixth grade simply too late? The doubters weren't alone. Across the country, there was a larger dialogue about class and cognitive development under way among a loosely connected group of scholars and scientists, all trying to find answers to the same perplexing set of questions: What kind of help was needed to set poor children on a more productive path? Which interventions really worked? And how early in a child's life did those interventions need to begin in order to succeed?

At the center of this ongoing investigation was James Heckman, the Nobel Prize–winning Chicago economist. Heckman's first real encounter with these issues came in the mid-1980s, when he led a group of researchers on a government contract to evaluate the Job Training Partnership Act (JTPA), a federal law passed in 1982 to fund local programs that helped disadvantaged young people enter the workforce. Heckman and his team looked through reams of wage statistics, and they also visited job-training centers around the country to see for themselves what the programs were doing to aid poor youth, and especially poor black and Hispanic youth. Heckman, then in his forties, had more than an academic interest in inner-city poverty; he was white, but as a student in 1963 he traveled through the segregated southern states with his college roommate, a black Nigerian, and he was pained by the discrimination his friend encountered. Ever since, his work had been motivated, in part, by a desire to better understand American inequality, both racial and economic.

Heckman's investigation of job training, which lasted several years, came during a time of rising public dissatisfaction with welfare programs. But the JTPA, which enjoyed bipartisan support in Washington, was seen as a hopeful alternative—the perfect antidote to the kind of cash handouts that many felt had turned welfare into a trap. Instead of giving men fish so that they could eat for a day, as the saying went, the JTPA was supposed to teach them to fish so that they could eat for a lifetime.

But when Heckman and his researchers took a close look at the data, they discovered, to their great surprise, that the JTPA simply didn't work. It wasn't just that it was an inefficient use of the $2 billion the federal government was spending on it each year; it literally had no discernable effect on the future wages of most of the young people enrolled. One study compared a group that went through job training with a demographically similar control group that didn't and found that young black males who got the training earned *less* than the ones who got no training at all. Heckman, baffled, began looking into other programs targeted at disadvantaged adolescents and young adults, like literacy classes and prisoner re-habilitation. With each one, he found the same result: none of the programs seemed to do much good at all. "I was staggered," he told me. "All of these programs that were being funded were basically disasters."

This was the same period that Heckman was embroiled in the controversy over *The Bell Curve,* writing his critique that disman-tled the authors' conclusions while embracing many of their prem-ises. Heckman was certain that Richard Herrnstein and Charles Murray were wrong in their claims for the genetic roots of intelli-gence, but he was equally convinced that they had uncovered some important new truths about the role of ability in the modern American economy. Their research clearly showed that it was not race or class but cognitive ability—the kind measured on stan-dardized tests—that best predicted socioeconomic success. Where Murray and Herrnstein went astray, Heckman believed, was in their claim that cognitive ability was immutable. In fact, he wrote, the data showed that the abilities that made such a difference in adult success were teachable.

So here was Heckman's quandary: He was sure ability mattered, and he was sure that it could be taught. But all the federal pro-grams that were designed to do just that, to teach the kind of skills that raise incomes—they didn't seem to be having any effect. What was going wrong? In the mid-1990s Heckman set out to solve that riddle, and in the years since, his quest has taken him into areas of study where he never expected to find himself, from the architec-ture of the brain to the life cycle of barn owls. It is only recently, he says, that he has begun to feel as though he has an answer.

Heckman is a curious figure, bookish and jowly, his eyes hidden behind large round tortoiseshell glasses. He is the antithesis of the best-selling new model of the modern economist: his subjects are broad and weighty, his papers abstruse and hard to read; just when you think you've got a handle on the point he's making, he'll un-spool a few pages of dense equations full of Greek letters that, to a non-economist, essentially translate as "Take my word for it, son." He has a logical, exacting personality, which is no doubt part of the reason that his public profile has remained relatively low, at least for a Nobel laureate. But his hyperrational approach has allowed him to collect and synthesize vast amounts of research from a wide range of disciplines and distill them into an intellectual framework that is original, coherent, and persuasive. More than any other figure in the academic world today, Heckman is constructing a grand unified theory of poverty in America.

The first relevant fact in Heckman's framework is the one he took away from *The Bell Curve:* skills matter. The more ability you have, the better you are likely to do in life.

The second is that significant skill gaps exist—by race, class, and maternal education—and they open up very early. At age one there is not a great difference between the cognitive abilities of the child of a college graduate and the child of a high school dropout, but by age two there is a sizable gap, and at three it's even wider. The "accident of birth," Heckman says, matters more than it ever has, and its effects can be seen even in very young children.

The third fact is that cognitive skills are not the only ones that matter. Heckman has for many years been studying the General Educational Development (GED) tests, which states use to bestow high-school-equivalency degrees on dropouts. He has discovered a curious phenomenon: GED recipients earn no more than high school dropouts, on average, even when their intelligence scores are higher. And why? Heckman says it is because they lack all of the *noncognitive* skills that a person must possess in order to make it through high school: patience, persistence, self-confidence, the ability to follow instructions, the ability to delay gratification for a future reward. Those skills, it turns out, are useful not only in school, but in the job market, too.

The fourth fact is that both cognitive and noncognitive skills are teachable—but it matters a great deal *when* you try to teach them. The main problem with the JTPA, Heckman concluded, was that its interventions came too late; by sixteen or seventeen, he says, a person's cognitive abilities are fairly stuck in place. But the same level of intervention at an *early* age can make a very big difference in a child's life. To demonstrate this, Heckman draws on two famous experiments in early-childhood development: the Perry Preschool program and the Abecedarian Early Childhood Intervention. From 1962 to 1967, the Perry Preschool in Ypsilanti, Michigan, enrolled black three-year-olds from disadvantaged families into a two-year prekindergarten program. The program itself was solid but not particularly remarkable: classes ran for two and a half hours each weekday and were supplemented by a weekly home visit. What was notable was the rigor of the experiment: 123 children were enlisted, and only half of them were randomly selected for the preschool; the others were left to their own devices. Both groups, the Perry preschoolers and the control group, were then followed and tested regularly, not just through elementary school but for decades. The Abecedarian Early Childhood Intervention enrolled 111 children from poor families in North Carolina during the 1970s and 1980s; again, half were randomly assigned to a control group, and again they were studied into adulthood. The Abecedarian program was more intensive than Perry had been: children were enrolled when they were just a year old; the preschool was in session all day and ran for fifty weeks out of the year; and the children received medical and nutritional services as well as language enrichment.

Both experiments showed a significant and lasting advantage for the preschool group over the control group. The Perry preschoolers were more likely to graduate from high school, less likely to receive public assistance as adults, and more likely to own a home. At age twenty-seven, they were earning more than their peers in the control group, and they had been arrested less. The Abecedarian graduates were less likely as children to be enrolled in special education or to fail a grade; as young adults, they were more likely to go to college and less likely to smoke marijuana. To Heckman, the evidence from both experiments is clear: early interventions can make a big difference in the lives of poor children.

The final critical fact for Heckman is that the skills that a child learns early on make it easier for him to master more complex skills as he grows up. If you intervene in a child's life early, later interventions will have more to build upon, which means that they will pay off more as well. But if you don't start early, the reverse happens: each year it gets harder and harder to have an effect on a child's development. As Heckman and a colleague, Dimitriy Masterov, wrote in a paper in 2007, "Skill begets skill; learning begets learning. Early disadvantage, if left untreated, leads to academic and social difficulties in later years. Advantages accumulate; so do disadvantages."

In person, Heckman is enthusiastic and animated, and it quickly becomes evident when you meet him that his research is motivated to a great extent by a strong desire to improve the lives of poor children. "This is a very exciting subject," he said when we spoke, sitting at an outdoor table at a Starbucks on the University of Chicago campus. "I really think this research is going to have the effect of reducing inequality in American society."

In his academic articles, though, he is ever sober, appealing not to the emotions of his readers but to the cool, rational accountant within. In the paper he wrote with Masterov, Heckman points out that pleas to help solve the problems of disadvantaged families are usually cast "as a question of fairness or social justice." But that's not *his* argument, he says. He wants instead to make his case on "productivity grounds"—a less heart-stirring angle, perhaps, but for Heckman a politically persuasive one. Yes, he argues, the nation will become more just and equitable if poor children have more opportunities for success—but it will also become wealthier, spending less on welfare and crime prevention and drug treatment and collecting more in taxes from the workers who otherwise might never find a job.

What Heckman proposes is "a policy of equality of opportunity in access to home environments (or their substitutes)." That in-nocuous parenthetical phrase has a somewhat magical effect: it turns a vague, sentimental nostrum—every child deserves a lov-ing and supportive home—into a plausible policy goal. In an ideal world, Heckman contends, every American child should have ac-cess to the same kind of nurturing, stimulating, language-rich early home life as every other American child. But since we know they're not all going to get that, we need to provide substitutes to those who don't get what they need at home. Heckman's point is that those substitutes exist, and we now know they can actually work quite well. His conclusions are in many ways similar to Geof-frey Canada's: the best and simplest way to prepare children for a successful life is for their parents to give them everything they need at home, in their earliest years. But if that doesn't happen, if they're not born lucky, all is not lost: with the right inputs, at the right time, you can compensate for any kind of childhood.

DURING PROMISE ACADEMY's first few years, while Canada was struggling to get the middle school on track, he was also deeply engrossed in the development of his early-childhood initiative, and he was increasingly preoccupied by a concept he was calling the conveyor belt. The point of the Harlem Children's Zone had always been to weave disparate programs into a seamless whole, but in practice, Canada knew, there were still plenty of seams in evidence, and sizable ones. The conveyor belt as it existed in 2004 and 2005 started with Baby College. But the next stop, the Harlem Gems prekindergarten, didn't come until age four. That left a lot of empty territory in the early years, after Baby College, and a lot of opportunities for parents to drop out or drift away. The transi-tion from Harlem Gems to Promise Academy wasn't working right yet, either—too many Gems graduates weren't going on to Prom-ise Academy, and too many Promise Academy kindergarten stu-dents started school without having experienced the benefits of Harlem Gems.

Part of the problem was a bureaucratic one: by law, admission to the charter school was determined by random selection. In the first lottery, in 2004, almost every child in Harlem Gems was admitted into Promise Academy kindergarten. But in the 2005 lottery, the cards fell a different way, and just fourteen of the forty Gems got in; the other twenty-six were forced to find slots elsewhere, usually in a regular public school in Harlem. This meant that Canada had just spent thirteen thousand dollars per child—the cost of a year of Harlem Gems—to educate twenty-six four-year-olds who were now being dumped back into the public school system.

So in the summer of 2005 Canada overhauled the lottery system. Instead of admitting kids each April for admission to the kindergarten the same fall, as he had done the first two years, he created a new, early lottery for the elementary school, to be held each year in August. In this lottery, only two- and three-year-olds would be eligible, and if they were chosen, they would start Promise Academy kindergarten not that September, not the following September, but the September after *that*, twenty-five months after their names were drawn in the lottery. Next, Canada made admission to the Harlem Gems prekindergarten program automatic for the winners of the charter school lottery. The three-year-olds chosen in the August 2005 lottery were put at the front of the line for the Gems class that started in September 2006, when they would be four. At the same time, he started work on expanding Harlem Gems, so that by the fall of 2007 there would be two hundred slots, one for every child admitted in the early kindergarten lottery.

That solved one problem. Next, Canada added another section to the conveyor belt: a brand-new program to precede Gems called the Three-year-old Journey, open only to parents whose children had been selected in the kindergarten lottery. The Three-year-old Journey was to be like the graduate school version of Baby College: parents would again meet every Saturday morning to talk about discipline and brain development and health, but the program would last longer than nine weeks, and the discussions would be more intense and the requirements more demanding. Canada had plugged another hole.

Together, these changes represented a complete rethinking of the Harlem Children's Zone's early-childhood system. Before, the path to Promise Academy kindergarten had been somewhat random and haphazard. Now it was direct and purposeful, with the same group of children progressing through four clear stops along the way, from Baby College to Three-year-old Journey to Harlem Gems to Promise Academy. What the changes meant in practice was that beginning in 2008, nearly every incoming kindergarten student would be a graduate of an intensive eleven-month prekindergarten program, and their parents would have been through two separate parenting programs. They would be prepared for kindergarten in a way that few children in Harlem ever had been.

THE DIFFICULTIES at the middle school, meanwhile, had given the conveyor-belt project a special urgency for Canada. On the surface, at least, Terri Grey's struggles proved a point that Canada had been making for years — the longer you wait to intervene with poor children, the harder your job is going to be. "Here's the problem with everything that we've been doing in this field," he told me. It was a chilly February morning, and we were sitting at the small round meeting table in his office. "For the last thirty or forty years, all of us have chosen to work in places where kids are behind, with the thought that we would be superheroes and we would go in and save these kids." This superhero method was often emotionally rewarding for those who practiced it, Canada said, even if it was also usually personally exhausting. It meant you were engaged in battle in the most hopeless neighborhoods, teaching or mentoring or otherwise rescuing desperate kids whom the system had written off, and if you were good at your job, it meant that you regularly performed miracles.

Canada had felt the sense of triumph that came with those successes. He knew it well, in fact. It could be exhilarating. "But the problem with that approach is you will always have more busi-ness than you can handle," Canada said. "You will never solve the problem. You will only save some small number of kids who are on their way to the dark end of things. We've all done it, and we all still do it, and we need to keep doing it. But it is what I've come to think of as the old-fashioned way of working in these commu-nities."

What the conveyor-belt idea represented to Canada was the hope of a new alternative. "The question is, can you build a system where kids in middle school won't need these kinds of interventions in order to be successful?" he said. "And my bet—I could be wrong, but this is my bet—is if we start with kids very early, and we pro-vide them with the kind of intense and continuous academic rigor and support that they need, then when they get to the middle school and high school level, we're not going to need those super-human strategies at all."

THIS WAS WHERE Canada's philosophy could get a little confus-ing, for me, at least. On the one hand, he believed that the only way to get kids to a high level of success was to start working with them at birth. If you waited till middle school to start, you would have to use a superhero strategy. But at the same time, he thought it was essential not to give up on the poorly prepared kids in Promise Acad-emy middle school—which meant he wanted Terri Grey and Glen Pinder to take the superheroic measures necessary to educate them.

To Canada, there was no contradiction at all; it was just a matter of timing. In the future, when the conveyor belt was fully opera-tional, carrying kids from birth right into and through the Prom-ise Academy school system, you wouldn't need to be a superhero in order to educate Harlem's middle school students. But the kids currently enrolled in his middle school hadn't had the good for-tune to get on the conveyor belt early, which meant that they needed exactly the kind of emergency measures that Canada was hoping someday to be able to do without.

"I want to get out of the business of trying to save failing students before their lives are destroyed," Canada said. "I've been in that business, and it's a tough business and a good business, and I'm glad some people are in it—but I really think it's the wrong place to focus."

He still believed it was possible to get every single one of Promise Academy's middle school students to college; he refused to believe that it was too late for any of them. But he also knew that because they had arrived in the sixth grade so far behind, getting them merely to a decent level of success and achievement would take such a high degree of expertise, resources, and effort, on the part of both the kids and the staff, that it would be hard to sustain and probably impossible to replicate on a large scale. The intensive rescue mission he had asked Glen Pinder to undertake might be the right answer for the 250 kids downstairs, in other words, but it couldn't possibly be the right answer for all of Harlem.

It was another quibble Canada had with the KIPP strategy. KIPP had started as a single middle school, and middle schools were still at the heart of the KIPP network. And to Canada, running a middle school in isolation made sense only if you were determined to stay a superhero forever. It really came down to a question of numbers. Canada knew that the KIPP middle school strategy could work very well with one important category of poor kids: the ones who were behind, but not too far behind. And no doubt some of KIPP's best educators could perform occasional miracles and save a few kids who were a *lot* behind. But it was impossible, Canada believed, for KIPP or anyone else to create a large-scale system that regularly took the middle school students who were furthest behind, the ones that Promise Academy was working with, and caught them up. There just weren't enough miracle workers out there. "If we continue waiting until middle and high school to intervene with poor students of color," he said, "I just don't think that we're going to change the numbers in America as a whole."

As it turned out, the people who ran KIPP had started to move toward the same conclusion. In Houston, where KIPP began, the middle school had recently expanded up into a high school and down into an elementary school—and the administrators had just opened the first KIPP prekindergarten as well. KIPP Houston had become a conveyor belt, too, in other words, running from age three to the end of high school.

As for Promise Academy's conveyor-belt kids, the ones who were now in first and second grade, Canada believed that when they arrived in middle school, they would be very different from the kids who were now attending Promise Academy middle school. "Instead of getting them two years behind or three years behind, these kids will be on grade level," he said. "But I'll still be doing an extended day. I'll still be doing an extended year. I'll still be pushing with the same intensity."

And at that point, Canada said, who knew where the conveyor belt might lead? "Usually what happens, starting in the fourth grade, is that test scores start going backward for these kids," he said. "The percentage of kids at or above grade level goes down every year from that point right through to eighth grade." He leaned forward in his chair. "But what if their scores are going *up?* What if you sent kids to the middle school who are *above* grade level, and you didn't let up, but you kept the same intensity, and you kept the same focus? What might happen to a place like Harlem then?" He leaned back, savoring the question for a moment. "The answer right now is that we don't know," he said. "No one has ever done it."

CANADA HAD BECOME convinced that he and his staff weren't pushing parents hard enough, especially in the earliest years of their children's lives. The parents were ready to do more, Canada believed, but no one had figured out yet how much to demand from them and just how to demand it.

In Baby College, parents were taught some basic principles of early cognitive development; they were encouraged to read and play and sing with their children, and they were told that those activities would stimulate a baby's growing brain. But because Baby College was designed to be welcoming and accessible, the parents weren't expected to absorb a lot of detailed information about the scientific knowledge that informed those ideas. Canada decided that the new Three-year-old Journey program, which got under way early in 2006, would be different. He and Caressa Singleton, the project manager who ran the Harlem Children's Zone's early-childhood programs, wanted to use the Journey process to give more explicit direction to parents, not only about parenting techniques, but also about the reasoning behind those techniques. Their belief was that parents—even those who had never graduated from high school—would be more likely to respond to encouragement to change their behavior if they understood that the changes they were being urged to make were rooted in solid research. So when Singleton and Canada spoke to parents, they began using phrases like "attachment theory" and "parental ambivalence" and "seriation language." At one meeting, Canada told the Three-year-old Journey parents about a new study on parental warmth and parental expectations that he had heard about from Ronald Ferguson, the Harvard economist. According to Canada, this advanced approach worked. "People just sort of got it," he told me later. "It is the kind of information that our parents usually find out about last—if ever. No one ever explains to them the science behind these behaviors, and so they never get a chance to use these tools. And you don't know what you're missing until someone points it out to you."

When Singleton went looking for instructors for the Three-year-old Journey, she wanted a level of expertise that went beyond what the typical Baby College instructor possessed. "I think we need to go deeper," Singleton told me—not just deeper into parenting skills, but deeper into parenting psychology as well. She hired a licensed social worker and a clinical psychologist, and in the first cycle of the program, she told me, things often got emotional. Parents talked about some intense and personal issues: their feelings toward their own parents, the ambivalence they sometimes felt about their kids, and the guilt that ambivalence provoked in them. Tears were frequent. On many Saturday mornings, the Journey could feel more like group therapy than a parenting-skills class.

Alongside the psychological discussions, Singleton and her instructors tried to give the parents a fuller understanding of the cognitive preparation their children would need for kindergarten. The Harlem Children's Zone used a popular early-childhood assessment called the Bracken Basic Concept Scale–Revised to measure the school-readiness of children before and after the Harlem Gems prekindergarten program. The Bracken scale gauges a child's understanding of 308 "functionally relevant educational concepts," broken down into 11 "concept categories," including colors, letters, numbers, size, shape, quantity, direction, and texture, and it measures whether a child has the ability to express those ideas. The Bracken isn't like the SAT, where each student is informed of his or her test score and percentile ranking. At most schools, it is used only as an internal evaluation, and parents are rarely told much about it. But Singleton wanted to make things more transparent for the Three-year-old Journey parents.

Harlem children tended to score below average on many of the Bracken subtests when they arrived in kindergarten, and it was likely that a big part of the reason could be found in the research that social scientists like Betty Hart and Todd Risley and Annette Lareau had done about how parents in different socioeconomic classes speak to and interact with their children. Many middle-class parents had been inculcated with the idea that it was part of their duty as parents to speak fairly incessantly to their one- and two- and three-year-old children about things like colors and letters and numbers and shapes. Most poor parents, though, had not received the same indoctrination. So Singleton decided to use the Bracken categories as a checklist for parents to consult: she told them that these were the very concepts and words and phrases that they should be teaching their kids. In some ways, it seemed like taking "teaching to the test" to an absurd extreme—could you really help your child drill for something as basic as the Bracken? But of course Singleton didn't want the parents to teach their kids about shape and number and direction just so they'd do well on the Bracken test; she wanted them to teach their kids about shape and number and direction so that they'd be better prepared for kindergarten. She just thought the test might give them a benchmark to shoot for.

One Saturday morning in December, Singleton stood in the cafeteria of PS 149, on 117th Street, talking to the assembled Three-year-old Journey parents about "teachable moments." The cafeteria doubled as the school's gym, and basketball nets hung down over the parents' heads as they sat in twos and threes at long white lunch tables. There were about forty-five parents enrolled in this three-month course, mostly mothers, a few fathers. Many of them had been through Baby College already, and those parents had noticed a difference as soon as Three-year-old Journey had begun. The new program felt much more bare-bones, even austere. "They're cheap now!" one mother told me with a laugh. There were no raffles and no gift certificates at Three-year-old Journey; Singleton wanted the only reward for participation to be a better-prepared child. Even the food was less bountiful. In place of the hot lunch that was served to the Baby College parents, there was a table set up against the front wall of the room with plastic bowls of apples and oranges, a few bags of SunChips, and a couple of cartons of Tropicana Berry Punch. Parents could help themselves.

Singleton, who was in her midfifties, wore a black turtleneck and slacks and black running shoes, and she had a black and white silk scarf knotted around her neck. A thick streak of gray ran back from her forehead, parting her dark hair. "When we talked about the assessment tools that we use, one of the things we talked about was the Bracken," she reminded the parents. "And we said that our children here in Harlem struggle around certain things. Do you remember? Texture, number, position, direction—they struggle around those things."

Singleton sipped from the large cup of take-out coffee she held in her hand. "If you know more about what those standards are and what those assessments are about, you're going to be more deliberate in terms of what you talk about with your children," she said. "I want you to think about how we can make sure that it happens. How does it become an intentional thing, a conscious process, so it is at the forefront of your mind all the time? So that instead of just saying, 'Go get your shoes,' it becomes 'Go get the *black* shoes. Go get the shoes that have the *shoelaces,* not the ones that have the buckles.'"

Singleton was preparing the class for a brief field trip across 117th Street to the Fine Fare supermarket on Lenox Avenue. Each three-year-old child had made up a shopping list by cutting pictures of grocery items out of advertising circulars and gluing them to sheets of brightly colored construction paper. Each family had a twenty-five-dollar budget for the trip—the one giveaway in the course was a voucher to pay for the groceries—and after Singleton had finished her talk, the families would all go over to Fine Fare together to shop. The point of the shopping trip wasn't food—it was language. The idea was for parents to look for teachable moments in the supermarket's aisles, to find ways to use the trip to talk with their children about the concepts the Bracken measured. "If your child has jelly on her list, then you can talk about whether the jar is *big* or *small,* whether the jar is *round,* if the surface is *smooth,*" Singleton suggested. "And then you're talking about the bread, and look, this loaf of bread is *soft,* but this roll is *hard.* When you go to get a bag of sugar, understanding what's *heavy* and what's *light.*"

The visit to Fine Fare was a little stressful for some of the parents. Grocery shopping with a strong-willed three-year-old is hard enough on its own; it adds an extra degree of difficulty when you have a clinical psychologist following you around with a notepad, observing your every move. But for most of the parents it was fun. They treated the whole thing like a game, talking with their kids about how many apples they should buy, and what color they were, and what color the carrots were, and whether they were hard or soft, long or short, bumpy or smooth. When the class regrouped back at PS 149 for a debriefing, Singleton and the other instructors offered feedback and a few more tips, praising the parents for redirecting their children when the kids became frustrated, suggesting that the checkout line was a good place to go through the contents of the cart with a child and find a few more adjectives to use. It was small stuff, maybe, but as Hart and Risley and other researchers had showed, it was the small stuff that added up to big gaps when children reached kindergarten.

ENLISTING THE HELP of parents was a vital part of Canada's conveyor-belt strategy, but he knew it wasn't enough on its own. Even with the most verbally intensive grocery shopping imaginable, most Harlem kids were still likely to arrive in kindergarten behind their peers; downtown, there were just too many museum visits and nature documentaries and Gymboree classes and Barnes & Noble story times, too many books and too much parent-child chatter. To fully prepare children for Promise Academy, Canada felt, it was essential to get them into an organized and intensive prekindergarten program.

There was plenty of research around that showed that poor children not only benefited from being in prekindergarten, but they benefited more than other children. For the four-year-old population as a whole, a year of pre-K would raise an average child's reading score from the fiftieth percentile to the fifty-fifth percentile, according to a 2004 study. But for disadvantaged children, a year of pre-K would bring an average child's reading score from the thirty-third percentile to the forty-fourth percentile—still behind her peers, but significantly closing the gap. Despite those findings, kids from disadvantaged homes in the United States attended preschool *less* than others, not more; a 2003 study found that children whose mothers had graduated from college were almost twice as likely to be enrolled in preschool as children whose mothers had never graduated from high school.

The Harlem Gems program was unusual in many ways. The state of New York required prekindergartens to run for two and a half hours a day for the ten months of the school year, but the Gems year lasted for eleven months, from the beginning of September through the end of July, and the day was extended, too, beginning at 8:00 A.M. and ending at 5:45 P.M. In the two Gems classrooms, at the end of a hallway in PS 149, the child-to-teacher ratio was 4:1, compared to the New York State standard of 9:1. The most significant difference, though, was in the way that the Gems kids spent their time. They did all the regular prekindergarten activities—imaginative play, music, building blocks, and recess, as well as a midday nap and three meals—but throughout the day, at every turn, the emphasis was on language.

On a typical morning in February—after breakfast, after circle time, after each child picked a job for the day (Serigne chose plant helper, Brianna picked mat helper); after Daeija, the calendar helper, stood up and spoke to her classmates about the day's date and Binta, the weather helper, led the discussion of the daily weather chart—Monica Lucente, the lead teacher in room 124, gathered the sixteen Harlem Gems in her classroom together on the blue rug for a vocabulary lesson. The kids on the rug had known each other for a while; every child in the room had been through Three-year-old Journey with their parents the previous year; the next year, they would all move together into kindergarten at Promise Academy. Now, one by one, Lucente held up six-by-eight-inch flashcards with a photograph in the middle and the word spelled out underneath, and the children raised their hands and identified the words. She started easy, with "car," which Serigne got right, and then Malaysia got "island" and Ezekiel got "cliff." The inflatable raft was a little harder: Tiara said "swimming pool," and Troy guessed "Santa's chair." "Canoe" was a stumper, too, with Mercedes guessing "boat," because of the picture, and Binta guessing "cot," because she recognized the c at the beginning of the word. Finally, Ezekiel guessed "a kazoo," which was either very close or very far off, depending on how you looked at it. And then three correct answers in a row: Brianna got "waterfall" and Ezekiel got "volcano" and Mikala got "mountain."

These weren't Harlem-specific words—far from it. In their daily life, Ezekiel and Troy and Tiara would likely not encounter canoes or volcanoes anytime soon. The theory behind Lucente's word selection, though—one that E. D. Hirsch Jr., the cultural critic, had written about extensively—was that part of what children in low-income neighborhoods are lacking early on is a general cultural vocabulary, the kind of core knowledge of the world and how it works that makes it easier for a child to go on and read independently about unfamiliar topics. So the Gems were learning about China for the next two weeks, and then they would switch to Italy; they learned about science and food and maps and sports.

Each class had a foreign-language teacher, and in room 124 that was Fatiha Amrani-Muhammad, who was from Morocco and wore a dark scarf to cover her head. After some outdoor play and lunch, it was time for Miss Fatiha's French lesson. Together, the children recited the days of the week and identified numbers up to one hundred, and then Miss Fatiha turned to a few brief one-on-one conversations.

"Comment tu t'appelles?" Miss Fatiha asked Jayde.

"Je m'appelle Jayde," she replied.

"Quel âge as tu, Jayde?"

"J'ai quatre ans."

"Et tu es une fille ou un garçon?"

"Une fille."

Together, the children held up their hands and recited the names for the five fingers—*le pouce, l'index, le majeure, l'annulaire,* and *l'auriculaire*—and then, using flashcards that Miss Fatiha displayed one by one, they read aloud weather terms like *vent,* meaning wind, and *brouillard,* for fog.

Spread out on the rug in front of Miss Fatiha, the students seemed so comfortable and confident that it took me a moment to remember that this was not normal: in the United States, most inner-city four-year-olds do not sit around talking about the weather in French. To the students in room 124, though, being surrounded by words—in many languages—seemed like the most natural thing in the world. Lucente and the other Gems teachers did their best to squeeze language enrichment into every spare minute of the day, whether they were asking children pointed questions about the food at lunch or leading songs and chants in the playground at recess. Being in Harlem Gems certainly looked like fun—there were plenty of toys and games and opportunities to dress up and cook make-believe food in a play kitchen—but it also seemed like a verbal hothouse, in which a child's vocabulary could not help but grow rapidly.

The children's scores on the Bracken test demonstrated just what a powerful effect the immersion in language was having on their developing brains. On average, over the three previous years, 18 percent of incoming Gems had arrived scoring "delayed" or "very delayed" on the Bracken scale for four-year-olds, while 17 percent of them scored "advanced" or "very advanced." At the end of their eleven months in Harlem Gems, they were tested again, this time on the Bracken scale for five-year-olds; on average, 51 percent of them scored advanced or very advanced. Most remarkably, over three years, not a single student was still considered delayed or very delayed after a year of Gems.

AS JAMES HECKMAN HAS noted, there is considerable research that shows that this kind of early verbal skill can make a great and lasting difference in a child's life. In the mid-1980s, a handful of researchers in the science of reading identified a phenomenon they called the Matthew effect, named after a fairly un-Sermon-on-the-Mount-like verse from the Bible: "To every one who has, will more be given, and he will have abundance; but from him who has not, even what he has will be taken away." What the researchers were trying to describe was a consistent rich-get-richer pattern that they had observed in the development of reading ability: with very few exceptions, good early readers become great readers, and limited early readers almost always wind up as poor readers. Late bloomers are, in fact, quite rare.

And in reading, as it turns out, the metaphorical rich overlap with the literal rich. Even as early as the beginning of kindergarten, children's level of ability with the printed word tends to correspond closely to the income level of their parents. As Susan B. Neuman, the education scholar, has reported, more than four out of five children at the highest socioeconomic level recognize the letters of the alphabet on the first day of kindergarten, compared to less than two of five children at the bottom of the socioeconomic scale. Half of all well-off kids can identify the beginning sounds of words when they start kindergarten, while just 10 percent of poor children can do the same.

And then after kindergarten, because of the Matthew effect, the disparities get even worse. The Matthew effect is a pretty common-sense phenomenon: Kids who are able to master "decoding," to grasp the strange fact that black marks on a page connect to sounds that you make with your mouth, and that those sounds and marks go together to convey information about, say, hopping on Pop—those kids think reading is fun. They do more of it. And the more they do, the easier it gets, and the easier it gets, the more they do. For children who have a harder time cracking the code early on, the opposite occurs, a grim process that one researcher calls "the devastating downward spiral." Those kids don't get the way letters go together, which means they can't figure out words they don't know, which means they never get to the stage where they're deriving actual meaning from the words on the page. They don't enjoy reading, so they don't do it unless they're forced to.

By middle school, the gap between avid readers and reluctant readers has grown into a chasm. If you rank fifth-grade students by how much time they spend reading on their own, outside of school, you find a huge range. A child at the ninetieth percentile—not the most book-crazy kid in class, but close to the top—

will spend an average of twenty-one minutes a day reading, according to a 1988 study, which means that she goes through more than 1.8 million words a year. A child at the tenth percentile—not the most reading-averse kid in class, but close—will spend an average of six *seconds* a day on independent reading, which works out to just eight thousand words a year. Not surprisingly, the six-seconds-a-day kids don't catch up with the rest of the class. In fact, they just keep falling further and further behind.

Joseph Torgesen, a researcher at the Florida Center for Reading Research at Florida State University, has studied attempts to reverse the spiral, and his conclusions are relevant not only to the efforts taking place in Harlem Gems, but to the struggles at Promise Academy middle school as well. In a study published in 2004, Torgesen looked at a dozen or so experimental studies of intensive reading interventions done in different parts of the country and targeted at different ages. When he analyzed the interventions aimed at nine- to twelve-year-old struggling readers, he found results that were mixed at best. With enough time and work, it seemed, it was possible to push these middle school-aged kids forward on the reading basics, like decoding, accuracy, and word comprehension. But the news was much more discouraging when it came to "fluency"—the ability to read with ease. Despite the fact that the middle school students in the studies were given as much as one hundred hours of one-on-one or small-group instruction, they made very little progress in fluency. Torgesen's conclusion: by the end of elementary school, "if children's impairments in word-reading ability have reached moderate or severe levels," catching kids up may simply be impossible.

But when Torgesen looked at *early* interventions with delayed readers—in first and second grade—his mood brightened. He cited dire statistics from the National Assessment of Educational Progress, the annual survey known as "the nation's report card," which showed that 37 percent of American fourth-graders had "below basic" reading skills, meaning they were significantly delayed. But, he said, new research had made it possible to envision a very different picture. "Once, this was inevitable, but no more," he wrote. "We now have the knowledge and the tools to bring this percentage down to a single digit." Torgesen examined six different studies, all intensive interventions aimed at accelerating first- and second-grade children who were at a reading level far below that of their classmates. The results were striking, and the implications were nothing short of stunning. The interventions were remarkably effective; each one brought at least half of the targeted students up to an average level of reading ability by the end of the grade, and in one study, 92 percent of them hit that level. According to Torgesen's calculations, if these early interventions were applied to delayed readers nationwide, at least four-fifths of the current population of problem readers—a disproportionate number of whom are poor and minorities—would move into the average ability range. Their reading problems would simply disappear.

The difference between the interventions that worked and the ones that didn't was as plain as day, according to Torgesen. Start early, the way Monica Lucente was doing with the Harlem Gems, and you can accomplish almost anything; start late, the way the reading teachers at Promise Academy middle school were trying to do, and it gets harder and harder to make an impact.

MORE THAN ANY other kind of intervention in the lives of low-income children, intensive prekindergarten programs have an impressive track record. In her book *Changing the Odds,* Susan Neuman describes one of the best and most thoroughly documented: Bright Beginnings, a pre-K program in the Charlotte-Mecklenburg, North Carolina, school district, which an ambitious new superintendent named Eric Smith introduced in 1997. Bright Beginnings is intended for the kids who are furthest behind; it is open to the four-year-olds in the city who score the lowest on a screening test of cognitive ability. The program has a disproportionate number of African American students and poor students. The thirty-one hundred children who are now enrolled get six and a half hours a day of instruction, focused on literacy skills. Each classroom of eighteen or nineteen students is led by a certified teacher and a teacher's assistant. Parents are enlisted in the effort to help their children read; at the beginning of the school year, they sign a "learning compact" that commits them to read at least one hundred books with their child at home during the year.

The total cost per child per year was $5,391 in 2002—less than Harlem Gems, but more than most pre-K programs—and the results are quite promising. After a year of Bright Beginnings, students not only score higher on a "kindergarten entry profile" test than a demographically similar control group; remarkably, they also beat the average for the city as a whole, despite the fact that low cognitive scores were a prerequisite for inclusion in the program. In just a single year, in other words, the worst-performing four-year-olds in Charlotte are able to erase their deficit altogether.

After a year of kindergarten, the scores for the Bright Beginnings students slip a bit, though they are still elevated; 72 percent of kids in the 2002 Bright Beginnings class were on grade level at the end of kindergarten, compared to 79 percent of non–Bright Beginnings kids. As they continued to make their way through elementary school, though, their scores continued to slide, and by third grade, 60 percent were on grade level, compared to 75 percent of non–Bright Beginnings students. There was still some encouraging news in those numbers—the control group, made up of students who were eligible for the program but didn't participate, had only 52 percent of students on grade level by third grade—but they showed disturbing evidence of the notorious fade-out effect.

Smith had paid for Bright Beginnings by taking almost all of the federal funding his district received for poor children—so-called Title I money—and putting it into the prekindergarten program. (Most superintendents try to spread the funding out over the length of a child's school career.) In many ways, Smith's strategy worked very well. The enriched environment that he was able to create for the district's most disadvantaged four-year-olds gave them a huge lift. But as those students returned to regular public school, and the enrichment ended, some of the benefits wore off—and at that point, there weren't resources available to help the low-income students hang on to or build on their gains.

A similar pattern is evident in the data from the Perry Preschool program. In the course of the two-year program, the participants' average IQ shot up from 80 to 96, but by the fifth grade, it was back down to 85, about the same level as the control group. In his writing, James Heckman uses that statistic to demonstrate how powerful noncognitive abilities can be—his point is that even after the IQ bump faded, the Perry children still went on to have more successful lives than their peers. But the fade-out effect is nonetheless a disturbing phenomenon, and one that leads to an intriguing set of questions: What would happen if a program like Perry or Bright Beginnings never ended? What if that same kind of support and intervention lasted for years?

That was exactly the question that Canada had set out to answer with the conveyor belt. And he would soon get the first indication of how well his new invention might work. In the fall of 2007, the first Promise Academy kindergarten class, the students chosen at the lottery in April 2004, would be going into third grade, where they would take their first statewide reading and math test. About a third of the class were Harlem Gems graduates, and a lot of them had gone through Baby College too, and so for many of the kids, it would be their fifth straight year of academic enrichment. It would be a moment of truth: If the third-grade scores looked like average Harlem scores, then Canada's conveyor belt wasn't working. But if they looked like average American scores, then Canada would have the first concrete evidence that he might be onto something; that he might finally have found the right strategy and the right tools not just to close the gap between poor kids and middle-class kids, but to keep it closed.

9 Escape Velocity

THE MAN RESPONSIBLE for guiding Harlem's children down the next stretch of the conveyor belt was Dennis McKesey, who became the second principal of the original Promise Academy elementary school in the summer of 2005, at the age of thirty-one. McKesey, who like almost all of his students was African American, grew up in a working-class neighborhood in one of New York City's northern suburbs. His first job was at the post office, which was something of a family tradition — his grandfather, mother, father, sister, and twin brother all worked for the U.S. Postal Service, too — but he soon concluded that he wasn't meant to sort mail, and he traded his postal sinecure for the life of a public school teacher. Now, with almost a decade in education behind him, he was living with his wife and two sons in New Windsor, a bedroom community sixty miles north of Harlem, where he woke every morning at 4:00 A.M. in order to arrive at Promise Academy, on West 134th Street, by 6:00 A.M. He liked to be the first person there, to open up the building himself, so that he had a few moments to collect his thoughts before the students began arriving at 6:45. It had become a necessary ritual for McKesey; if his schedule was off or if he hit some predawn traffic and one of his teachers somehow beat him to work, he spent the rest of the day feeling like he was trying to catch up.

Most days, though, McKesey seemed unflappable, an oasis of placid confidence. He kept a radio on his desk tuned to CD 101.9, a smooth-jazz station, with the volume down low, and he seemed sometimes to exist in a serene bubble filled with the mellow, soulful hits of Marvin Gaye, Sade, and Stevie Wonder, with the occasional Kenny G instrumental thrown in. Unlike Glen Pinder at the middle school, McKesey never raised his voice, never seemed anywhere near the end of his rope. Aggrieved parents, discipline problems, staff complaints; he received them all with the same even demeanor. His look was meticulous and self-possessed, his four-button jackets always crisp, his hair and mustache and beard carefully trimmed—even his eyebrows, two thick dark stripes hovering above his large brown eyes, seemed precisely calibrated.

The position at Promise Academy was McKesey's first as a principal, but he gave the impression that he had been preparing for it for a long time. He was a believer in leadership with a capital L, that mysterious concept that has been the subject of countless business seminars and CEO memoirs. Prominently displayed on the bookshelf in his office was a copy of *Good to Great,* the bestselling management handbook by Jim Collins, alongside a collection of the Dalai Lama's teachings on Buddhism and compassion. McKesey referred to his administrative staff as his "leadership team," and once a week he gathered them around the conference table in his office to discuss their own personal development as managers. McKesey would hand out photocopied selections from books with titles like *The 21 Irrefutable Laws of Leadership,* and in his low and measured tones he would talk with his staff about sacrifice and character and the importance of learning from your mistakes.

In many ways, McKesey resembled a younger version of Geoffrey Canada, self-assured and driven, intent on his goals. He was less quick to anger than his boss, though, motivated not by the personal ghosts and historical injustices that gave Canada his passion but by a strong desire to prove himself, to accomplish more than anyone thought possible. He rarely spoke in the grand way Canada did about education and race and poverty; he never talked about saving his people or righting wrongs. The way McKesey saw it, he had been given a job to do, and he meant to do it very well. He was clearly devoted to the students at Promise Academy, but it wasn't difficult to imagine that he would be applying the same single-minded intensity if his task was to meet quarterly sales forecasts or launch a new product line.

McKesey arrived at Promise Academy at the very end of its inaugural year, when the elementary school consisted of a single kindergarten class. The school's first year had been an uneven one. Terri Grey's middle school, just a few floors down from the Harlem Children's Zone's executive offices, had absorbed almost all of the attention and energy of the board and of Geoff Canada; the elementary school, a dozen blocks away to the northwest, often seemed to escape notice altogether, a relative afterthought. Like many new charter schools in New York, the elementary school occupied a few classrooms inside an existing public school, and sharing space wasn't easy. Some mornings, just after 9:00 A.M., tinny speakers in each classroom broadcast several minutes of announcements from the host school, all at deafening volume and all entirely irrelevant to the Promise students. The Promise Academy teachers had no choice but to stop their lessons and grind their teeth until the squawking had subsided. The bathrooms were often filthy, and after a construction project started across the street, the school building was invaded by mice and rats. The first year brought a disorienting amount of personnel turnover, too, as the principal, Jesse Rawls Jr., tried to find staff with the right mix of dedication and skills; by Christmas break, some kids were on their third teacher.

Testing data was spotty and hard to come by that first year, and what numbers did emerge weren't very reassuring. The point of Promise Academy was to catch kids up, but in the elementary school they seemed to be slipping further behind. When the first cohort of students took the Iowa standardized math test at the beginning of kindergarten, 42 percent of them were above the average national score; a year later, 36 percent of them hit that mark. When the TerraNova reading test was given to students at the beginning of kindergarten, thirty-six children out of the class of about seventy-five scored below average; ten months later, forty-eight scored below average. Although those numbers in isolation might seem like a clear cause for concern, they were mostly ignored or misunderstood, buried as they were in a bewildering mound of data: In addition to the Iowa and TerraNova numbers, the children were regularly given a third set of tests called Developmental Reading Assessments, or DRAs. Each one of these evaluations had a different standard, and no one was quite sure how to coordinate and analyze the results. When the school board met, the trustees and administrators admitted they had little idea how the kindergarten class was doing. At one meeting, in the fall of 2005, Stan Druckenmiller said to the board that from what he could tell, it looked like the math scores at the elementary school had gone up in the first year. In fact, they had fallen.

While Promise Academy limped through its first year, McKesey was working as an assistant principal at PS 30, a tough public elementary school in East Harlem with a student population that drew heavily from local homeless shelters and housing projects. He was well regarded by the parents and the principal, but halfway through the year, he decided he was ready for a bigger challenge, and that winter, he sent out a batch of resumés, one of which found its way onto the desk of Doreen Land, the Promise Academy superintendent. When Jesse Rawls resigned in July 2005, McKesey got the call, and the position.

In McKesey's first year, Canada and the school board remained preoccupied by the ongoing problems at the middle school, and the elementary school stayed mostly off the radar screen. Some of McKesey's teachers felt slighted by the lack of attention, but McKesey was glad to be ignored. He had changes he wanted to make, reforms to put in place, and he felt he could work best with a minimum of oversight and interference from above. He hired new teachers, let a few others go, instituted a new focus on instruction, and worked to develop a unified school culture. He was proud of the school's arts programs—in music, the kids were learning violin, and in art they were studying abstract painting—but his real targets were reading and math. And by the end of McKesey's first year, the children's test results had started to turn around, slowly. The percentage of first-grade students scoring above the mean on the Iowa math test had crept back up to 43 percent, and on the Iowa reading test the figure stood at a more impressive 60 percent. Scores on the Developmental Reading Assessment showed improvement as well: thirty kids in the first-grade class were classified as below grade level in November 2005; by the following March, that figure had fallen to twenty-one.

BY THE MIDDLE OF his second year as principal, in early 2007, it was clear to McKesey that the benign neglect his school had been enjoying wasn't likely to last much longer; like it or not, Geoffrey Canada and the rest of the board of trustees were bound to start paying attention to him soon. In New York State, the first official evaluation that a student receives comes in the winter of third grade, and the inaugural Promise Academy kindergarten class was now in second grade, just a year away from that statewide exam. From afar, McKesey had been observing the troubled progress of the middle school, and he'd seen the disappointment and the recriminations that had followed the results of each year's statewide tests. For a year, he had attended board meetings side by side with Terri Grey, his counterpart at the middle school; now she was gone, a casualty of inadequate test scores. McKesey knew that if his own school's numbers weren't high enough when the third-grade results were posted, he could easily meet the same fate.

Of course, no one had told him exactly how high "high enough" might be. But McKesey had heard Canada say to a variety of audiences that with the conveyor belt fully in place, he saw no reason why 100 percent of Promise's third-grade students couldn't score at grade level. McKesey could think of a few reasons, starting with the fact that perfect scores were basically unheard of, especially in inner-city neighborhoods. In New York City's school district five, whose boundaries roughly approximated those of Harlem, just 36 percent of third-grade students scored at grade level—a 3 or above—on the 2006 reading test, as did 57 percent on the math test. In the state as a whole, the numbers were higher—69 percent in reading and 81 percent in math—though they were still a good distance from 100 percent. Even in Scarsdale, one of the city's wealthiest suburbs, where the public schools were beacons of excellence and parents shelled out as much as four hundred dollars an hour for private tutors, perfection was elusive: 92 percent of the town's third-grade students scored a 3 or above in reading, and 96 percent in math.

McKesey knew that if the third grade fell short of Canada's ideal by a few points—if they pulled in merely Scarsdale-level numbers, let's say—he wouldn't be fired; he might even get a parade. But there was something in the 100 percent challenge that appealed to McKesey's overachieving nature. There were only about ninety students in the current second grade, after all, the class that would be taking the third-grade test the following winter. Most of them had been in the school since the first day of kindergarten, and by now his staff had a pretty good idea of each child's strengths and weaknesses. He and his teachers had a full twelve months to prepare them. He had faith in his team, and almost unlimited resources to draw on. Why *couldn't* they get every single student to grade level?

First, though, McKesey needed to know more precisely where the second-grade class stood. The students had already faced a battery of exams—Iowas, DRAs, internal assessments—but while McKesey believed each test had some diagnostic value, he didn't really trust any of them completely. At PS 30, he had been responsible for the students from the third grade through the sixth grade, and he had watched a lot of them struggle with the statewide evaluations, including students who had scored reasonably well on other assessments. In the third grade, especially, students seemed caught off-guard by those first statewide tests, tripped up by unexpected instructions, making unforced errors, unable to finish on time.

In Harlem, the solution for struggling students is often remediation, going back over easier, more basic material until it is perfectly clear. McKesey, though, decided to go in the opposite direction. He announced to his staff that beginning in January, they would start giving practice versions of the third-grade test to the second-grade students, even though it was still a year before the real test—and not just once, but repeatedly. Some parents and members of his administrative team questioned the decision, McKesey told me, worried that subjecting fragile seven-year-olds to a demanding test a year beyond their reach would only frustrate and upset them. But McKesey thought that might turn out to be a good thing. "People react to frustration in one of two ways," he said. "They can feel so overwhelmed that they stop performing, or they can take that frustration and use it to push themselves to be better. Many of our communities are filled with people who got frustrated and stopped. These children need to get frustrated and keep going. I *want* the children to be frustrated at this point. I don't want them to be comfortable with where they are."

McKesey's plan had a twofold purpose. First, he wanted to make the students so familiar with the style and structure of the third-grade test that taking it became second nature to them. By the time they encountered the real test, he figured, all the anxiety would have been leached out of it, and the students would react to it with a shrug rather than a whimper. The second reason was to give the school's administrators and teachers more precise data about which students were having difficulty with which subjects, so each kid could receive help that was tailored to his or her needs. Mc-Kesey and his staff had already created a variety of specialized interventions for students, from one-on-one tutoring and small-group sessions during the school day, to afterschool instruction, to a morning literacy program for advanced students called Stretch Out and Read. In addition, for those kids who were behind, the school offered catch-up sessions on Saturday mornings, as well as classes two afternoons a week at Harlem's newly opened Kumon Center, a private tutoring franchise, based on a Japanese model, that had become popular with Asian American families across the country. McKesey looked at this array of options as the equivalent of a doctor's medicine chest. He wanted to use the practice tests to diagnose which students suffered from which ailments, and then cure them, one by one, with the appropriate prescriptions: a dose of small-group reading instruction here, a shot of Kumon math classes there.

The students were given the first practice test at the end of January 2007, with little fanfare and no special preparation; McKesey wanted to find the raw baseline that the second grade was starting from. As with all New York State tests, the results were tabulated in four levels: 1 and 2 meant below grade level; 3 and 4 were on and above grade level. McKesey expected that on this early practice test the students would mostly score 1s and 2s, with a few precocious 3s, and, indeed, on that first math test, there were thirty-eight kids on level 1, forty on level 2, and ten on level 3 (meaning they had mastered third-grade material a year early). On the reading test, scores were somewhat lower: fifty-six kids were on level 1, twenty-seven were on level 2, and four were on level 3.

McKesey knew that if he turned in scores like that a year later, in the middle of third grade, it would mean his job. But given that the real test was still twelve months away, the results struck him as relatively good news. The 3s, obviously, were going to be fine. The 2s didn't concern him much, either; he felt confident that he could get them all to a 3 in a year. The kids he had to worry about were the 1s, and on the reading test, especially, there were too many of them for McKesey's comfort. He scheduled a second run-through of the third-grade test for April, and a week before the test, he called a meeting in his office of the five second-grade teachers. Four of them were young, under thirty, some of them on their first teaching job, but one, Beverly Bristow, was a twenty-two-year veteran of the Department of Education, a gray-haired African American woman who McKesey sometimes called "Mama B." Bristow had worked with McKesey at PS 30, and when he moved to Promise Academy, she gave up her seniority in the public school system to move with him.

After McKesey laid out his goals to the second-grade teachers, Bristow asked him about one student in her class, a special-needs student who had been diagnosed with a learning disability. Under the laws of New York State, the girl had been issued an Individualized Education Plan, or IEP, which meant that she was granted certain accommodations in school. She was given special tutoring and more time to complete tests, and she could be promoted to third grade with lower marks than her classmates. Her score on the statewide test, though, was calculated in the same way as everyone else's, and it would be included in the school's overall total. What about this girl, Bristow asked McKesey. Did she need to get a 3, too?

Yes, McKesey answered, she did. "The idea is that Geoff wants 100 percent of our third grade at or above grade level," he said. "That means students with IEPs, that means high achievers, that means everybody in between. So with this particular student, I want to make sure that I'm giving her everything she needs. She comes to school and she tries very hard. She has an inner drive. If we give her the same level of support we give everyone else, I believe she can make it."

The teachers looked a little skeptical.

"There's an answer out there to this age-old question of how to get children who are struggling in school to achieve proficiency,"

McKesey told them. "I think we're on the right path, I really do. I just think we need to take a greater responsibility, a greater role in making sure that the children who need help get help. When your students take this test, I want it to be something you really take personally. If the children don't do well, for real, you really should be mad at yourself." He paused. "I don't mean that you need to go out and start drinking and stuff like that."

"Too late." That came from Ryan Sparzak, one of the young teachers.

McKesey laughed and continued. "Listen, the stakes are high. No one is accepting anything less than 100 percent on grade level. That might sound unrealistic, but we just have to identify the ones who need the help. Those parents who are not involved, we've got to get them involved. With all these resources, there's no reason why these children can't make it. There's none."

MCKESEY'S BELIEF WAS that on tests like the one the second-grade students were practicing to take, knowledge was only one part of the equation, and a fairly small part, at that. It wasn't that he didn't believe in teaching content—in the classrooms the kids were learning about seed germination and Chinese culture and the U.S. Constitution—it was just that he thought that when a child sat down to take a standardized test, knowing a lot of information wasn't necessarily all that helpful. What mattered more was having mastered certain test-taking strategies and tricks, the kind that allowed students to understand what the exam was really asking.

The reading test for the third grade consisted of four written passages and one spoken passage, about subjects like how robins build their nests or the adventures of Mole and Troll; each passage was followed by a few multiple-choice questions that required students to understand and, in some cases, to extrapolate from the information in the passage: "Which title would be another good title for this article?" "What is the main purpose of this article?" "Which sentence from the story gives the most important information?" Children in the third grade often panicked when they took the test for the first time, because they couldn't get past the idea that tests measured what you already knew. So if a student didn't know anything about robins, and she was faced with a passage and a series of questions about robins, she'd freeze up. The test, of course, was designed to measure reading ability, not ornithologic knowledge, and that was one of the main ideas that McKesey and his teachers were trying to hammer home. They wanted students to believe they had the necessary tools to read and understand any text, no matter how foreign it might seem at first.

One rainy April morning a few days before the second practice test, the twenty-two children in Ryan Sparzak's second-grade class were going over a sample worksheet that followed the patterns of the third-grade test. (It was, in essence, a practice test for the practice test.) Together, they read a brief six-paragraph story about chipmunks. ("A chipmunk is a small animal with a loud voice. Its fur is grayish brown with stripes from head to tail. When it is alarmed, it may duck into a hole in the ground.") Working alone, each student circled his or her answers for a half-dozen questions about the passage, and then Sparzak led them through a discussion.

"All right, question number eleven," Sparzak said. "'Why would a chipmunk run away from a cat?' This is called *inference*, where you come up with an answer based on what you know. You put it together and make a guess. Sydney, read the options."

Sydney Mannette, a quiet boy with braids in his hair, read aloud: "F, the cat might eat the chipmunk. G, the cat might ruin the burrow. H, the cat might fall into the burrow and sleep." A few kids laughed at the image, while Sydney continued: "I, the cat might steal the chipmunk's food." More laughter.

"OK, now, you're laughing, and that's a good clue," Sparzak said to the class. "Usually, if you laugh at an answer, you can cross it out. Those answers are just silly. So cross out those two you just laughed at. That's called *process of elimination*. Now we have two left: G, the cat might ruin the burrow, or F, the cat might eat the chipmunk. Raise your hand if you think it was F."

Almost every hand went up. "And if you answered F, you would be wrong," Sparzak said. The kids looked confused. "No, just kidding, you're right," Sparzak said. "F is the right answer. Pat yourself on the back."

Everyone cheered.

Sparzak was one of the youngest teachers in the school, hired when he was twenty-six, and he was also one of the few white people on staff. In the summer of 2005, Geoffrey Canada gave the commencement address at Wheelock College in Boston, where Sparzak had just completed a master's degree in urban education, and delivered a rousing call for the graduates to "join the losing team"—to steer themselves away from comfortable jobs and instead do the hard work with the kids who had fallen behind. Sparzak was inspired, and later that summer, he took a Greyhound bus down to New York to drop off a resumé with McKesey, who had just been hired himself. McKesey called him back for a demonstration lesson and an interview, and the two young men found a quick and easy bond.

Sparzak hadn't grown up in a particularly urban environment or around many minorities—his father, a conservative Baptist minister, had kept the family moving around the Midwest during Ryan's childhood, from Scranton, Pennsylvania, to Lacrosse, Wisconsin, to Grand Rapids, Michigan. But Sparzak felt drawn to work in a low-income, inner-city community like Harlem or Dorchester, the Boston neighborhood where he had done his practice teaching. It was hard for him to put into words why—when he did, it usually started with his faith, his belief in the gift of grace and a corresponding duty to serve others however possible. But even that explanation came reluctantly; he didn't like sounding pious. At Wheelock, his fellow students had mostly been African American women, and in class discussions, they had "disabused" him, he told me, "of the mentality of being the white guy coming in to save the poor black kids."

Sparzak's first few months at Promise Academy had disabused him of a lot of other things, including any confidence that he knew what he was doing as a teacher. He and his wife lived that fall at a friend's house a few blocks north of the school, sleeping on a mattress on the floor. Sparzak would regularly arrive at school at 6:00 A.M. and stay till 8:00 or 9:00 at night, then work on the couch at his friend's house until 2:00 in the morning, planning the next day's lesson, trying not to panic. There was one advantage to his long hours, which was that he had a lot of contact with the parents of his first-grade students: he was there when they dropped their kids off in the morning and he was there when they picked them up at night. Some were skeptical at first that Sparzak was qualified to teach their kids, not because he was white, but because he was green; this was his first real teaching position, and the parents wanted someone who knew what he was doing.

Gradually, though, Sparzak found his footing. He asked the parents for help, and he leaned heavily on his teaching assistant, a young, no-nonsense African American woman named Jovon Lewis, and by the middle of his first year, parents of his students had started to ask McKesey if Sparzak could continue to teach their kids when they moved up to second grade. Sparzak and his wife had found an apartment of their own in Lenox Terrace, a giant complex a block away from the school, and he was beginning to feel at home in Harlem.

Sparzak had an introspective nature, and he often seemed to be trying to plumb the deeper meanings of the work he and his colleagues were doing at Promise Academy. Part of his job, he believed, was to train his students in appropriate behavior for the mainstream working world, so that down the road they could compete for college admissions and jobs with the kids who were growing up in the city's wealthy and middle-class neighborhoods. In class, he reminded them to use "school words" and correct pronunciation: "that" instead of "dat" and "going to" instead of "gonna." He started each day with a "morning circle," where students practiced greeting each other and looking each other in the eye. When a conflict erupted between two classmates, they would stand in the middle of the circle the next morning and resolve things publicly, usually by apologizing and shaking hands. Sparzak taught his students that the best way to absorb information when listening included nodding and following the speaker with their eyes. This was similar to the system known in KIPP schools as SLANT; in Sparzak's class, though, the practices were referred to as the Urindisky Method. It was an inside joke—the class had had a substitute teacher named Ms. Urindisky, and Sparzak had mentioned that he thought her name sounded like a scientific theory. So when they needed a name for their listening system, Sparzak called it the Urindisky Method, and the name stuck.

At the parents' request, McKesey did keep Sparzak with the same cohort of kids for a second year; he graduated with them from first grade to second grade, and as the months had gone by, Sparzak had become quite close to many of the students and to their parents. When one of his students, Jason Williams, joined the Abyssinian Crusaders, the youth football team of the Abyssinian Baptist Church, Sparzak showed up at a game to cheer him on, an event that so impressed Jason's mom that she was still talking about it months later. Sparzak took his students on field trips to expose them to life outside Harlem: a fishing trip in Central Park, classical music concerts in Bryant Park, an excursion to Philipsburg Manor, a Revolutionary-era site north of the city where the kids could watch women in historically accurate costumes churn butter.

Most days, Sparzak's classroom had a tranquil, studious feel to it. While the students worked at their desks on math problems, Sparzak would fire up his laptop and play a little background music—sometimes Vivaldi, sometimes Cab Calloway or Ella Fitzgerald. McKesey liked to joke that Sparzak was trying to turn his kids into nerds, and Sparzak didn't shy away from the idea. He had friends whose children were in competitive private schools, and at those schools, he knew, being smart was highly valued. "So that's what I'm trying to instill in my kids," Sparzak told me. "That it's OK to be really smart. It's even OK to be kind of nerdy when you're in the classroom, to compete on that level. Because that's something that is being instilled in their peers in other parts of New York."

THE RESULTS FROM the April practice test were on the whole encouraging. On the reading test, the number of children at level 3 jumped from four to thirty-one, and the number of level 1s dropped from fifty-six to twenty-one. More than a third of the second-grade class was now working at a third-grade level. There was a similar bump in the math scores—twenty-three students were now at level 3, and just sixteen remained at level 1. Sparzak's class had done particularly well: on the first reading test, in January, nine children in his class had scored at level 1; in April, none of them did. His students were now all at level 2 or higher, all within striking distance of third-grade proficiency, with nine months still to go until the real test.

For McKesey, the new data meant that it was time to get more serious and more specific about the interventions the school was aiming at the second grade. He gathered the second-grade teachers together again and asked each of them to draw up a list of the students in their class who needed the most help, the ones who might not make it to a 3 on the third-grade test without special assistance and extra attention. "I'm going to keep this list in my office, and I'm going to highlight the students on the list at every opportunity," McKesey told the teachers. "Those children are going to get everything." He and his staff would develop an action plan for each child that specified which supports the child would receive. The teachers' assistants would be responsible for doing pullouts during the day, working one-on-one with the struggling students, and the math coach and the literacy coach would oversee each child's progress.

McKesey said he also wanted to use the list as a spur to motivate the parents. He planned to meet with the parents of each second-grade student individually in the coming weeks. "And if their children are on that list," he explained, "I'm going to tell them that I expect those kids to be here for afterschool. I expect them to be here on Saturday. I expect that their attendance will be 95 percent or better from now till the end of the school year. I need to really just up the ante with some of the parents, make sure they understand what is expected."

The staff of the elementary school wrestled constantly with the question of parental involvement—as did the staff of every other program in the Harlem Children's Zone. They tried to follow Geoffrey Canada's two somewhat conflicting principles. The first one held that uninvolved parents couldn't be used as an excuse for a child's failure: the organization needed to have strategies in place to lift *every* kid to success, no matter how disengaged or unhelpful the child's parents might be. The second principle held that even if parental involvement wasn't indispensable, it was still invaluable: the more a child's parents participated in his education, the easier it would be to get him on grade level and keep him there. What that meant in practice was that if you were running one of the organization's programs or schools, you did everything you could to get the parents onboard. McKesey considered inadequately engaged parents to be his own responsibility, the same way that well-organized classrooms and healthy lunches were his responsibility. If parents weren't doing as much to further their children's education as he needed them to be doing, it was his job to figure out how to turn them around.

McKesey had two goals for Promise Academy parents. First, and most important, he wanted them to feel connected to the school and involved in their children's education. On that level, he felt, he was mostly succeeding. He estimated that he personally saw and greeted about three-quarters of the parents every day, when they dropped off and picked up their children. He had created a special outreach for the fathers of Promise Academy students, a monthly get-together of twenty or thirty men that he had named Dinner with Dads. And he made sure each teacher worked hard to develop close relationships with the parents of their students. Sparzak regularly exchanged e-mail with his parents, punching messages into his BlackBerry on his lunch break, and he took calls on his cell phone throughout the school day and into the evening.

The second thing McKesey wanted from the parents was active help with their children's academic development. And so far, at least, he had found that harder to accomplish. He would have liked for all of his parents to be reading with their children every day, but his guess was that that was happening in only a few homes. Ideally, his parents would fill their children's weekends with educational activities: trips to the library, the bookstore, the museum. But again, he thought that was probably pretty rare. Still, McKesey figured it was his job to try to change that situation—and he knew it wasn't a straightforward thing to do. "I can't just say, 'Go read to your child,'" he told me. "It's my responsibility to explain why it's so important. If they don't understand what it takes for their child to be successful, it's my responsibility to tell them. It's my responsibility to educate them on that."

AS THE MONTHS WENT by, it seemed that the pieces of the puzzle were beginning to fit together at the elementary school. In contrast to the middle school, where progress came haltingly, McKesey's plan unfolded smoothly and deliberately, the parents helping with homework, the assistants doing pullouts, the teachers reminding students about inference and the importance of showing their work on their test papers. The students took another practice test in June, at the end of second grade, and then another at the beginning of October, after summer vacation, and the numbers continued their steady ascent. When the students finally sat down to take the tests in the winter of 2008, they seemed, for the most part, calm and confident. Preliminary results released by the state late that spring showed about 70 percent of the school's third-grade students scoring on or above grade level in reading—not quite Scarsdale levels, but most likely topping the state average—and, more remarkably, about 95 percent scoring on or above grade level in math. Almost as important, McKesey said, was that not a single student had scored at level 1 on either test. For a school in Harlem—a school anywhere in New York City—they were impressive results.

The numbers took on even more significance when you compared them to the numbers that the first Promise Academy sixth-grade class posted on that first Iowa test, back in the fall of 2004—the test that showed that more than half of the sixth-grade class was reading at a second- or third-grade level. Almost all of McKesey's third-grade students had hit or surpassed that same level already, with three years of education ahead of them before they reached Promise Academy middle school. The future that Canada had predicted suddenly seemed all but inevitable: in a few years, the middle school would look and feel very different than it did today.

And the conveyor belt was just beginning. Only about a third of the students in that first third-grade class were graduates of Harlem Gems. But the kindergarten class that would arrive in the fall of 2008 would be nearly 100 percent Gems graduates, with almost every parent a graduate of the Three-year-old Journey as well. If McKesey was able to keep honing and improving his system, it seemed likely that those students would soon be passing the third-grade test in even higher numbers.

Canada was, of course, pleased with McKesey's results. After such a long run of disappointing news from the middle school, it was a relief, even a thrill, to see something working the way it was supposed to work. But even so, he felt it was too soon to become complacent, or even comfortable. These ninety kids might be successful eight-year-old scholars, but, he reminded me when we spoke that fall, they weren't saved yet. If he didn't keep watch over them, Canada believed, if he didn't keep up the pressure on their parents and didn't keep giving them all the additional supports he thought they needed, then they would most likely slip back toward mediocrity.

"It's my belief that the longer a child is with us, the stronger that child's resistance to becoming a failing student," Canada explained. "If a child goes to Baby College, goes to Gems, and stays with us at Promise until the second grade, we think we've got a child who is at or above grade level in reading and math. The child probably has a parent who is pretty decently connected to the school, with high expectations of what school is going to be. If that kid then transfers to an average Harlem public school, I think that child would be good for a year or two years. By middle school, though, I think you're going to see it all fall apart."

Canada told me that he had recently read an article that had given him a new way of thinking about what the Harlem Children's Zone was trying to achieve; oddly, it was an article about Isaac Newton's discovery of gravity. When Newton wanted to get people to understand the concept of gravity, Canada explained, he told them that if you fired a cannon from the top of the highest mountain in the world, the cannonball might travel a long way, but it would eventually fall to earth because of the power of gravity. And the faster you shot the cannonball, the farther it would travel before falling to earth. "What that article didn't say is that if you shoot the cannonball fast enough, it will actually escape earth's gravity and go into orbit," Canada said. "The question is what it takes to achieve escape velocity."

This was the latest metaphor that Canada had embraced for the work he and his colleagues were doing. "In communities like Harlem, people tend to think that a single decent program for poor children is enough to provide escape velocity, to give the children the momentum to orbit around their communities and not be damaged," he said. "But they're wrong. The programs are just not powerful enough. The gravity of the community always pulls the child back down. They might stay in the air for a year, but then

lousy schools, lousy communities, the stresses of being poor all begin to weigh on that child and that family, and they begin to fall
closer and closer back down to the values and the performance
levels of the community."

Canada went on: "I am convinced that the longer a child remains with us, the longer they will be able to orbit around the
community without the gravity pulling them back in. And I don't
know exactly when they would reach that escape velocity. I would
dare say if we got a kid to fourteen or fifteen, and he's a good student, we about got him. That would be my thought. We about got
him. He would have the momentum he needs to make it through
the last three years of high school. But if we let him go much earlier than that, I think we fail."

In some ways, Canada's whole project, the entire Harlem Children's Zone, was an attempt to answer that one question: What
would it take? What would it take to get an entire community of
mostly poor children, born mostly to poorly educated, overbur-
dened parents, to college, to turn them all into fully functioning
members of the American middle class? Canada believed he had
found part of the answer already: It would take parenting programs like Baby College and Three-year-old Journey to give parents the knowledge and the confidence to engage with their children's education from birth. It would take intensive, language-rich
prekindergarten classes to compensate for the advantages middle-
class children had in their first few years of life. In elementary
school, it would take extra time in the classroom, plus the kind of
focused, personalized attention to each student's needs that Dennis McKesey was trying to provide.

And those sections of the conveyor belt were working, it seemed,
or at least they were well on their way. Canada now had programs
in place that he believed would produce fifth-grade students from
poor families in Harlem who were academically indistinguish-
able from middle-class fifth-grade students downtown. If he was
right—and the scores from the elementary school indicated that

he was—that alone was something of a miracle. But as Canada saw it, producing class after class of perfectly educated fifth-graders wouldn't in fact amount to much of an accomplishment. Perfectly educated fifth-graders wouldn't change Harlem; it was more likely, in fact, that Harlem would change those perfectly educated fifth-graders, and for the worse.

In order for his project to succeed, Canada knew, the conveyor belt had to keep going, to sixth grade and seventh grade and beyond. And that meant that somehow, and soon, he had to solve the problems of the middle school.

10 Graduation

O N T H E A F T E R N O O N of Tuesday, March 27, 2007, every child in the eighth grade at Promise Academy middle school was handed an envelope and instructed to take it home that night to his or her parents. This wasn't so unusual, on the face of it—the kids were always carrying word home about one thing or the other, usually a note from the principal, Glen Pinder, about a parent conference or a school trip or new and dire consequences for student misbehavior. But this letter was different. It was from Geoffrey Canada, not from Pinder. And the news it carried was weightier and more troubling than anything Pinder had ever sent home. Things were going to change at the middle school, the letter announced. The annual lottery for incoming students, scheduled for that Thursday, had been canceled, and there would be no new sixth grade arriving that fall. More important, the entire eighth grade would be leaving Promise Academy at the end of this school year. They were going to "graduate," as the letter put it, into high schools around the city. Instead of expanding to four grades next year, as planned, the school would shrink to two: the current sixth and seventh grades, which next year would become the seventh and eighth.

Canada's letter tried to put a positive face on things. The changes, he wrote, would "permit us the opportunity to focus our efforts on making the middle school the best possible environment for a child to be educated." To the students in the eighth grade, though, the message seemed a lot simpler: "They're kicking us out." That was Julien Coutourier's analysis at 7:30 the next morning. He was sitting at one of the round tables in the school's cafeteria, sharing an iPod shuffle with a friend, each boy taking one earbud, their two heads joined by a thin white cord. They were listening to Young Dro's "Shoulder Lean," and the song, a celebration of girls, diamonds, and tricked-out cars, had them bobbing their heads and tapping out beats on the tabletop in front of them. Julien had been growing fast, and he was now one of the biggest kids in the eighth grade, five foot eight and heavyset. Somehow, though, the extra bulk he carried made him look dominating rather than doughy. He was still moody, often sitting alone in the cafeteria, the hood on his Bad Boy sweatshirt pulled low over his forehead, looking down at the ground or off into space, warding off inquisitors with an aura of sullen menace. But other days he could be loud and outgoing, the center of attention, exchanging hugs with the girls and shouting out greetings and jokes to classmates and teachers.

It was Julien whose theatrical sighs had provoked such an angry response from Pinder during the showdown with the bad apples, way back in September, on the first day of school. Now, though, six months later, Julien was doing a lot better. He did get an F in drama for the last marking period, and a D in math, but overall his grades were looking up, and his behavior had improved too. Despite his poor showing in math class, he had done well, he thought, on the New York State math exam, which he and his classmates had taken two weeks earlier. And though he still struggled with reading, he felt that the state English test, back in January, had gone all right too. He had joined the poetry club as part of the afterschool program, and one of his poems, titled "See Me," was posted in the second-floor hallway:

> When I see myself I see
> a black man trying to make
> it in the world.
> Trying to dodge what the
> white man says about us.
> Trying to make it in
> the streets of Harlem.

In his three years at Promise Academy, he had changed, he told me that morning. In sixth grade, he hadn't applied himself to school at all, and he was constantly getting in trouble. Terri Grey suspended him every week, it felt like. But then in seventh grade something switched for him. Some close friends, fellow misbehavers, were expelled, and that, for Julien, was a reality check. "I started taking things more serious," he said. But the letter from Canada made him wonder just what the point of all that hard work had been. "Now that I'm taking it more seriously, they're going to kick us all out," he said. "I just don't think it's fair. I've worked too hard to be getting kicked out of school."

A couple of tables away, Xavier Patterson sat with his own group of friends, the academic stars of the eighth grade. "This is crazy," he said, shaking his head. Xavier had always been a skinny kid, but adolescence had recently hit him and he was broad-shouldered now, with an easy smile and a fresh spray of acne across his cheeks and chin. He had a sharp mind and a quick wit, but he wasn't always the most attentive student, and his grades often didn't reflect his natural intelligence. He seemed unsettled a lot of the time, restless, a seeker. His father was Billy "Spaceman" Patterson, an old-school jazz and funk musician who had played guitar with Miles Davis and Sly and the Family Stone, and Xavier had inherited some of his dad's wandering-artist tendencies. It was easy to imagine Xavier at an Ivy League college in a few years, studying math or engineering, but it was just as easy to imagine him dropping out of school to join an experimental theater group or to hitchhike across India.

The other boys at the table were more devoted to their studies. Elijah Baber was generally considered the top student in the eighth grade, and Brandon Bacon wasn't far behind him. The other two, Shaquille Carter and Joel Hernandez, were among the select group of fourteen eighth-grade students who had been chosen to take a weeklong school-sponsored spring-break trip to the Galápagos Islands. Twenty-four hours earlier, their academic futures had all seemed secure. Next September, they had assumed, they would be advancing from eighth grade to ninth grade at Promise Academy. Technically, they would be moving from middle school to high school, but the transition would barely have been noticeable: the same building, the same principal, and many of the same teachers. Now they had no idea where they would be next year. Rumors flew around the table, from Carter to Bacon to Hernandez and back.

"All of the high schools are full already," Joel said.

"All of the *good* schools," Shaquille clarified. "That's why they say that we've got to go to our zone schools."

"Oh, forget that," Xavier said, waving his hands in front of him as if he was trying to dispel a bad odor. "If I go to my zone school, I'm going to lose my life."

"Oh my God," Joel said. He was suddenly forced to contemplate his own zone school—the local high school that the city's Department of Education would make him attend if he couldn't find a place at a specialty school somewhere. "They want to kill my family at that school," he said, half-serious. "I'm scared."

"This is crazy, yo," Xavier said again. In the past, teachers had threatened that if the students didn't shape up, the school would shut down, but Xavier had assumed they were just being dramatic. "Didn't they say that it depended on our eighth-grade grades to see if they'd keep the high school open or closed?"

"So it's obvious that half the school failed," Shaq said with a laugh. "More than half the school."

As they ate breakfast, the young scholars traded ill-formed notions about where they might end up—an all-boy charter school that Shaquille had heard about, a Catholic school nearby, an alternative school for artsy kids called Bread & Roses that offered classes in yoga and mural painting. Now and then, another student would wander by to hear what Xavier and his friends had to say about the situation.

"We're not having no ninth grade," Xavier announced to one kid. "This is it. It's over."

"We're not doing well enough academically," Joel explained. "We're not up to the standards."

"Basically," Shaquille said, "they're kicking us to the curb."

A few minutes before 8:00 A.M., Pinder raised his hand over his head, the signal that the students should stop talking and do the same. The cafeteria grew quiet, and everyone raised a hand except Julien. Pinder stared at him.

"Please don't make a bad situation worse," he said.

"Why not?" Julien was defiant. "You're kicking us out anyway."

"We're not kicking you out," Pinder said, a little wearily.

But it still wasn't clear to the students just what the school was doing to them, and Pinder wasn't answering any questions. There would be an assembly at 8:30 A.M., he told the kids, but for now, they should go to their homerooms, like they always did at 8:00 A.M., and act natural. Business as usual.

Xavier, Shaquille, Brandon, and Joel all had homeroom up in 304 with Lisa Ramos, a young, energetic English teacher. She talked to the students for a while about their upcoming "Profiles in Courage" project, and she wrote two quotations on the board, one from Lao Tzu and the other anonymous: "The person who removes a mountain begins by carrying away small stones." She asked each student to choose one quotation and then write a paragraph explaining how it related to courage.

Most of the students started writing, but Xavier, in a back corner of the room, was too distracted to concentrate. He could barely look at the sheet of blank paper in front of him. He turned to Brandon. "So we have five months left of school?"

"Xavier, focus on your work," Ramos said.

"Can't we talk about the school?" Xavier asked.

"We're going to talk about it all day. You're still here for the rest of the year."

"Are you upset that it's closing?"

"We'll talk about it later, Xavier."

"It's not closing," a girl in the front row reminded Xavier.

"OK, not closing," Xavier said. "But there won't be a ninth grade."

"Xavier, Xavier!" Ramos said, talking over him. "Right now you're getting points for doing what you're doing. This is for your grade. We'll talk about it, I promise, after the meeting."

"SO THE FIRST QUESTION I imagine you're asking is why," Canada said from behind the lectern. "Why this sudden and dramatic change?"

While the students were up in homeroom, the tables in the cafeteria had been rolled to one side and the chairs rearranged into rows. Now the eighth-grade students sat facing the front, silent, watching Canada speak.

"When we first talked about opening this school, I made one promise, that we would not have a lousy school," he said. "I promised that our school would be better than the other schools around us. And I think that we have all tried hard to make that happen. But the truth of the matter is, when we look at how our school is doing, we're not doing better."

He looked down at his hands. "That's not your fault," he went on. "A lot of you in here have worked very, very hard. A lot of you are doing terrific. You're great students. You're really focused. But there's a group of kids that, as hard as we try, we have not been able to get them to a level where I can look at myself in the mirror and say, 'I'm running a better school than other schools in this neighborhood.' And there are too many times in Harlem when people have allowed schools that aren't doing their job to continue. The kids don't get an education, and later on they can't get jobs and take care of their families. That's what happened in Harlem for a long time. And I promised everybody that we would never do that."

Canada looked a little unsteady; he was wearing his reading glasses, which made him seem older than usual. And in truth, he felt awful. Up until just a few weeks earlier, he had believed that the middle school was back on track. He liked Glen Pinder, and from walking the halls of the school he could tell that in the school's third year, things were more orderly than in the previous two, more together. As always, though, it was hard to know how much the kids were actually learning. They had taken the state English test in January, but the results wouldn't come back until late spring at the earliest. Canada didn't want to wait that long. He felt he needed a more immediate indication of how much progress the students had made. So he asked the school's administrators to do their own unofficial analysis of the students' answer papers from the multiple-choice section of the state English test and then give him a rough idea of how well they might have done.

Although Pinder had done his best all year to tamp down expectations for the state tests, Canada was hoping for a big jump in scores—fifteen or twenty percentage points. But when the English-test numbers landed on his desk in the middle of March, the estimates were mediocre across the board, showing no movement at all for the eighth-grade students, more or less the same disappointing scores they had received in seventh grade, when only 24 percent of them were on grade level. Canada was crushed. It wasn't just that there was no improvement. He knew Pinder had had only a few months on the job, and it was always hard to turn an underperforming school around quickly. The truly disheartening fact was that the scores had been so consistently low for so long. For three years now, if these new estimates were accurate, his middle school students had been falling short of expectations on standardized tests. Canada couldn't quite believe it, but he also knew that he couldn't let it continue.

With the help of Betina Jean-Louis, the Harlem Children's

Zone's director of evaluation, and Kate Shoemaker, the head of the afterschool program, Canada pulled together a presentation for the school's board of trustees: some charts and tables showing data on the middle school's performance and an annotated list of four different options for how to proceed. He met with his main advisers on the school board—Stan Druckenmiller, Ken Langone, and Mitch Kurz—and presented them with the alternatives, as he saw them.

Option one was to continue with the status quo. Option two was to close the middle school altogether and ship all three grades off to other schools in September. Option three was to graduate the eighth-grade students into other schools, cancel the sixth-grade lottery, and ask KIPP or another charter entity to take over the middle school charter—something like what Langone and Druckenmiller had suggested to Canada more than a year earlier. But that option, Canada thought, would create a serious morale problem among the school's current staff. He had had some preliminary discussions with David Levin, the head of KIPP's New York schools. Levin had told him that it would take KIPP at least a year to train a new principal to take over the school, and at that point, Levin said, KIPP would want to start fresh with a new crop of kids, beginning with a fifth grade. In that case, Canada knew, the only role for Glen Pinder and his teachers would be as caretakers during a gloomy transition, overseeing the outgoing seventh- and eighth-grade students while KIPP prepared to take over. It was a job with "no hope of redemption," as Canada put it. No matter how well Pinder performed, he would be rendering himself obsolete, watching his school disappear, and Canada knew that Pinder was too ambitious to accept such a depressing role.

That left one option, the one Canada favored: a last chance for Glen Pinder. In many ways, it resembled option three: suspend the lottery, graduate the eighth grade, and continue negotiations with KIPP. The only difference was that under this option, Pinder would in fact have some hope of redemption. If during the

2007–2008 school year he could significantly raise the scores for the two grades remaining in the middle school, then he would keep his job and the school would remain under the sole control of the Harlem Children's Zone. But if the scores didn't improve, then in September 2008 Pinder would be out and KIPP would be in.

It didn't take long for the board to agree to the plan.

In the nine-page summary of alternatives that Canada had prepared for the board, he had identified nine "constituents" whose reactions he thought it was important to consider, including students, parents, staff, funders, and the city's Department of Education, and for each alternative, he had drawn up a chart predicting the response from each constituent. Most of the constituents weren't going to be happy with any of the options, he knew. Even under the plan Canada preferred, students would be "upset," according to the chart; parents would be "very upset"; staff would be hit by "low morale"; and the community would experience a "loss of confidence in HCZ short-term."

Once the decision was made, though, it was Canada's job to try to explain the situation to each of those unhappy constituents. He was due to speak to the parents at 6:00 P.M., and he was sure they wouldn't hold back in expressing their disappointment. But for now it was the students that he was most worried about, and particularly the eighth grade. These were children he had known for almost three years, and he cared about them deeply. In the end, he thought, they would be just fine; he had worked out a plan to get them all into decent high schools, and he believed there was a way to use the other programs of the Harlem Children's Zone to continue to support them all the way through college. But on a personal level, he felt that they had put their trust in him, and he had failed.

After Canada finished his speech in the cafeteria, the students were divided into small discussion groups, and each group retreated to an empty classroom with an administrator or two and a handful of social workers. Canada led one group up to room 404,

Xavier and Jasmine and Tiffany and a dozen other kids. He was concerned about the students' emotional state and concerned too that their natural inclination would be to refuse to talk about it. Abandonment issues were common among Promise students; only a few of them still lived with both parents. At Promise, they had already lost a principal, a superintendent, and plenty of teachers. Now, Canada feared, they would feel abandoned by him and the Harlem Children's Zone as well.

"Let me just get a sense of how people feel now," Canada said. He was sitting next to the bank of windows that looked out on 125th Street. The room was bare except for the circle of straight-backed chairs where the students were sitting. "I imagine if I were some of you I'd be in shock, angry, maybe a little sad. What's the general sense?"

No one said anything.

"All right, who's angry?"

Xavier and a couple of other students raised their hands.

"Who's sad, besides me?"

A few more hands.

"How else are people feeling?"

There was an uncomfortable silence, and then Xavier spoke up. "The thing I don't get is, why didn't you give us some warning?"

Canada didn't say anything, only nodded, so Xavier went on. "I mean, I guess we had a feeling ever since the end of last year that there was a big possibility that things here wouldn't work. So why wouldn't there be some type of warning, so we could prepare? We haven't really thought about the application process for other high schools, stuff like that."

"That is a very legitimate question," Canada said. "And I think the answer to that is that I really believed that it wouldn't come to this." He shifted in his chair. "That was probably naive on my part," he admitted. "I probably should have thought it through and probably should have said to people, you know, 'This may not work out. So you should think about what the options are.'" He looked over at Xavier. "But even up till the exam, I really thought we were going to do much better." He shrugged. "I just did. And I was really, really shocked to see that we didn't. So that was basically my fault. If I had honestly thought that we weren't going to do better, then I would have said something much earlier. I just didn't think that was going to happen."

AFTER A FEW MORE questions, the group meetings broke up. The social workers stuck around to talk to any students who wanted to discuss their feelings, but not many of them did. Canada didn't, either, but his staff were worried about him, and as the day went on, they kept stopping by his office, one by one, to check on him. He tried to close his door and stay busy, hoping his assistant, Tuere Randall, would keep him occupied with phone calls and meetings, and for the most part she obliged.

For Xavier, the day was just plain weird. He moved from class to class as usual, and his teachers went on and on about polynomials and the Underground Railroad, but personally, he couldn't see the point of talking about anything but the school and the uncertain future that faced the eighth grade. Xavier had neglected to give Geoffrey Canada's letter to his mother the night before; his excuse, after he finally called to tell her about the 6:00 P.M. meeting she was supposed to attend, was that it had somehow got lost in his "black hole of a book bag." She wasn't very happy, but she said she'd be there.

Xavier's mom, Christine Patterson, had always been somewhat skeptical of Promise Academy. She had entered the initial lottery, back in 2004, on a whim, but Canada's words that night inspired her, and when her number was pulled, she enrolled not one but two children; Xavier's younger brother, Tabara, was now in Ryan Sparzak's second-grade class at the elementary school. Although she liked Sparzak, she had been only intermittently satisfied with the Promise education overall; at various moments over the last three years she had considered pulling both of her sons out and transferring them to different schools. She and her husband were artistic types—she had a MySpace page where she offered self-improvement classes and sold all-natural skin-care products—but when it came to their children's education, they thought more like buttoned-down professionals, always looking for the best opportunities, exploring every possible option. Their diligence had paid off for their first child: Xavier's older brother was now attending Amherst College in Massachusetts. They expected great things from Xavier as well.

Patterson was eight months pregnant, and when she arrived at the school for the evening meeting, she wore a big purple paisley maternity dress, her long braids held back with a thin maroon headband. The cafeteria was set up like it had been for the eighth-grade meeting, and Patterson took a seat in the very first row, right in front of Canada's lectern. Xavier sat next to her.

JoAnn Coutourier, Julien's mother, was a couple of rows back, on the right-hand side, wearing dark jeans and a leather jacket over a pale green sweater. Coutourier knew that her son wasn't on the same academic level as Xavier and his friends. She wasn't aiming for Amherst. But, like the Pattersons, she was deeply involved in her son's education. When it had first become clear that Julien was behind in reading, she had sought out private tutoring and enrolled him in a diagnostic course at a local college's school of ophthalmology. And though she had a hectic life, working for the city and raising two kids on her own, she made a point of attending every parent meeting Promise Academy offered—one of the few parents who did. Just two days earlier, on Monday night, she had come to a two-hour brainstorming session in the cafeteria, trying, along with fifteen or twenty other mothers, to think up new ways to involve more parents. Now, looking around the cafeteria, she saw dozens of parents who never showed up at regular meetings. The good turnout made her feel depressed. Where was this crowd on Monday night, when they might still have made a difference?

When Canada spoke, he told the parents many of the same things he had said to their children that morning. He had been sure that the scores were going to go up this year, he said, and he was stunned when he found out that they hadn't. But it wasn't the kids' fault, he assured parents. "I'm not blaming students for the failure to get good scores," Canada said. "That's our job and our responsibility. That's what we get paid for."

Canada changed the subject to the question of what was going to happen next for the students in the eighth grade. He said he knew it was late in the year to be thinking about high school. "We are behind the eight ball," he admitted. "But I have called everybody I know, including the chancellor, to say that we want to make sure that parents and students aren't penalized by us getting a late start on this." He had assembled a team of experts and advocates from around his agency, he said, who would spend the next several weeks consulting with the families of the eighth-grade students on how to get their kids into the high school of their choice. As he spoke, members of his staff handed out blue folders to each parent, each one stuffed with information about applying to New York City high schools: application forms, charter school lottery deadlines, timetables, and an outline of the official appeals process.

"Another question that I am sure you have is, 'Didn't you promise that you were going to support our kids through college?'" Canada said. A few parents nodded. "I absolutely did make that promise," he said. "And I'm not backing away from it. But I am changing it." The Harlem Children's Zone ran a number of programs for high-school-aged children, Canada explained, from afterschool tutoring to an investment club to a drop-in arts center, and all of them were directed at getting kids into college. He said he wanted the students leaving Promise Academy this year to take part in as many of those programs as they could in the years to come. "This is our core business at the Harlem Children's Zone," he said. "Helping young people do well and getting young people into college."

This was a mode Canada was more comfortable with—telling

people what his organization had to offer, finding solutions, promising that he would pull every string he could to help fix things. But many of the parents weren't ready to move past the recrimination stage. When Canada opened the floor for questions, the first parent to speak was Shaquille Carter's father, a disgruntled-looking man in the second row in a blue sweater and glasses.

"You said you were going to talk to the chancellor," he said. "Well, my son wants to go to St. Xavier. He wants to go to Bronx Science." These were two of New York's selective high schools, one Catholic and one public, each with a demanding entrance exam that had taken place months earlier. "Those schools are gone," Shaquille's dad said. "There are no makeups. What are you going to do about that?"

Canada looked uncomfortable. "The specialized schools that have test requirements to get in, there's no way I know of that we can help kids get into those schools," he said. "That's the one area that I don't think we can be of any real help."

"So my son lost his opportunity to get into those schools." It was an accusation, not a question.

"My understanding is that those schools are closed now."

"That's all I wanted to know." He turned to Shaquille. "I'm ready to go. I don't have nothing else to say. Let's go."

The Carters stood and walked out of the cafeteria. From the lectern, Canada watched them go.

There were more questions, some of them pointed—Xavier's mom wanted to know if Canada would make calls for students who wanted to apply to private schools, and a mother who worked at Louis D. Brandeis High School, a notorious local zone-school with metal detectors and security guards, wondered if Canada could at least guarantee that none of the Promise kids would wind up there—but no one else walked out.

"We will spare no cost or expense around this issue," Canada reassured the parents after he had answered the final question. "That doesn't mean this is going to be easy. I'm not in a fantasy world. I know this is going to be hard and frustrating. We're just simply going to go through it." He tried to sound upbeat. "We're going to stay on top of it, and we're going to do everything we can to help support your young people now and in the future."

Then he paused and looked down at the lectern. "Let me just say one more thing." Suddenly, though, he couldn't find the words. He didn't want to seem like he was looking for sympathy; he knew it was his day to be the bad guy. But still, he wanted the parents to understand how he felt. After a long moment, he looked up, his eyes watery. "As upset as you all are, some of you must have *some* idea of how upset I am," he said. "You just need to know that." His voice cracked. "I am very upset and disappointed. Your kids know it. I want you to know it too."

AFTER THE MEETING, parents gathered in small clusters to talk or went to track down their assigned advocate in order to begin the long process of finding a high school. There were tables set up at the back of the room, and some of the parents were there already, looking through their paperwork. JoAnn Coutourier hadn't moved from the third row, where she sat alone, dabbing at her eyes.

A tall man wearing tinted blue sunglasses and a denim shirt walked over to where Geoff Canada was standing. He extended his hand. "My heart is breaking, Mr. Canada," he said. His name was Edward Mollette, and his daughter, Jasmine, was one of the students who had been chosen for the Galápagos trip. "I am truly heartbroken over this. There's no way, no how, that anything can be done for the school?"

Canada shook his head.

"When Jasmine came home with that letter yesterday, I just can't tell you what was going through my mind," Mollette said. His voice was deep, a double bass. "I'm hoping something amazing will happen, like a miracle."

After a few more encounters like that one, the only person Canada wanted to talk to was his friend Alfonso Wyatt, the minister who had roused some of these same parents three years earlier with his call-and-response at the lottery. Together, the two men quietly slipped out of the cafeteria through a back door that led into the closed-up kitchen. A few minutes later, Wyatt emerged from the kitchen alone and closed the heavy metal door behind him, leaving Canada inside, alone, to reflect in peace.

Out in the cafeteria, Glen Pinder was angry. He didn't like that Canada had said that the problems at the school weren't the fault of the students. That let them off the hook too easily, he told me. It sent the wrong message. "Yes, we failed them," he said. "But they failed themselves as well. It can't just be us. The way it came across was like we didn't do what we were supposed to do. The truth of the matter is we've got great teachers, we've got great staff, and if we had willing participants, we would have great students."

When I spoke to Pinder three weeks later, he was feeling more optimistic and more sympathetic to the way Canada had expressed things in the meeting with the parents. "I understand from a political standpoint that that was the right thing to say," he told me when I met with him in his office. "One way to interpret this is we're getting rid of the riffraff so we can move forward. That's how I feel. They were a cancer on the whole school. But you don't want to communicate that to the parents. So, yeah, 'We failed your child.' A lot of people failed the child. The parents failed the child, the child failed the child, and so did we, to a certain extent."

When I spoke to Stanley Druckenmiller the following week, he identified one very specific mistake that he and the rest of the board had made: starting the school with sixth grade instead of fifth grade, the way KIPP did. "It's not just that the kids are two or three grades behind at that point," he said. "It's that there is a culture that is largely formed by that age. Lack of parenting, lack of discipline. And when they come in, it is an extraordinary task to turn that around. I still don't know whether we're capable of it."

The school's administrators and trustees continued to engage in

an informal postmortem that spring, exchanging theories and explanations. But the process was suddenly made more complicated
in May, when the official scores on the state English tests were released. As it turned out, the eighth grade had done better than the
preliminary estimates had indicated. Their reading scores hadn't
stayed where they were the previous year, after all; they jumped
from 24 percent on grade level to 33 percent on grade level. Those
weren't stellar scores, but they were a significant improvement over
the previous year; the students had gone from being twenty points
behind the city average to nine points behind.

And then when the math scores came out in June, they showed
an improvement that was downright startling. Back in sixth grade,
just 9 percent of Julien and Xavier's class had scored on grade level
in math. In seventh grade, 34 percent of them did. Now, in eighth
grade, the number had jumped all the way to 70 percent. The
eighth-grade scores weren't just impressive when compared with
the abysmal place the class had started from; they were impressive
by any measure. Julien and Xavier and their classmates beat the
state average on the math test by twelve points, and they beat the
city average by twenty-four points. Of the 409 New York City
public schools that took the eighth-grade math test in 2007, including KIPP schools, magnet schools, and schools that specialized
in math, only 70 did better than Promise Academy, putting Julien
and Xavier's class in the top fifth of all eighth-grade classes in the
city, a truly elite level. When the departing students and their parents, some of whom were still scrambling to find a slot in an acceptable high school, saw the scores, they couldn't help but feel
exasperated. Wasn't scoring in the top fifth of all schools good
enough? Just how much better would the kids have had to do in
order to be allowed to stay at Promise Academy? (To top off these
accomplishments, when the city issued report cards late that fall
for each school in the city, Promise Academy middle school received an A, the highest score a school could get, in part because of
the big jump in the eighth grade's test results.)

That spring, after Druckenmiller had seen preliminary math results indicating a sizable jump, he told me he still felt that the board had made the right decision. "We haven't decided to end the middle school," he reminded me. "We've just decided to suspend it and get it right. I don't think it's such a bad thing that Glen is going to be working with two hundred kids instead of four hundred kids next year. And if we get it right, we'll do the lottery again and proceed the way we were."

When I spoke to Mitch Kurz, the board member, about the decision, he told me he looked at it through a slightly different lens. You had to remember that Druckenmiller and Langone were famously successful stock pickers, he said. And the decision to cut the school's losses and send off the eighth grade displayed "a very typical trader's instinct." He explained what he meant. "When a trader makes a bet on a commodity, and the trader starts losing money, then he or she closes the bet out. Unless hubris takes over. Then you've got Long-Term Capital Management." He was referring to an early hedge fund, run by an elite group of traders and math savants, that had collapsed in spectacular fashion in 1998, nearly taking a corner of the stock market down with it.

Kurz's history as a marketer also played into his thinking on the board's decision. Pulling back the way they had done looked bad, he admitted. But if the board hadn't trimmed the sails, and a year later the school was still in trouble, it could have been a disaster for the agency's public profile. "Right now, on a continuum from perfect to terrible, we have a significant hiccup," he told me. "We stubbed a toe, and it continues to hurt. But we don't have a failure. If we had continued for another year and were unable to show dramatic progress, then the middle school would have been placed in a failing bucket. Not failure, but a failing bucket. Which would have made it extremely difficult for us, because it would have affected the Harlem Children's Zone brand, and that is a very important brand to protect."

At the school itself, no one had much of an appetite for rehashing the decision. For Chris Finn, the dean of students, the year had just been too exhausting. "Overall, I would say the biggest feeling is a failure kind of feeling," he told me at the beginning of June. "It does feel a little like a loss, where something didn't happen right." There were some eighth-grade students who he felt really bad for, he said, the ones who had found a sense of belonging at Promise Academy, and he worried about how they would do at their new schools. But at the same time, if Finn was honest about it, there were plenty of others he wouldn't miss—the bad apples who had plagued him all year. No matter what the state-test results said, many of them were undeniably a negative influence, apathetic about school and disruptive in class, and Finn couldn't help but feel that the school would be better off without them.

"I'm excited about the opportunity to kind of press reboot," he said. "I feel good about this next year. I am really optimistic about it."

WHEN CANADA FIRST told the eighth-grade students they were leaving the school, several of them asked him if they could have a graduation ceremony to mark their departure. Pinder, for his part, thought it was a bad idea. If you make a big deal over graduating from middle school, he said, you send kids the message that an eighth-grade education actually means something. But Canada said yes. He figured it was the least he could do.

And so on Friday, June 22, at 10:30 A.M., the eighth-grade students walked into the gymnasium for the last time. They entered to the strains of "Pomp and Circumstance," walking slowly, the girls in red dresses, some unsteady in high-heeled shoes, the boys in black suits. Each child's outfit was topped with a mortarboard and tassel. Xavier grinned sheepishly when he saw his parents standing and applauding with all the others, his mother holding his new baby sister. A handful of jumbo Mylar balloons hovered over the crowd, saying "Way to go, grad!" and "You did it!"

Pinder spoke first, offering congratulations tempered by a note of caution. "It is my hope that eight years from now, in June of 2015, you will all be participating in your college graduations," he said. "There is no doubt that you have the ability. We all agree that you are a very talented group. The question remains: do you have the desire to do whatever it takes to have a successful life?"

Elijah Baber had ended the year with the highest marks in the class, and he delivered a one-minute valedictory address, gripping the microphone with one hand and reading from his speech without looking up or smiling. A solemn-faced girl named Nashakeem Uzzell came second, and Brandon Bacon was third.

Xavier didn't win any special awards, but he was feeling pretty good. He had been admitted to Cardinal Hayes, an all-boys Catholic high school in the Bronx with a good academic reputation and a list of illustrious former students that included George Carlin, Don DeLillo, and Regis Philbin. The graduate who most impressed Xavier was Martin Scorsese, who had recently endowed the Martin Scorsese Video Center at the school. Xavier already had plans for his first movie, a documentary about the two separate groups of friends that he had been spending time with in recent months. One group was the ballers, black kids from Harlem and the Bronx whose recreational lives revolved around pickup basketball games. The other was the skaters, white boys from the Upper West Side who hung out in a park near Grant's Tomb, on the Hudson River, riding rails and popping kickflips. Xavier's plan was to bring his skater friends and his baller friends together one afternoon and just roll the cameras and see what happened.

Julien Coutourier had been admitted to Cardinal Hayes, as well, and most of the rest of the eighth-grade students had found a home, too. Some parents were more satisfied than others at the outcome—some were still quite angry about what had happened and how it was handled—but at least it looked like no one was going to end up at Brandeis High.

As for Geoffrey Canada: try as he might to emulate the cool decision-making abilities of his fellow board members, the trader's instinct didn't come naturally to him. The middle school had always been a questionable investment, and he knew it. From the start, his experience and the research told him that starting early was the smarter angle, that poorly educated sixth-grade students in Harlem were always going to be a risky bet. But he still believed it was entirely possible to educate children like the ones leaving the school to a high level of success—and the 70 percent result on the math test only confirmed that for him.

He didn't regret the decision to pull back for a year. The one hundred students who had entered the school in 2004—now a class of just sixty-five, after three years of steady attrition—had required an enormous amount of attention and time, not to mention a significant portion of his organization's financial resources and staff. And in reality, they represented a tiny fraction of what the Harlem Children's Zone was accomplishing. Removing them, and letting Pinder and Finn and the rest of the staff concentrate on just two grades next year, could only improve the odds of long-term success—and it would buy Canada time to convince the more skeptical members of the Promise Academy board that they should stay the course with the middle school.

It was only when he thought about the graduates themselves that he hesitated. He told me he was confident that they'd turn out well, that they'd all end up in college, but in his heart, he admitted, he thought that they would have had a better shot at success if they could have stayed at Promise Academy. When it came down to it, he was making a tradeoff: he was reducing the students' individual chances of success in order to improve the odds for the school as a whole. It might have been a shrewd tradeoff, but for Canada it was not a happy one. And unlike Pinder and other administrators, Canada wasn't able to comfort himself with the notion that the fault lay with the departing students—that the kids were the ones who had blown a great opportunity. "It's not the kids," he told me in his office on the morning of the graduation ceremony. "It's us. The kids are middle school kids from Harlem who come from troubled environments and have lots of problems. That's who they are. Yes, they're difficult. If they were not difficult, I'd be quite shocked. But we didn't do our job. Inside the classroom, good, solid instruction was not going on in a way that could drive results, and that's what we have to deal with. We didn't have the teachers prepared and organized in a way that they could deliver the outcomes on the English test. Saying it was the behavior, that something was wrong with the eighth-graders, that is just a cop-out. The evidence doesn't support it."

Down in the gymnasium, Canada took to the stage and introduced Rev. Wyatt, the keynote speaker for the graduation ceremony. Wyatt gave a spirited address, pacing the stage, thanking the parents and the faculty for all they had done and telling the outgoing students that they were "the children of the promise." He warned them against the snares and seductions of high school. "There are some people who are going to try to convince you to lower your IQ to fit in with them, and they can't even spell IQ!" he said. "My sisters, you are going to meet some brothers that just can't handle the fact that you're gorgeous *and* smart. They're going to be intimidated by your preparation. And my brothers, there are some folk who will try to convince you that the only thing you can do is bounce a basketball and let your pants hang down. You don't have to be a basketball player! Make some money and buy the team!"

For the parents who had been at the lottery three years earlier, it was, all of a sudden, an oddly familiar moment—another school, another stage, another fiery speech by Wyatt. Christine Patterson had been there that rainy April evening, waiting for her child's name to be called, and so had JoAnn Coutourier. ("It was a fantastic night," Coutourier recalled, a little wistfully. "The energy level was just so high.") Back then, they were anxious about whether their boys would get into Promise Academy. Now they were anxious about what would happen to them after they got out.

Still, as they watched their sons file across the stage to collect their diplomas, they couldn't help but feel proud. The boys looked handsome and wise and somehow a little more grown-up. After all the graduates had returned to their seats, Sakina Gabriel, the school's parent coordinator, asked them all to stand and led them through the Promise Academy creed. "I promise to always dream out loud," the students recited together. "To lift my head and be proud. And never end up a face in the crowd." In unison, grins on their faces, they made a show of shifting the tassel on their mortar-boards from left to right. And then, with a shout, they all tossed their caps straight up in the air, as high as they could throw them.

11 What Would It Take?

VICTOR ANTHONY PREMIERE BORIA, all six pounds, four ounces of him, came into the world on a cold March morning in 2007, a little before dawn. For sixteen hours, his mother, Cheryl Waite, had labored in the maternity ward of Harlem Hospital, with her twin sister and her mother and her new husband, Victor Boria, by her side. Victor was now twenty. Cheryl was eighteen. They had been married for three months. The ceremony, brief and simple but tearful nonetheless, took place at City Hall in December, just a few days after Victor's showstopping marriage proposal during their graduation from Baby College.

After the delivery, the mood in Cheryl's hospital room was happy and festive. She was a little dazed still, from the pain and the epidural, but all the aches and cramps of pregnancy had vanished. Victor sat in a chair by the foot of her bed, wearing blue antibacterial scrubs and a surgical mask, and held his son, whose big brown eyes seemed to search the room.

It wasn't until Victor and Cheryl left the hospital two days later that the weight of their situation really hit them. In the cab going down Lenox Avenue, with Victor Sr. on one side of her and Victor

Jr. in his car seat on the other, Cheryl started to cry. "I was feeling very nervous and very scared," she said. "I was thinking, 'We have to spend the rest of our lives with this baby. What are we going to do?'"

When I met up with Cheryl and her new family two and a half months later, in an International House of Pancakes restaurant a couple of blocks west of Harlem Hospital, her fears seemed to be fading. The family's problems weren't over; to begin with, they still didn't have a stable place to live. They had applied for a Section 8 voucher from the federal housing department, which would help them pay rent on a place of their own. For now, while they were waiting to make it off the program's long waiting list, Victor Jr. was shuttling with his parents between one grandmother's place, a house in New Jersey, and the other's, an apartment on the second floor of a public housing high-rise in Harlem. Still, despite their frequent moves, Cheryl and Victor seemed to be enjoying parenthood and marriage. "We're very bonded," Cheryl said with a smile. "We have a fun relationship. We learned to talk about our differences. We argue like normal people, but at the end of the day we make up and we still love each other."

Victor and Cheryl were doing their best to follow the lessons they had learned in Baby College. They put Victor Jr. to bed early each night and got up when he woke at 5:00 A.M. Almost every day they pushed his stroller to the local library, where they sat and read picture books with him, pointing out colors and shapes, and they had already taken family field trips to Central Park and the Museum of Modern Art and the Museum of Natural History and the Bronx Zoo. Like many new parents, Victor and Cheryl had made a few mistakes along the way. They started Victor Jr. on solid food too early, thinking that a little cereal might help him sleep through the night, and his weight had shot up too fast. But when they visited their pediatrician, the felicitously named Dr. Love, she told them to stop, to keep him on formula for another few months, and they dutifully followed her instructions.

WHAT WOULD IT TAKE? • 259

At IHOP, Victor wore a blue T-shirt with a skull logo on the front, and after demolishing a bacon and egg cheeseburger, he took his baby son in his arms and made faces, hoping to be rewarded with a smile. "You've got to keep peeking at him," he told me. "You'll look over and he'll all of a sudden be cracking up."

Victor Jr. and his young father represented two separate generations of Harlem youth, and looking at them together was a way to grasp the full scope of Geoffrey Canada's project. Because Victor Sr. was just twenty years old, he was still in the upper age range of the Harlem Children's Zone target population, while Victor Jr., as the child of Baby College graduates, was, de facto, one of the agency's youngest clients. Canada's staff had one program that would help Victor Jr. complete all his immunizations and another to help Victor Sr. complete high school.

But while the Harlem Children's Zone was prepared to work with both Borias, it didn't take a Nobel Prize–winning economist to recognize that the prospects of the infant and those of the young man were very different. Victor had spent two years in Job Corps, the federal program that was intended to prepare wayward teenagers for the GED, but at twenty, he still hadn't earned his equivalency degree. He wanted to work—he liked the idea of supporting his family—but he had a hard time holding on to employment. Just before his son was born, Victor was hired as a stocker at a ShopRite supermarket in New Jersey. It was a good job, covered by a union contract and paying more than minimum wage, but it didn't last long. Victor worked the shift from 11:00 P.M. to 7:00 A.M., and he had one main task: breaking down the cardboard boxes that the store's deliveries came in. But he couldn't keep up. The boss expected him to break down 240 boxes in a shift, and Victor found it hard to complete more than 120.

Victor was young still, and there were more job-training programs open to him, but James Heckman's research made it hard to be optimistic about how much those programs could improve his chances. Victor had always struggled with the printed word, and in the economy of the twenty-first century, that meant it would be difficult for him to find a job with decent pay. Victor had the bad fortune of being short on marketable cognitive skills at a moment in economic history when the premium on those skills was higher than ever.

His infant son, by contrast, was an eleven-pound bundle of pure possibility.

If you looked only at the statistical patterns of recent decades, Victor Jr.'s future could seem just as bleak as his father's. He was an African American boy born to an unemployed teenage mother in the ghetto, and his father was an unemployed high school dropout with an arrest record. Through the "accident of birth," as Heckman put it, Victor Jr. had entered life saddled with almost every risk factor you could think of.

But there was another route open to Victor Jr. Watching him giggle with his dad, it was easy to believe what the neuroscientists and psychologists had concluded, which was that at this moment in his life there was no cognitive difference whatsoever between him and an upper-middle-class white infant growing up in a good neighborhood downtown. Victor Jr. could babble and coo and stare and smile with the best of them. If things went the way they usually went in Harlem, his cognitive trajectory would diverge from the upper-middle-class path soon, in the next twelve months or so, and he would begin to fall further and further behind. But Victor and Cheryl—and Geoffrey Canada—now had the tools to stop that from happening.

What would it take for Victor Jr. to succeed? For the next few years, it would take his parents continuing to do what they were doing: raising him in a home (two homes, for now) that provided him with love and stability and attention. They would need to read to Victor Jr. every day, as Cheryl did already; to keep taking him to the library and the zoo and the museum; to give him decent nourishment; to continue to follow their pediatrician's advice. And then Victor Jr. would need a spot on the conveyor belt. He will be eligible for the Promise Academy lottery in August 2010, when he will be three, for admission to kindergarten in 2012. If he is accepted, his parents will be enrolled in the Three-year-old Journey, and Victor Jr. will have a slot in the 2011–12 Harlem Gems prekindergarten class. When Victor Jr. turns five, Dennis McKesey and his staff will take over. If Victor Jr. needs remedial help at that point, Promise Academy will make every effort to catch him up. But more likely, he will never have fallen behind his peers.

In the years that follow, the cognitive and noncognitive skills that Victor Jr. develops will have the potential to offset the disadvantages of his birth and his family's finances, and the opportunities open to him will multiply. As a teenager, he may still live in public housing. His family may still be broke. But those facts will no longer necessarily represent an insurmountable obstacle for Victor Jr. With a little luck, he will be headed toward a very different future than the one that faces most children growing up in America's ghettos.

IF YOU STAND ON the roof of the headquarters on 125th Street, you can see the entire Harlem Children's Zone, extending south to 116th Street, just a few blocks from the northernmost reaches of Central Park, and reaching north past the towering Abraham Lincoln projects to 143rd Street, where the Harlem River curves west and the island of Manhattan narrows. The Zone quadrupled in size during the years that I spent reporting in Harlem, growing from twenty-four blocks to sixty blocks to ninety-seven blocks; the final stage, known as the northern expansion, opened in 2007, funded by a $25 million grant from Hank Greenberg, a former insurance-company CEO, and a matching grant from Stan Druckenmiller. As of the beginning of 2008, more than seven thousand children were being served each year by one or another of the organization's programs. Baby College was pushing into the northern expansion, hiring new outreach workers to canvass the Lincoln projects and graduating about four hundred parents a year. Harlem Gems had just expanded to two hundred slots, which meant that every child admitted to Promise Academy in the early lottery would now be able to attend a year of intensive prekindergarten on the way to elementary school. Promise Academy middle school had of course shrunk temporarily to fewer than two hundred students. But the two elementary schools were together educating almost eight hundred students. There were still plenty of young people in Harlem who couldn't get into Promise Academy, but they now had several other options; many of them were attending other charters or academies in the neighborhood, and Canada was trying to provide afterschool options for those children, as well. The Zone's offerings for Harlem's teenagers—afterschool arts workshops, tutoring help, an investment club—had expanded, and each fall, about 150 of the high school seniors enrolled in those various programs went on to college.

What was most important to Canada, though, was not the individual successes of each of these initiatives; what mattered to him was the way they fit together. There were two separate strategies at work in the Harlem Children's Zone, and Canada believed them both to be essential to the success of the project. The first was the intensive conveyor-belt strategy, the smooth and continuous path that led kids from Baby College into Promise Academy and all the way through high school. The second strategy, for the kids who didn't get into Promise Academy, was more improvised and less orderly. It was the teenager strategy, the it's-never-too-late strategy, and its ambitions were less lofty. The goal with those programs wasn't to elevate kids to the top rungs of academic achievement; it was to steer teenagers toward a moderate degree of success: away from crime, toward achievement, into some kind of college program.

Toward the end of my reporting, sitting with Canada in his office, I asked him to explain the point of the second strategy. I had been spending a lot of time at Harlem Gems and at the elementary school, and I had been immersed in the writings of scholars like

James Heckman and Joseph Torgesen, who made a strong case for intervening early. By that point, I was thoroughly convinced by the conveyor-belt idea. Heckman, in particular, made what seemed to me to be an airtight case for the start-early approach; his papers included chart after chart proving that investing resources in babies and young children from low-income communities usually paid off in a big way, while investing in adolescents and young adults usually did not. And it wasn't just what I was reading; I was able to see the evidence firsthand. In the elementary school, kids were moving ahead in great strides, accomplishing amazing things, while at the middle school, every step forward seemed to be followed by a step back. The epitome of the second strategy was TRUCE, the afterschool arts center for teenagers. When I visited, it seemed fun and engaging and productive, but not very scientific; in fact, it seemed exactly like the kind of scattershot program Canada had been running ten years earlier, the kind he grew disenchanted with.

So why not put all your resources on the front end, I asked Canada, into the early-childhood programs? Why spend time and money reaching a few self-selected teenagers here and there, when you could use those resources to perfect the conveyor belt, to give kids like Victor Jr. even more support?

Canada said he agreed that TRUCE was an example of the superhero approach that he was trying to get beyond: working with poorly educated middle school and high school students, trying to save them from ruin. It was much less efficient than the conveyor-belt strategy, he acknowledged; the penetration rate was much lower, and success depended less on predictable and replicable methods and more on the personal connections between Canada's staff and the children they were working with—not to mention a healthy dose of luck.

But having said all that, Canada told me that in fact, he believed the non-Promise strategy was at least as important as the conveyor-belt strategy, possibly more so. Without it, he believed, he would never be able to truly change Harlem's culture—he would never successfully infuse it with a new set of values. As of the fall of 2007, he told me, there were 284 kids in college who had come through TRUCE and the other drop-in and afterschool programs for teenagers. If, a few years from now, those young men and women graduated and returned to Harlem, they would become a part of the "contamination" of the neighborhood that Canada liked to talk about.

"Imagine growing up in a community where your cousins, your uncle, your father, everybody has gone to jail," Canada said. "That's just been the normal experience. Now, you're nine years old, and you're trying to figure out what it means to be a nine-year-old in Harlem. Well, pretty quickly you're going to come to believe that going to jail is no big deal. If my third-graders grow up"—the ones Dennis McKesey was just then preparing for their first statewide test—"and things stay the same in Harlem, meaning that every other man they run into has gone to jail, we're going to lose a huge number of those kids. They're going to look up to these guys, and they're going to end up being sucked into that same kind of environment very easily."

On the other hand, Canada said, "if you've got all these hundreds and hundreds of kids who've gone to college, then at least you have a competing vision of what it means to grow up poor in Harlem. So this second strategy, the middle school strategy, the superhero strategy, it is essential. If you get enough of these adolescents to do well, they'll prepare your community for those third-graders."

The first strategy, the conveyor-belt strategy, had no shortage of scholarship and data to back it up. Canada's second strategy, though, had very little research behind it, if any; there, he was relying much less on science and much more on instinct. It was his contamination theory in action, and that was something that social scientists hadn't yet found a way to measure.

But he was no less certain of its validity. "If you just do the early childhood and you don't have a separate strategy to reach large numbers of adolescents in your community," Canada said, "then those individual kids will do well, but it will have no impact on the community at all."

A hundred college graduates arriving in Harlem every year, though—that could really change things. "When my grandparents first moved to Harlem in the 1920s, it was a community where people had a lot of pride," Canada said. "Folks valued education. Everyone was working; there were jobs to be had; people had dreams that Harlem was a launching pad to making it in America. My belief is that in ten years, Harlem could be that kind of place again."

CANADA HAD FOR MANY years been a sought-after public speaker, but in 2007 his calendar was especially full, as he traveled from one American city to another—Rochester, New York; Columbia, Missouri; West Palm Beach, Florida—explaining the Harlem Children's Zone's methods, usually at the invitation of a civic or business group that wanted to try to emulate the Zone. At the same time, a steady stream of community leaders from around the country were visiting the headquarters on 125th Street, attending a three-day workshop called the Practitioners' Institute, run by Rasuli Lewis, Canada's co-conspirator since Bowdoin College.

That July, Barack Obama, then a rising presidential candidate, gave a speech in Washington, D.C., on urban poverty, in which he held up the Harlem Children's Zone as a model for the strategy he would follow as president. "The philosophy behind the project is simple," Obama explained. "If poverty is a disease that infects an entire community in the form of unemployment and violence, failing schools and broken homes, then we can't just treat those symptoms in isolation. We have to heal that entire community. And we have to focus on what actually works."

If he were elected president, Obama went on to say, "the first part of my plan to combat urban poverty will be to replicate the Harlem Children's Zone in twenty cities across the country. We'll train staff, we'll have them draw up detailed plans with attainable goals, and the federal government will provide half of the funding for each city, with the rest coming from philanthropies and businesses." Obama acknowledged that such an undertaking wouldn't be cheap. It would cost the federal government "a few billion dollars a year," he estimated. "But we will find the money to do this, because we can't afford not to."

Geoffrey Canada didn't return Obama's endorsement. He was always careful to keep his political preferences to himself; the various members of his organization's board were backing just about every major presidential candidate, both Democratic and Republican, and so Canada couldn't afford to be too closely affiliated with any one candidate or party. Mitt Romney came to take a tour of the Zone with him a couple of months later, as it happened. And Canada enjoyed continuing good relations with the Clintons, as well; Bill Clinton had written about the Harlem Children's Zone in his book *Giving,* and in September 2007, he held his book launch in the Promise Academy gymnasium.

But in fact, Canada thought that Obama had got it exactly right. He agreed that it was time to expand the model to other cities. He thought twenty sounded like the right number. And he thought that a public-private partnership was the only way to succeed.

Obama's speech served as something of a watershed. For the first time, Canada's strategy was on the table at the highest level of American politics. For the first time, a potential president was seriously discussing replicating his work—and not just offering vague promises, but digging down into the specifics: how many cities, how the budget would be divided, how much it might cost. It was an exciting moment. "If the stars align," Canada told me that fall, "there could be a real conversation developing in America about a new strategy on poverty. If it happens, I think it would give Americans a belief again that not only can you do something, but we *should* do something—that there's a self-interest involved in helping these kids. In the end, it's going to make America a stronger country."

Meanwhile, there was still Victor Jr. to think about—and thousands of kids in Harlem just like him, and millions more in the country as a whole. There were plenty of signs of hope out there, and Victor Jr. was one of them. But at the same time, every individual success only highlighted a collective failure: why did Victor Jr. get to be one of the potentially lucky ones, while a baby born into similar circumstances in Detroit or Oakland or Camden, New Jersey, still had so little chance of faring well?

It was the question that Canada had been thinking about—that he'd been obsessed with, really—for almost fifty years, since he was in the fourth grade at PS 99 in the Bronx, watching a handful of kids be tracked with him into the successful classes, while the rest of his friends were designated to fail. It was the question that had motivated his life's work: Why not give *every* child the tools to succeed? Why not level the playing field for real? In the past, there had always been someone there with an answer, an explanation for why it couldn't be done, or why the question didn't make sense, or why the time wasn't right to ask it. But Canada had a feeling that things might be changing. There were more and more people who were asking the question right along with him. And the explanations for why things couldn't change seemed to be running out at last.

Acknowledgments

Notes on Sources

Index

Acknowledgments

I owe debts of gratitude to the many people who helped in the creation of this book. The first and largest one is to Geoffrey Canada, who over the course of almost five years of interviews and conversations displayed a level of self-awareness and candor and a depth of insight and knowledge that never ceased to amaze me. From our first meeting, he gave me the freedom to write about him and his organization without restrictions or oversight, and for that I will always be grateful. Here's one representative story: In March 2007, on the day before Canada announced to the students and parents of Promise Academy that he was taking steps that would profoundly alter the school, he called me on the phone and, in a subdued voice, said that he thought I should probably come up to the school the next day, as it might be useful for my book. He was right; the events of that day made up the bulk of chapter 10. What made Canada's call so remarkable to me is that he knew the day of the announcement was going to be a low point in his career—he later called it the worst day of his professional life. But he invited me to trail him anyway, on a day when most people would want the media to be far, far away, because he knew it would help me paint a more complete portrait of his work.

I am grateful, as well, to the friends and colleagues who volunteered (or were conscripted) to read different parts and drafts of this book along the way. Matt Bai read many of these chapters early and often and helped me rethink everything from structure to punctuation. Ira Glass was the first person to encourage me to report on the Harlem Children's Zone, and five years later, he gave me crucial advice on the manuscript, especially the concluding chapters. Over the course of many years, Vera Titunik guided me through the material in this book with a steady hand and a sharp pencil. Kira Pollack gave me valuable input on some of my earliest drafts and later applied her keen eye and judgment to the selection of photographs for the book. Robert Gordon read chapter 2, and shared with me his considerable expertise on the history of poverty policy and education policy. Heather O'Neill offered the perspective of a poet and a novelist; her own writing about children is so finely observed that I felt lucky to have her weighing in on mine. And Allen Tough read many drafts of many chapters and gave me not only heartfelt support but also the benefit of his long years of study in education.

It was a stroke of good fortune that I was able to collaborate on this book with Alex Tehrani, a photographer I have known and admired for many years. His photographs not only captured much of what I was trying to convey in my writing, they also allowed me to see details and nuances that I hadn't been able to see on my own. The book is much richer for Alex's contributions, and his friendship helped make the process of reporting it a great pleasure.

My colleagues at the *New York Times Magazine* gave me both encouragement and insight. I owe special thanks to Aaron Retica, Ilena Silverman, Scott Malcomson, Jamie Ryerson, Rob Hoerburger, and Alex Star for their suggestions and ideas. Two articles I wrote for the *Times Magazine* served as the basis for the book, and I'm grateful to Adam Moss, Gerry Marzorati, and Joel Lovell for assigning those to me, to Vera Titunik for editing them, and to Kira Pollack, Cavan Farrell, Lia Miller, and Robert Mackey for the work they did to improve them on the way to publication. Kira was also responsible, along with Kathy Ryan, for negotiating the complex logistics behind the great Jeff Riedel portrait of Geoff Canada (and several hundred energetic children) that appeared on the cover of the magazine and now appears on the cover of this book. Finally, I'm grateful to my boss, Gerry Marzorati, not only for his counsel and encouragement but also for giving me the latitude to report much of the book while working for him as an editor, and for allowing me to take a leave of absence to finish writing.

My agent, David McCormick, had faith in my ability to write this book long before I did, and his support, advice, and friendship along the way were essential to its completion. At Houghton Mifflin, I owe a debt to Eamon Dolan, the editor who first expressed interest in the project and who gave me some invaluable suggestions early in the course of my writing, and to Deanne Urmy, the patient and painstaking editor whose hard work and careful attention brought the book into being. Thanks, too, to Deanne's assistant, Nicole Angeloro, who handled the countless details of publication with professionalism and good humor.

I count myself lucky that Charles William Wilson agreed to fact-check much of the manuscript. He is an exacting researcher, and he quickly mastered a lot of complex material. His conscientious and careful work saved me from more errors than I'd like to admit.

The leadership and staff of the Harlem Children's Zone invited me into their offices, classrooms, and staff meetings, and they spoke candidly and thoughtfully with me about their work and their lives. I'm grateful to them all, but I need to single out for special thanks George Khaldun, Tuere Randall, Caressa Singleton, Rasuli Lewis, Kate Shoemaker, Marty Lipp, Will Norris, Betina Jean-Louis, Shirley Brown, Adrienne Daniels, Ron Carlos, Monica Lucente, and Alyson Gilbride.

At Promise Academy, my thanks go to Efiom Ukoidemabia, Glen Pinder, Dennis McKesey, Ryan Sparzak, Terri Grey, Doreen Land, Sakina Gabriel, Jesse Rawls Jr., Sarah Snyder, Shondell James, Rudy Forbes, Shelly Klein, Selby Gaylock, Edward Landry, Shakira Brown, Lisa Ramos, and Chris Finn, all of whom were generous with their time and their insights. Many students from Promise Academy shared their thoughts with me over the years, and I'm grateful especially to Tiffany Vargas, James Stevens, and Neville Plummer, and to Julien Coutourier and Xavier Patterson and their families, including Christine Patterson, Billy Patterson, and JoAnn Coutourier.

The nine weeks that I spent at Baby College were a unique and unforgettable experience. I'm grateful to Marilyn Joseph and her staff for opening their doors to me and for sharing their expertise and their reflections. In particular, I want to thank Francisca Silfa, Mark Frazier, Carol Grannum, Wanda Osorio, Anthony Santiago, Shanta Chapman, Abasi Clark, and Jasmine Tumma. I owe an even more profound debt to the 103 parents of cycle 21, who let me listen in on their classes and conversation and, week after week, shared with me their hopes and fears for their children's futures. I'm especially grateful to Darryl Reaves and Damita Miles-Reaves, Stridiron Clark, Angelique Vasquez, and Shauntel Jones. And I owe an extraspecial thanks to Victor Boria and Cheryl

274 ▪ ACKNOWLEDGMENTS

Waite. More than anyone, they helped me understand the potential of Baby College to transform parents and children.

There were countless parents and caregivers in other programs who took the time to speak with me about their interactions with the Harlem Children's Zone, including Yasmin Scott, Varainia Utley, Wilma Jure, Shawniqua Adams, Gail Witt, Gloria White, Laverne Palmer, Aisha Tomlinson, and Edward Mollette. I'm grateful to Precious Bonaparte and Derek Owens, who spoke to me at great length about their experience in the Three-year-old Journey program and the difficult decisions they were confronting about their daughter DePre's education.

I received valuable assistance from many people at Bowdoin College as I sought to understand the changes that took place at the school in the 1960s and 1970s. Scott Hood, of Bowdoin's communications office, and Richard Lindeman and Caroline Moseley, of Bowdoin's archives, provided me with a rich trove of documents. Catrina Cartagena, an undergraduate at the college, dug through back issues of the school newspaper, the *Orient,* to pull together a documentary history of that era for me. Daniel W. Rossides, a retired professor, offered a valuable perspective on Bowdoin's past. And I owe a special thanks to the Bowdoin alumni who spoke to me about those days, including George Khaldun, Rasuli Lewis, Robert Johnson, Horace Lovelace, Michael Owens, Richard Adams, and Dennis Levesque.

I'm grateful to the members of the Promise Academy board of directors, including Mitchell Kurz, Alfonso Wyatt, and Kenneth Langone, who gave me their behind-the-scenes perspectives on the progress of the school. Stanley Druckenmiller was an especially valuable and generous source; while he is not a man eager to see his name in print, he spoke with me at length about the process of building not only the school but the entire Harlem Children's Zone.

I benefited from the intelligence and hard work of many scholars, and I am especially indebted to those who spoke to me about their research. James Heckman and Susan B. Neuman were instrumental in helping me understand recent developments in the science of intervention. Ronald Ferguson enriched my understanding of issues of class, race, and education, as did several of his colleagues at Harvard, including William Julius Wilson, Richard Weissbourd, Roland Fryer, Katherine Newman, and Thomas Kane. At Columbia, Jeanne Brooks-Gunn and Rebecca Ryan illuminated their parenting research for me. Glenn Loury shared with me his thoughts and research on the achievement gap. Annette Lareau, Martha Farah, and Angela Duckworth each took the time to help me better grasp their ideas. Robert Gordon, Doug Harris, Richard Rothstein, Abigail Thernstrom, and Stephan Thernstrom gave me insights into the politics of schools. And I benefited as well from conversations with Robert J. Sampson, Ruby Payne, Julie Petersen, and Lei-Anne Ellis.

I owe a debt to the many people who helped guide me through the world of education reform, including David Levin, Michael Feinberg, Aaron Brenner, and Steve Mancini at KIPP; Dacia Toll, Matt Taylor, and Jon Valant at Achievement First; and John King and Norman Atkins at Uncommon Schools. Joel Klein was a great help, as was his communications director, Julia Levy. Margaret Spellings kindly shared with me her thoughts on No Child Left Behind.

I had the help and support of many friends and allies, including Joel Lovell, Kate Porterfield, Jonathan Goldstein, Ann Clarke, Kim Temple, Elana Fremerman, John Hodgman, Stephen Dubner, Chuck Klosterman, John K. Samson, Cathy Rand, Evan Harris, Starlee Kine, Adrian Nicole Leblanc, and Jack Rosenthal. The congregation and clergy of Middle Collegiate Church gave me indispensable moral support at the same time as they enriched my understanding of issues of race, class, and justice; I'm grateful especially to Jacqui Lewis, Gordon Dragt, Freeman Palmer, and Kendall Thomas. Michael Pollan was generous with his advice and encouragement at the book's earliest stages. Jack Hitt and Lisa Sanders provided not only support and friendship but also their thoughtful answers to my questions about medicine, education politics, and the craft of writing.

One last round of thanks: to my parents, Anne Tough and Allen Tough, my sister, Susan Tough, and my cousin Hilary Wood for their love and aid; to the people of Montauk, for helping to create the ideal writers' retreat; to the employees of Apple, Amazon, Google, Olympus, and Starbucks, for a variety of innovations that helped make this book easier to report and to write; to Georgie, for her constant support, even if she did fry my laptop that one time by walking across the keyboard; and most of all to my patient and loving wife, Paula, who makes everything more fun, even writing a book. I promise that our next honeymoon won't be a trip to an education conference.

Notes on Sources

The information in this book was collected in three different ways: interviews, direct observation of events, and research online and in books and academic papers. The notes below refer only to the third category. Some chapters depended entirely on interviews and observations, especially the chapters about Promise Academy. So there are no notes below for chapters 6, 7, and 9.

Further information, including links and a bibliography of useful books and papers, can be found at www.paultough.com.

1. The Lottery

7 *The charter idea was born in Minnesota:* Chester E. Finn Jr., Bruno V. Manno, and Gregg Vanourek, *Charter Schools in Action: Renewing Public Education* (Princeton, N.J.: Princeton University Press, 2000), p. 18.

18 *The average white family:* Sam Roberts, "In Surge in Manhattan Toddlers, Rich White Families Lead Way," *New York Times,* March 23, 2007.

2. Unequal Childhoods

21 *One notorious study:* C. McCord and H. P. Freeman, "Excess Mortality in Harlem," *New England Journal of Medicine* 322, no. 3 (January 18, 1990); see also Steven A. Holmes, "Conference on Black

Males Finds Many Problems but No Consensus," *New York Times,* May 25, 1991.

the homicide death rate: McCord and Freeman, "Excess Mortality in Harlem."

22 *two police precincts:* There were sixty-six homicides in the Thirty-second Precinct and forty-one in the Twenty-eighth Precinct. See www.nyc.gov/html/nypd/html/crime_prevention/crime_statistics .shtml.

In just three years: Roland G. Fryer Jr. et al., *Measuring Crack Cocaine and Its Impact* (Cambridge, Mass.: National Bureau of Economic Research, April 2006).

gunshot wounds had become: Daniel Goleman, "Black Scientists Study the 'Pose' of the Inner City," *New York Times,* April 21, 1992.

"It really is getting worse": Geoffrey Canada, *Fist, Stick, Knife, Gun: A Personal History of Violence in America* (Boston: Beacon Press, 1995), p. x.

23 *Those two Harlem precincts:* See www.nyc.gov/html/nypd/html/ crime_prevention/crime_statistics.shtml.

24 *For more than a century:* This history of poverty policy in America draws on many books, including Susan E. Mayer, *What Money Can't Buy: Family Income and Children's Life Chances* (Cambridge, Mass.: Harvard University Press, 1997); Michael B. Katz, *In the Shadow of the Poorhouse: A Social History of Welfare in America* (New York: Basic Books, 1986); John Iceland, *Poverty in America: A Handbook* (Berkeley: University of California Press, 2003); Nicholas Lemann, *The Promised Land: The Great Black Migration and How It Changed America* (New York: Knopf, 1991); Ken Auletta, *The Underclass,* rev. ed. (Woodstock: Overlook Press, 1999); Jason De-Parle, *American Dream: Three Women, Ten Kids, and a Nation's Drive to End Welfare* (New York: Viking, 2004); William Julius Wilson, *The Truly Disadvantaged: The Inner City, the Underclass, and Public Policy* (Chicago: University of Chicago Press, 1987); David T. Ellwood, *Poor Support: Poverty in the American Family* (New York: Basic Books, 1988); and Mickey Kaus, *The End of Equality* (New York: Basic Books, 1992).

25 *Early in his presidency:* This history of the War on Poverty is informed by many of the above books, and also by Daniel P. Moynihan, *Maximum Feasible Misunderstanding: Community Action in the War on Poverty* (New York: Free Press, 1969); Kenneth P. Clark, *Dark Ghetto: Dilemmas of Social Power* (New York: Harper & Row,

1965); Jeffrey L. Pressman and Aaron B. Wildavsky, *Implementation: How Great Expectations in Washington Are Dashed in Oakland; or, Why It's Amazing That Federal Programs Work at All, This Being a Saga of the Economic Development Administration as Told by Two Sympathetic Observers Who Seek to Build Morals on a Foundation of Ruined Hopes* (Berkeley: University of California Press, 1973); Tom Wolfe, "Mau-Mauing the Flak Catchers," in *Radical Chic and Mau-Mauing the Flak Catchers* (New York: Farrar, Straus and Giroux, 1970); Harlem Youth Opportunities Unlimited, *Youth in the Ghetto: A Study of the Consequences of Powerlessness and a Blueprint for Change* (New York: Orans, 1964); Christopher Jencks, *Rethinking Social Policy: Race, Poverty, and the Underclass* (Cambridge, Mass.: Harvard University Press, 1992); and Charles Murray, *Losing Ground: American Social Policy, 1950–1980* (New York: Basic Books, 1984).

"the professionalization of reform": Moynihan, *Maximum Feasible Misunderstanding*, p. 23.

26 *"a total attack on the problems"*: Ibid., p. 71.

a confidential internal memorandum: See Lee Rainwater and William L. Yancey, *The Moynihan Report and the Politics of Controversy* (Cambridge, Mass.: MIT Press, 1967).

27 *"at the heart of the deterioration"*: Ibid., p. 5.

The second report: See Adam Gamoran and Daniel A. Long, "*Equality of Educational Opportunity: A 40-Year Retrospective,*" Working Paper No. 2006–9 (Madison: Wisconsin Center for Education Research, December 2006); Frederick Mosteller and Daniel P. Moynihan, eds., *On Equality of Educational Opportunity* (New York: Random House, 1972); Deborah W. Meier, "The Coleman Report," *Integrated Education* 5, no. 6 (December 1967–January 1968); Barbara J. Kiviat, "The Social Side of Schooling," *Johns Hopkins Magazine* (April 2000); and William Ryan, *Blaming the Victim* (New York: Random House, 1971).

28 *"the controversy surrounding"*: Wilson, *The Truly Disadvantaged*, p. 4.

But all of that progress: Murray, *Losing Ground*, p. 245.

serious expenditures on Great Society: Ibid., pp. 57–58.

total government spending: Jencks, *Rethinking Social Policy*, p. 76. I rounded Jencks's statistics to the nearest whole number.

29 *a third of poor African Americans:* Murray, *Losing Ground*, p. 263.

unemployment rate among black teenagers: Ibid., p. 247. The figures are for eighteen- and nineteen-year-olds.

violent crime rates: Ibid., p. 256.

"scrapping the entire": Ibid., pp. 227–28.

"Some people are better": Ibid., p. 234.

30 *"sharp increase in social pathologies":* Wilson, *The Truly Disadvantaged,* p. 6.

Harlem was an affluent white neighborhood: This brief history of Harlem's demographic shifts comes mostly from Gilbert Osofsky, *Harlem: The Making of a Ghetto* (New York: Harper & Row, 1966).

Between 1970 and 1984: Wilson, *The Truly Disadvantaged,* p. 40.

31 *the national employment rate for black men:* Ibid., p. 43. The statistics here are for "blacks and others," the designation that the Census Bureau used at the time when data were not available for blacks alone. As Wilson explains, "Because about 90 percent of the population so designated is black, statistics reported for this category generally reflect the condition of the black population."

In the five largest American cities: Ibid., p. 46. The number increased by 182 percent.

two-thirds of all poor whites: Ibid., pp. 58–59.

"mainstream role models": Ibid., p. 56.

"the chances are overwhelming": Ibid., p. 57.

32 *"program of economic reform":* Ibid., p. 122.

"a nationally oriented labor-market strategy": Ibid., p. 154.

"changes in cultural norms": Ibid., p. 159.

34 *all treated with "dignity":* Richard J. Herrnstein and Charles Murray, *The Bell Curve: Intelligence and Class Structure in American Life* (New York: Free Press, 1994), p. 551.

Writing in the New Republic: Steven Fraser, ed., *The Bell Curve Wars: Race, Intelligence, and the Future of America* (New York: Basic Books, 1995), p. 130.

In the New Yorker: Ibid., p. 11.

35 *Heckman argued:* James Heckman, "Lessons from the Bell Curve," *Journal of Political Economy* 103, no. 5 (October 1995).

including Robert Reich: See Robert Reich, *The Work of Nations: Preparing Ourselves for 21st-Century Capitalism* (New York: Knopf, 1991), p. 219ff.

The authors used as a measure: Herrnstein and Murray, *The Bell Curve,* p. 73, and also pp. 119–20.

young people's scores on the test corresponded closely: Ibid., p. 136.

37 *"the world has changed":* Christopher Jencks and Meredith Phillips, eds., *The Black-White Test Score Gap* (Washington, D.C.: Brookings Institution Press, 1998), p. 4.

higher-skilled black men: Ibid., p. 6.

Beginning in 1991: This data on the economic recovery and its effect on Harlem comes mostly from Katherine S. Newman, *Chutes and Ladders: Navigating the Low-Wage Labor Market* (Cambridge, Mass.: Harvard University Press, 2006).

38 *Across the country:* Paul A. Jargowsky, *Stunning Progress, Hidden Problems: The Dramatic Decline of Concentrated Poverty in the 1990s* (Washington, D.C.: Brookings Institution, May 2003).

41 *"changing the way parents deal":* Jencks and Phillips, *The Black-White Test Score Gap*, p. 46.

The first scholars: The description of Hart and Risley's research is taken almost entirely from their book: Betty Hart and Todd R. Risley, *Meaningful Differences in the Everyday Experience of Young American Children* (Baltimore: P. H. Brookes, 1995).

44 *a method for evaluating parental behavior:* See Vasiliki Totsika and Kathy Sylva, "The Home Observation for Measurement of the Environment Revisited," *Child and Adolescent Mental Health* 9, no. 1 (2004).

The parents were judged: See Christy Brady-Smith et al., "Early Head Start Research and Evaluation Project: 24-Month Child-Parent Interaction Rating Scales for the Three-Bag Assessment" (New York: National Center for Children and Families, Teachers College, Columbia University, September 14, 1999).

46 *A researcher named Martha Farah:* My knowledge of Farah's research comes from personal communications with Farah and from two papers: Martha J. Farah, Kimberly G. Noble, and Hallam Hurt, "Poverty, Privilege, and Brain Development: Empirical Findings and Ethical Implications," in *Neuroethics: Defining the Issues in Theory, Practice, and Policy,* ed. Judith Iles (Oxford: Oxford University Press, 2006); and Martha J. Farah et al., "Childhood Poverty: Specific Associations with Neurocognitive Development," *Brain Research* 1110, no. 1 (2006).

"as an ivory tower pursuit": Farah et al., "Poverty, Privilege, and Brain Development," p. 277.

48 *This was the question:* My understanding of Annette Lareau's research comes from personal communications with Lareau and

from her book *Unequal Childhoods: Class, Race, and Family Life* (Berkeley: University of California Press, 2003), from which I also borrowed the title of this chapter.

50 *"intense labor demands on busy parents"*: Lareau, *Unequal Childhoods*, p. 13.
"learn how to be members of informal peer groups": Ibid, p. 67.
"Central institutions in society": Ibid., p. 3.
"children's leisure activities": Ibid., p. 83.
"things that are important to children": Ibid., p. 82.
51 *"seem to be fully understood by parents"*: Ibid., p. 64.
"skills children learn in soccer games": Ibid., p. 64.

3. Baby College

56 *"we are beginning to hear the rumblings"*: Carnegie Task Force on Meeting the Needs of Young Children, *Starting Points: Meeting the Needs of Our Youngest Children* (New York: Carnegie Corporation of New York, 1994).
57 *Bill and Hillary Clinton*: Sarah Moughty, "The Zero-to-Three Debate: A Cautionary Look at Turning Science into Policy," *Frontline*, www.pbs.org/wgbh/pages/frontline/shows/teenbrain/science/zero.html.
93 *A study published in 1999*: Deanna S. Gomby, Patti L. Culross, and Richard E. Behrman, "Home Visiting: Recent Program Evaluations—Analysis and Recommendations," *Future of Children*, 9, no. 1 (spring/summer 1999), p. 6.
In her forthcoming book: Susan B. Neuman, "Changing the Odds: Breaking the Bleak Cycle of Poverty and Disadvantage for Children At-Risk," unpublished manuscript, 2007.
A fourth program: LaRue Allen and Anita Sethi, "Bridging the Gap Between Poor and Privileged," *American Educator* (summer 2004), p. 3.
94 *the Nurse-Family Partnership spends*: See David Olds, "Prenatal and Infancy Home Visitation by Nurses: Recent Findings," *Future of Children* 9, no. 1 (spring/summer 1999); and Katherine Boo, "Swamp Nurse," *New Yorker*, February 6, 2006.
the Parent-Child Home Program costs: Linda Jacobson, "Home Visiting Program Helps Toddlers Fill Learning Gaps," *Education Week*, March 6, 2002.

95 *"As a practical matter"*: Jencks and Phillips, *The Black-White Test Score Gap*, p. 46.

4. Contamination

98 *the official poverty rate among blacks:* Carmen DeNavas-Walt, Bernadette D. Proctor, and Jessica Smith, *Income, Poverty, and Health Insurance Coverage in the United States: 2006* (Washington, D.C.: U.S. Census Bureau, 2007), p. 13. The exact figures (for 2006) are a poverty rate of 24.3 percent for blacks and 8.2 percent for non-Hispanic whites.

consistently poor for a long period: Iceland, *Poverty in America*, p. 49. *Downward mobility is more common:* See Michael A. Fletcher, "Middle-Class Dream Eludes African American Families," *Washington Post*, November 13, 2007; and *Economic Mobility of Black and White Families: Executive Summary* (Washington, D.C.: Economic Mobility Project, 2007).

more likely to live in high-poverty neighborhoods: Iceland, *Poverty in America*, p. 56.

if you look only at children who grow up in long-term poverty: Don Winstead et al., *Indicators of Welfare Dependence: Annual Report to Congress, 2003* (Washington, D.C.: U.S. Department of Health and Human Services, 2003). See Table Econ 6, at aspe.hhs.gov/HSP/indicators03/ch3.htm#tecon6.

103 *a TV in their bedroom:* Ronald F. Ferguson, "Racial and Ethnic Disparities in Home Intellectual Lifestyles" (paper presented at the Achievement Gap Initiative conference, Harvard University, Cambridge, Massachusetts, June 19–20, 2006).

twice as many children's books in their homes: Ibid.

107 *Canada reached for an analogy:* N. R. Kleinfield, "Living at an Epicenter of Diabetes, Defiance and Despair," *New York Times*, January 10, 2006.

109 *"Unemployment in the underclass":* Charles Murray, "The Hallmark of the Underclass," *Wall Street Journal*, September 29, 2005.

"people with their hat on backwards": "Dr. Bill Cosby Speaks at the Fiftieth Anniversary Commemoration of the *Brown vs. Topeka Board of Education* Supreme Court Decision," transcript available at www.eightcitiesmap.com/transcript_bc.htm.

117 *a long and troubled history:* Kenneth Chenault, "The Blackman at Bowdoin," unpublished paper, 1973.

118 *the black painter Dana Chandler:* Greg Nevens, "Black Arts Discussed," *Bowdoin Orient,* May 1, 1970.

"meet its commitment of a minimum of eighty-five black students": Jay Sweet, "Afro-Am Presents Statement; Faculty Meets Late Thursday," *Bowdoin Orient,* February 20, 1970.

121 *"The society will no longer permit our ideals to be stifled":* Doug Lyons, "Afro-Am Center Declares Restrictions," *Bowdoin Orient,* October 23, 1970.

5. Battle Mode

129 *"influence of social class characteristics":* Richard Rothstein, *Class and Schools: Using Social, Economic, and Educational Reform to Close the Black-White Achievement Gap* (Washington, D.C.: Economic Policy Institute, 2004), p. 5.

"Lower-class children, on average, have poorer vision": Ibid., p. 3.

"Sure, some kids are easier to teach": Abigail Thernstrom and Stephan Thernstrom, *No Excuses: Closing the Racial Gap in Learning* (New York: Simon & Schuster, 2003), p. 43.

131 *"not typical lower-class students":* Rothstein, *Class and Schools,* p. 74.

"simplistic remedy": All of the quotations in this paragraph are taken from "'Must Schools Fail?': An Exchange," *New York Review of Books,* February 24, 2005.

136 *an article in the business section:* Tracie Rozhon, "Before Christmas, Wal-Mart Was Stirring," *New York Times,* January 5, 2005.

143 *Grey and Land had both read Monroe's inspirational book:* Lorraine Monroe, *Nothing's Impossible: Leadership from Inside and Outside the Classroom* (New York: Times Books, 1997).

152 *"Our reforms are working":* David W. Herszenhorn, "Student Scores Climb Strongly Across the City," *New York Times,* June 2, 2005.

153 *A story in the* New York Post: David Andreatta, "'Charter' Kids Outpace Other Students," *New York Post,* June 6, 2005.

8. The Conveyor Belt

189 *One study compared a group:* See Jason DeParle, "Debris of Past Failures Impedes Poverty Policy," *New York Times,* November 7, 1993; and Jason DeParle, "Volunteers: Pro and Con," *New York Times,* April 26, 1997.

191 *Heckman is constructing a grand unified theory:* See, for instance, Eric I. Knudsen et al., "Economic, Neurobiological and Behavioral Perspectives on Building America's Future Workforce," NBER Working Paper No. 12298 (Cambridge, Mass.: National Bureau of Economic Research, June 2006); James J. Heckman, "The Economics, Technology, and Neuroscience of Human Capability Formation," *Proceedings of the National Academy of Sciences* 104, no. 33 (August 14, 2007); and Flavio Cunha and James Heckman, "The Technology of Skill Formation," NBER Working Paper No. 12840 (Cambridge, Mass.: National Bureau of Economic Research, January 2007).

192 *two famous experiments in early-childhood development:* See Robert G. Lynch, *Exceptional Returns: Economic, Fiscal, and Social Benefits of Investment in Early Childhood Development* (Washington, D.C.: Economic Policy Institute, 2004), and James J. Heckman and Alan B. Krueger, *Inequality in America: What Role for Human Capital Policies?* (Cambridge, Mass.: MIT Press, 2003).

193 *"Skill begets skill":* James J. Heckman and Dimitriy V. Masterov, "The Productivity Argument for Investing in Young Children," lecture given at the Allied Social Sciences Association annual meeting, Chicago, January 5–7, 2007, p. 3.
"as a question of fairness": Ibid., p. 2.
"a policy of equality of opportunity": Ibid., p. 4.

204 *For the four-year-old population as a whole:* Katherine A. Magnuson, Christopher J. Ruhm, and Jane Waldfogel, "Does Prekindergarten Improve School Preparation and Performance?" NBER Working Paper 10452 (Cambridge, Mass.: National Bureau of Economic Research, 2004).
Despite those findings, kids from disadvantaged homes: Jay Bainbridge et al., "Who Gets an Early Education? Family Income and the Enrollment of Three- to Five-Year-Olds from 1968 to 2000" (New York: National Center for Children in Poverty, 2003).

207 *In the mid-1980s, a handful of researchers:* Keith E. Stanovich, "Matthew Effects in Reading: Some Consequences of Individual Differences in the Acquisition of Literacy," *Reading Research Quarterly* 21, no. 4 (fall 1986).

208 *Late bloomers are, in fact, quite rare:* See, e.g., "Waiting Rarely Works: 'Late Bloomers' Usually Just Wilt," *American Educator*, 28, no. 3 (fall 2004).

more than four out of five children at the highest socioeconomic level: Susan B. Neuman, "From Rhetoric to Reality: The Case for High-Quality Compensatory Prekindergarten Programs," *Phi Delta Kappan* 85 (December 2003).

"the devastating downward spiral": Joseph Torgesen, "Avoiding the Devastating Downward Spiral," *American Educator* 28, no. 3 (fall 2004).

A child at the ninetieth percentile: R. C. Anderson, P. T. Wilson, and L. G. Fielding, "Growth in Reading and How Children Spend Their Time Outside of School," *Reading Research Quarterly* 23 (1988), cited in Anne E. Cunningham and Keith E. Stanovich, "What Reading Does for the Mind," *American Educator* 22 (spring/summer 1998).

209 *"if children's impairments in word-reading ability":* Torgesen, "Avoiding the Devastating Downward Spiral," p. 12.

210 *"Once, this was inevitable":* Ibid., p. 3.

Bright Beginnings, a pre-K program: Most of my information on Bright Beginnings comes from Eric J. Smith, Barbara J. Pellin, and Susan A. Agruso, *Bright Beginnings: An Effective Literacy-Focused Pre-K Program for Educationally Disadvantaged Four-Year-Old Children* (Arlington, Va.: Educational Research Service, 2003).

10. Graduation

250 *To top off these accomplishments:* Jennifer Medina, "Charter Schools Outshine Others as They Receive Their First Report Cards," *New York Times,* December 20, 2007.

11. What Would It Take?

265 *"the first part of my plan":* See www.barackobama.com/2007/07/18/remarks_of_senator_barack_obam_19.php.

Index

Abecedarian Early Childhood Intervention, 192–93
"Accomplishment of natural growth," 49
Achievement Gap Initiative, 102
Alston, George, 120
  See also Khaldun, George
Amistad Academy in New Haven, Connecticut, 130, 157, 160, 175
Amrani-Muhammad, Fatiha, 206
Armed Forces Qualification Test (AFQT), 35–36, 37
Avance program, 93
Avedon, Richard, 153

Baber, Elijah, 237–38, 253
Baby College
  baby showers at, 60–61
  beginnings of, 58, 66
  budget/spending, 58, 94
  conveyor belt concept and, 194–96
  cultural imperialism and, 95–96
  culture/atmosphere of, 94–97
  description, 13, 58, 66, 199–200
  discipline class, 75–84
  expansion, 261
  funding, 58
  goal/mission, 79, 87, 96–97
  growth, 58

outreach workers, 58–60, 64–66, 94, 96
twenty-first cycle beginnings, 61–63, 64–66
twenty-first cycle graduation, 90–92
young-adult class at, 78–79
Baby College stories
  Cheryl Waite, 59–61, 71, 72, 73–74, 75, 79, 84, 87–88, 90–91, 92, 94, 257
  Darryl Reaves/Damita Miles-Reaves and son, 67–69
  Shauntel Jones, 59, 69–71
  Stridiron Clark, 62–65, 66
  Victor Boria, 60, 71–72, 75, 77–78, 79, 81–84, 87–88, 90–91, 94, 257
Bacon, Brandon, 237–38, 253
Bell Curve, The (Murray and Herrnstein)
  controversy over, 33–37
  criticism of, 34–36, 37, 190
  standardized tests and, 35–36, 37
  thesis/observations in, 33–34, 35, 37, 190, 191
Bernstein, Leonard, 25
Black Panthers, 114
Black-White Test Score Gap, The (Jencks and Phillips), 41
Bloomberg, Michael, 6, 152, 169
Bonner, Jasmine, 139, 140
Boria Jr., Victor Anthony Premiere birth, 257

Harlem Children's Zone and, 259,
  260–61
possibilities for, 257–58, 260–61, 267
Boria, Victor
  Baby College and, 60, 71–72, 75, 77–78,
    79, 81–84, 87–88, 90–91, 94, 257
  background, 60, 71–72, 74–75, 92
  discipline vs. punishment, 75, 77–78,
    81–84
  as father/husband, 257–59, 260
  possibilities for, 259–60
  problems with police, 88–89
  proposal by, 75, 90–91, 257
Bowdoin College, 53, 54, 115, 116–23
Bracken Basic Concept Scale–Revised
  Harlem Gems and, 207
  Three-year-old Journey program and,
    201–4
  use of, 201
Brazelton, T. Berry, 58, 66, 81, 163
Bright Beginnings, 210–12
Brinnard, Dijon, 16
Bristow, Beverly, 221
Brown, Michelle, 151
Brown, Patrice, 142
Brown, Taylor, 150, 152

Canada, Dan, 54, 100, 112
Canada, Geoffrey
  "contamination" concept, 4–5, 124–25,
    162, 263–66
  coverage in press, 153
  description, 1, 11–12, 123–24, 136
  education views of, 134, 135, 136
  KIPP schools and, 7
  on public schools, 131–32
Canada, Geoffrey/background
  ancestors, 99–100
  birth, 99
  black activism, 14–19, 18–19, 99, 113–14,
    120–22
  Bowdoin College, 53, 54, 115, 116–17,
    119–23
  childhood, 11, 38, 99, 100–102, 109–13,
    169–70
  Dix Hills and, 114
  education, 18–19, 53–55, 112–15, 134
  first marriage/children, 53–55
  with grandparents in Wyandanch, 53,
    54, 112–15

second marriage/son, 55–57
sense of mission beginnings, 114–15
State University of New York, Stony
  Brook campus, 115–16, 118
as teacher, 19, 133
Vietnam and, 116
Young Disciples and Union Avenue,
  110–12
Canada, Geoffrey/Harlem Children's Zone
  at Baby College graduation, 90, 91–92
  escape velocity concept, 231–32
  ideas for, 3–5, 19
  office of, 168–69
  "saving each child" philosophy, 2, 4–5,
    9–10, 18, 19, 20, 86–87, 162, 163,
    169–70, 262–67
  See also Conveyor belt concept; Harlem
    Children's Zone; specific programs
Canada, Geoffrey/Promise Academy
  beginning second year, 156
  business model, 135, 136
  eighth-grade graduation, 252, 255
  KIPP model vs. Canada's model, 159–64,
    186–87
  lottery, 1–2, 9–10, 11–12, 16–18, 20
  middle school changes, 234–35, 239–49,
    252, 253–55
  middle school opening, 127, 128
  student data, 184–85
  student deficits/citywide tests, 133–34,
    135–36, 143–45, 147, 152, 153, 165, 172–73
  See also Promise Academy
Canada, Geoffrey/Rheedlen Centers for
    Children and Families
  analysis of programs, 2–5
  martial arts programs, 22, 169
  waiting lists and, 2, 20
  See also Rheedlen Centers for Children
    and Families
Canada, Jerry, 54, 56, 123, 124
Canada, John, 54, 100, 112
Canada Jr., Geoffrey
  birth, 56
  education of, 104, 105, 106, 122, 163–64
  majority culture and, 123, 124
Canada, Jr., Geoffrey (first son), 54
Canada, Mary
  childhood, 99–100
  education and, 100, 101, 108
  marriage, 99, 100

Canada, Mary (*cont.*)
  as single mother, 54, 100–102
  See also Williams, Mary
Canada, McCalister, 99, 100
Canada, Reuben, 100
Cardinal Hayes high school, 253
Carlin, George, 253
Carlos, Ron, 169–70
Carter, Shaquille/father, 237–38, 247
Cartwright, Amber, 66
Century funeral home, 21, 23
Chandler, Dana, 118
Changing the Odds (Neuman), 93, 210
Chapman, Shanta, 71
Charter School Athletic Association, 150
Charter schools
  2002 numbers/description, 7
  citywide tests and, 134, 153, 157, 160–61
  controversy over, 7
  counseling parents out, 166
  principles of, 159
  successes, 153, 157, 159
  See also KIPP schools; *specific schools*
Child development and language use
  early intervention and, 209–10
  Harlem Gems emphasis on, 205–7, 209,
    210
  Heckman's research, 193–94, 207
  language and intellectual development
    studies, 41–44, 94, 201
  lasting differences and, 193, 206–10
  Matthew effect, 207–10
  reading fluency and, 209
  socioeconomic status and, 42–43, 208
  spiral with, 207–10
Childhood inequalities
  addressing black parenting, 102–9
  before schooling, 41, 191
  culture transmission and, 48–52
  deficit areas, 46–47
  equality of opportunity and, 193–94
  gap description, 191
  life expectancies, 21–22
  murder statistics, 21–22
  noncognitive skills and, 191
  obstacles summary, 40
  role models and, 31–32, 264
  The Bell Curve views and, 33–37
  See also Education for poor children;
    Home (poor) environment; Poverty
    causes; Socioeconomic status

Childhood inequalities effects
  Abecedarian Early Childhood
    Intervention and, 192–93
  Heckman's studies, 190–94
  Perry Preschool program study and,
    192–93
  productivity and, 193
  See also Home environment and
    children's achievement
Chutes and Ladders (Newman), 38
Cisse, Kasim-Seann, 16
Civil Rights Act (1964), 27
Clark, Stridiron
  Baby College and, 62–63, 64–65, 66
  background, 62, 63–64
  daughter Adonya, 62, 64
Class and Schools (Rothstein), 129
Clinton, Bill, 6, 57, 169, 266
Clinton, Hillary, 57, 266
Cognitive abilities
  gap description, 191
  Heckman's research, 190–94, 212, 259,
    260
  home language use and, 42–43
  as malleable, 34, 35–36
  socioeconomic status, 190, 191
  standardized tests and, 35–36
  as teachable, 191
  zero-to-three movement, 56–58
  See also Bell Curve, The (Murray and
    Herrnstein); Child development and
    language use; Home environment
    and children's achievement;
    Intervention, early; Noncognitive
    skills
Coleman, James S., 27, 129
Coleman Report (*Equality of Educational
  Opportunity*), 27, 128–29
Collins, Jim, 214
Committee on Juvenile Delinquency and
  Youth Crime, 26
Community Pride, 14, 66–67
"Concerted cultivation," 49–51
Congress of African People, 120
"Contamination" concept, 4–5, 124–25, 162,
  263–66
Conveyor belt concept
  as continued intervention, 212,
    262
  early-childhood initiative and, 194–96,
    230–31, 232

middle school and, 197–99, 232–33
vs. superhero method, 196–97
Cosby, Bill, 109
Coutourier, JoAnn, 245, 248, 255
Coutourier, Julien
middle school changes and, 235, 253
school success, 235–36, 245
warning to "bad apples" and, 181, 182,
235
Crime
alternatives to, 22
decrease (beginning 1993), 23
drugs and, 22
increase (1965–1980), 29
See also Murders
Curtis, Jamie Lee, 88

Daggett, Athern P., 118
Davis, Cecilia/Jason, 59, 84–85
Davis, Miles, 236
"Deficit model" of poverty, 39–40
DeLillo, Don, 253
Developmental Reading Assessments
(DRAs), 216
Diabetes epidemic, 107–8
Diop, Marceline, 182
Discipline
Baby College class on, 75–84
description of, 81
time-out method, 13, 57, 80, 96
See also Punishment
Druckenmiller, Stanley
background, 9, 10, 157–58
business model for Promise Academy,
135
as Canada's friend, 105, 123, 173
citywide test results and, 156–58, 159
commitment of, 9, 10
elementary school and, 216
KIPP schools model and, 159, 161, 163,
164
middle school changes and, 241, 249, 251
statewide tests and, 170, 183, 251
student deficits and, 136
truancy issue, 135
wealth/contributions of, 9, 10, 261
Drug problems, 22

Early Head Start, 93
Early intervention. See Intervention, early
Eastern Star, 67

Economic inequalities
opportunities and motivation, 36–37
population divisions and, 18
The Bell Curve and, 33–34, 35, 36
See also Poverty
Education for poor children
choices, 12
Co-leman Report findings, 27, 128–29
debate on solutions, 188
noncognitive skills and, 191
poor parents views of, 104–7
preschool benefits, 204
schools vs. home environment debate,
128–32
See also Intervention, early; specific
programs; specific schools
Education of mother
abilities gap and, 191
preschool enrollment and, 204
End of the Weak Productions, 177
Escape velocity concept, 231–32
Excellence Charter School cofounders,
158–59

"Fade-out" effect
Bright Beginnings example, 211–12
description, 3
early intervention, 211–12
Head Start (government program), 3
Perry Preschool program, 212
Family environment. See Home (poor)
environment; Parenting
Farah, Martha, 46–48
Feinberg, Michael, 130, 160, 172
Ferguson, Ronald, 102–4
Finn, Chris
background, 175–76, 177
demands on students, 176, 178–82
middle school changes and, 252
warning to "bad apples," 178–82
Fist, Stick, Knife, Gun: A Personal History
of Violence in America (Canada), 22
Fonseca, Jaylene, 13, 16
Forbes magazine, 9, 157
Forbes, Rudy, 143
Foster care, 81
Frazier, Mark, 59
Frederick Douglass Academy, 143, 175

Gabriel, Sakina, 256
Garcia, Devante, 140, 141

Gardner, Linda, 66
General Educational Development (GED)
  tests, 191
George X, 120, 122
  See also Khaldun, George
"Ghetto, The" (Hathaway), 122
Gillis, Yanice, 13
Giving (Bill Clinton), 266
Good to Great (Collins), 214
Gould, Stephen Jay, 34, 36
Grannum, Carol, 76–79, 81–84
Grant, Yvonne
  background, 108, 123
  pregnancy/becoming mother, 55–56, 57
Great Depression, 25
Greater Allen Cathedral, Queens, 14
Greenberg, Hank, 261
Gregg, Dashaan, 139
Grey, Terri
  background, 134–35
  beginning second year, 155–56
  citywide tests and, 137, 156
  college promise and, 127–28, 167–68
  discipline problems, 166, 236
  dismissal, 156, 170–71
  education views of, 134–35, 147–48,
    165–67
  Promise Academy's inclusiveness and,
    166–68
  statewide tests and, 217
  student deficits/citywide tests, 137,
    143–44, 147–48, 150, 151, 165
  superhero method and, 197
  truancy issue, 135–36
Gun-control laws, 22–23

Hall, Keith, 141, 142
Harlem Children's Zone
  Barack Obama and, 265–66
  black America and, 95, 99
  description, 5, 66–67
  expansion of, 261–62
  incentives, 5
  location, 5, 261
  lottery system changes, 195
  mission, 99
  non-Promise strategy, 262–65
  recruitment, 5
  TRUCE, 263, 264
  working with principals, 5–6
  See also Canada, Geoffrey/Harlem

Children's Zone; *specific individuals;*
  specific programs
Harlem Gems
  Bracken test and, 207
  conveyor belt concept and, 194–96
  description, 13, 66, 205–7
  foreign languages and, 206–7
  language emphasis, 205–7, 209, 210
  New York state standards and, 205
Harlem Village Academy, 150, 153
Hart, Betty, 41–44, 94, 201
Hathaway, Donny, 122
Head Start (government program)
  description, 3, 68
  Early Head Start, 93
  "fade-out" effect, 3
Head Start (Harlem Children's Zone), 66
Heckman, James
  background, 34, 189, 190–91
  cognitive/noncognitive abilities
    research, 190–94, 212, 259, 260
  early intervention importance, 212, 259,
    263
  equality of opportunity proposal,
    193–94
  JTPA investigations, 189, 191–92
  on *The Bell Curve,* 34–35, 36, 190, 191
  understanding inequalities, 189
Henderson, Joyce/daughter Melina, 53, 54,
  55, 56, 115
Hernandez, Joel, 237–38
Herrnstein, Richard J., 33–34
  See also Bell Curve, The (Murray and
    Herrnstein)
Hip-hop music, 102–3
Hirsch Jr., E. D., 206
Home (poor) environment
  Canada's hope for, 86–87
  Coleman Report and, 27, 128–29
  ghetto families and, 31–32, 33, 166
  Moynihan Report and, 27
  Promise Academy students and, 166–67,
    185–86
  schools vs. environment debate, 128–32
  single mothers, 27, 29
  zero-to-three movement and, 57–58
  See also Parenting
Home environment and children's
  achievement
  encouragement/discouragement effects,
    42–43

HOME inventory and, 44, 47
minority underachievement and, 41
parental behavior effects, 42–48
Three-Bag Assessment, 44
vocabulary use effects, 42, 43
See also Cognitive abilities; Parenting;
    Socioeconomic status
Home Observation for Measurement of
    the Environment (HOME) inventory,
    44, 47
Human capital, 39
Human-capital perspective, 39, 40

Individualized Education Plan (IEP), 221
Inequality (Jencks), 36–37
Intelligence. *See* Cognitive abilities
Intervention, continuing. *See* Conveyor
    belt concept; Harlem Children's
    Zone
Intervention, early
    Abecedarian Early Childhood
        Intervention, 192–93
    Bright Beginnings preschool example,
        210–12
    child development and language use,
        209–10
    cognitive abilities and, 191–93
    "fade-out" effect and, 211–12
    Heckman on, 212, 259, 263
    noncognitive skills and, 191–92
    Perry Preschool program study, 192–
        93
    preschool benefits, 204
    Torgesen on, 209–10, 263
    zero-to-three movement, 56–58
    See also Baby College; Child develop-
        ment and language use; Harlem
        Gems; Head Start; Three-year-old
        Journey program
Iowa standardized tests, 132–33, 136, 144,
    153–54, 216, 217

Jackson, Janet, 91
Jean-Louis, Betina, 136, 240–41
Jencks, Christopher, 36–37, 41, 95
Job Training Partnership Act (JTPA/1982)
    description, 189
    failure of, 189–90, 191–92
Johnson, Lyndon B., 26
Johnson, Robert, 118
Jones, Paul Tudor, II, 157–58

Jones, Shauntel
    Baby College and, 59, 69, 70–71, 85–86,
        87, 91, 92
    background, 69–70, 85–86
    Treasure Lee and, 70, 71, 85, 86, 87, 92
Jones, Ymani, 180–81, 182
Joseph, Marilyn, 62, 69, 71, 88, 91, 96
Journal of Political Economy, 34
JTPA. *See* Job Training Partnership Act
    (JTPA/1982)
Jure, Wilma, 13, 16
"Juvenile delinquency" committee
    investigation, 25, 26

Kaus, Mickey, 34
Kennedy, John F., 25–26
Kennedy, Robert, 25
Khaldun, George
    Baby College and, 58, 90, 91
    background, 169–70
    at Bowdoin (as George Alston), 120
    as Canada's friend, 123
    Rheedlen, 122
King Jr., Martin Luther, 14, 26, 113–14,
    117–18
KIPP Academy in the Bronx, 7, 157, 160–61,
    162
KIPP schools
    Canada's model vs., 159–64, 186–87
    citywide test scores, 7, 160–61
    criticism of, 131
    discipline and, 159–60
    expansion beyond middle schools,
        198–99
    history of, 7–8, 130
    lottery and, 161
    rules of conduct, 130, 131, 172
    self-selection and, 161, 166
    SLANT system, 160, 226
    students as elite/separate, 161–62
    targets of, 7
Klein, Joel, 6, 7–8, 157, 170
Knowledge Is Power Program. *See* KIPP
    schools
Kumon Center, Harlem, 220
Kurz, Mitchell, 10, 241, 251

Land, Doreen
    citywide test results and, 156, 157
    dismissal and, 156, 170
    at lottery, 16

Land, Doreen *(cont.)*
  McKesey and, 216
  resignation, 172
  student deficits/citywide tests, 136–37,
    143, 144, 145
  truancy issue, 135–36
  welcoming students, 126–27
Langone, Kenneth
  background, 10–11
  as Canada's friend, 123
  citywide test results and, 157, 159
  KIPP schools model and, 159, 164
  at lottery, 10, 14
  middle school changes and, 241, 251
  statewide tests and, 170
  truancy issue, 135
Language. *See* Child development and
    language use
Lareau, Annette
  culture transmission effects, 48–51, 52,
    106
  parenting and, 48–51, 52, 106
Lauer, Matt, 153
Levin, David
  KIPP schools and, 7, 130, 160, 161, 163,
    172
  Promise Academy and, 170, 241
  Teach for America and, 7, 130
Lewis, Gerald (Rasuli)
  at Bowdoin, 120
  Practitioner's Institute and, 265
  Rheedlen, 122–23
Lewis, Jovon, 225
Lewis, Sharnea, 59
Lopez, Victor, 175
Losing Ground (Murray), 28–29, 33
Louis D. Brandeis High School, 247, 253
Loury, Glenn, 102, 103
Lucente, Monica, 205, 206, 207, 210

Malcolm X, 113
Mannette, Sydney, 223
Martial arts lessons, 22, 169
Masterov, Dimitriy, 193
Matthew effect, 207–10
Mayer, Susan, 24
McKesey, Dennis
  background, 213, 216
  description, 214–15, 218
  parental involvement and, 227–29

Promise Academy elementary school
    and, 213–15, 216–22
  statewide test practices, 219–22, 222, 227,
    229–30
  statewide tests and, 217–22
  test-taking strategies and, 222–23
Microsoft antitrust case, 6
Miles-Reaves, Damita/son, 67–68, 69,
    70–71, 92
Mollette, Edward/daughter, 248
Monroe, Lorraine, 143–44, 147, 175
Moynihan, Daniel Patrick, 25–27
Moynihan Report (*The Negro Family: The
    Case for National Action*), 26–28
Murders
  drugs and, 22
  gun-control laws and, 22–23
  statistics on, 21–22, 23
Murray, Charles
  background, 38
  poverty causes, 28–29, 33
  social Darwinism views, 29
  solutions proposed, 29, 32–33, 37
  underclass unemployment, 109
  views on intellectual differences, 33–34
  War on Poverty effects, 28–29
  See also Bell Curve, The (Murray and
    Herrnstein)

Nailor, Kaaryn, 66–67
National Assessment of Educational
    Progress, 209–10
Nation of Islam, 120
Neuman, Susan B., 93, 208
New Deal, 25
New England Journal of Medicine, 21
Newman, Katherine S., 38
New Republic, 34
Newton, Isaac, 231
New York City, citywide and statewide
    tests
  results, 152–53, 218
  scores explanation, 144–45, 220
  See also specific schools
New York City public high schools, 112,
    234, 237–38, 242, 246, 247, 247–48, 253
New Yorker, 34, 153
New York Post, 153
New York Review of Books, 131
New York Times, 107, 129, 136

New York Times Magazine, 153
No Excuses: Closing the Racial Gap in Learning (Abigail and Stephan Thernstrom), 129–30, 157
Noncognitive skills
    description, 191
    early intervention and, 191–92
    importance of, 191, 212
    as teachable, 191
North Star Academy in Newark, New Jersey, 130, 157, 160, 175
Nurse-Family Partnership, 67, 93, 94

Obama, Barack, 265–66
Oliver, Russell, 62–63, 84, 95
Opportunity Charter School, 153
Osorio, Wanda, 95–96
"Outdoor relief," 24–25

Parent-Child Home Program, 93, 94
Parenting
    addressing black parenting, 102–9
    Bracken Basic Concept Scale and, 201–4
    cultural imperialism and, 95
    "Ferberizing" tactics, 57
    home-visiting programs summary, 93–94
    middle-class values and, 108–9, 125
    Promise Academy student problems and, 166–67, 185–86
    quantifying effects, 45–48
    racial achievement gap discussion and, 102–4
    zero-to-three movement, 56–58
    See also Baby College; Home (poor) environment; Home environment and children's achievement; Three-year-old Journey program
Patterson, Billy "Spaceman," 236
Patterson, Christine, 244–45, 255
Patterson, Tabara, 244
Patterson, Xavier
    eighth-grade graduation, 252
    middle school changes and, 236–38, 242–44, 245, 253
    potential of, 236–37, 253
Percy, Jean, 138, 142
Perry Preschool program study, 192–93
Philbin, Regis, 253
Phillips, Meredith, 41, 95

Pinder, Glen
    background, 170, 177
    demands on parents/students, 171–72, 177–78, 179–80, 181, 182–83
    discipline problems and, 174–75, 179–80, 181, 182–83, 183, 235
    eighth-grade graduation, 252–53
    first day of school, 176–78, 179–80, 181, 182–83
    KIPP schools and, 170, 172
    middle school changes and, 238, 241–42, 249, 254
    Promise Academy interview, 170
    rules of, 172
    success of, 240
    superhero method and, 197, 198
    warning to "bad apples," 179–80, 181, 182–83
Porter, Thomas, 147, 152
Poverty
    1990s economic boom and, 37–38
    blacks vs. whites, 98–99
    population divisions by, 18
    race and, 98–99
    statistics on, 98–99
    See also Childhood inequalities; Economic inequalities
Poverty causes
    "deficit model," 39–40
    economic forces and, 24, 29, 30–31, 32
    government aid and, 24–25, 28–29
    historical debate on, 23–52
    middle-class black mobility and, 30, 31–32
    "moral failings" and, 39–40, 45, 109
Poverty cycle, 38–39
Poverty solutions
    community values and, 4–5, 124–25
    conflicting emotional reactions with, 39
    economic solutions, 31, 32
    human-capital perspective, 39
    Murray on, 29, 32–33, 37
    Wilson on, 32, 33, 37, 38
    See also specific projects
Practitioner's Institute, 265
Preschool
    benefits, 204
    See also Intervention, early; *specific programs*

Programs for disadvantaged youth/adults
    failure of, 189–90
    welfare vs., 189
    See also Job Training Partnership Act
        (JTPA/1982); specific programs
Promise Academy
    basketball at, 150
    college promise difficulties, 167–68
    creed of, 256
    culture/atmosphere of, 143
    disengaged parents/students and,
        166–67
    foster-care children and, 81
    inclusiveness effects, 166–68
    lottery, 1–2, 8–9, 10, 11–14, 15–18, 20, 255
    new building description, 143
    outreach workers, 8–9, 132
    outside assessment of, 158–59
    promises of, 12
    special-needs students and, 166, 167–68
    system of enrollment/growth, 8
    waiting list for, 17–18, 20
    See also Canada, Geoffrey/Promise
        Academy; specific individuals
Promise Academy elementary school
    classroom location description, 215
    first year, 215–16
    individualized help, 219–20, 227
    lack of attention to, 215, 216–17
    parental involvement and, 227–29
    special-needs students and, 221
    staff changes, 216, 217
    statewide test practices, 219–24, 227,
        229–30
    Stretch Out and Read, 220
    test scores, 215–16, 217, 218–19
    test-taking strategies, 222–23
    truancy, 135–36
    See also specific individuals
Promise Academy II, 155
Promise Academy middle school changes
    board members and, 241, 251
    Canada's meeting with parents, 245–49
    Canada's meeting with students,
        239–40, 242–44
    eighth-grade graduation, 252–53, 255–56
    Harlem Children's Zone programs and,
        246–47
    high school and, 234, 237–38, 242, 246,
        247–48, 253
    letter to parents, 234–35

options, 241–42
plan, 234–35, 241–42
staff reactions, 249–50, 252
student reactions, 235, 236–39
test scores and, 250–51
Promise Academy middle school first
    year
    citywide tests day, 150–52
    citywide tests preparation, 133–34, 137,
        138–42, 143, 145–50
    citywide tests scores, 152, 153–54, 160–61
    first day, 126–28
    math work, 138–41, 142, 143, 145–47,
        148–50
    middle school beginnings, 126–28
    remedial work, 134, 137, 138–42, 143,
        145–50
    standardized test results and, 132–34,
        135, 136–37, 144, 153–54, 230
    student deficits, 133–34, 144
    student racial composition, 132
Promise Academy middle school second
    year
    beginnings, 155–56
    statewide test preparation, 165
    statewide test results, 172–73
Promise Academy middle school third
    year
    changes in staff, 170–72, 175, 186
    demands on students, 176–82
    discipline problems and, 174–76, 179–
        83
    home life/emotional problems, 185–
        86
    statewide tests preparation, 183–86
    tutors and, 183–86
    warning to "bad apples," 179–83
Punishment
    ACS actions and, 80–81, 82
    ACS definition of child abuse, 80–81
    cultural history, 79–80
    See also Discipline

Quilles, Diamond, 150, 152

Race riots, 26, 113
Ramos, Lisa, 238, 239
Randall, Tuere, 244
Rawls Jr., Jesse
    elementary school and, 133, 215, 216
    kindergarten class and, 135

truancy issue, 135–36
Ready to Learn, 88
Reaves, Darryl, 67–69, 91, 92
Reaves Jr., Darryl, 67, 68–69, 92
Reformers in 1960s, 25–26
Reich, Robert, 35
Reiner, Rob, 57
Renteria, Bianca, 148–49
Rheedlen Centers for Children and
    Families
    description, 2–3
    Robin Hood Foundation and, 9
    See also Canada, Geoffrey/Rheedlen
      Centers for Children and Families
Ricard, Sophie, 184, 186
Richardson, Roshauna, 148, 149
Risley, Todd R., 41–44, 94, 201
Robin Hood Foundation, 9, 58
Romney, Mitt, 266
Rothstein, Richard, 129, 131
Roxbury Prep school, Boston, 157
Russwurm, John Brown, 117

Santiago, Anthony, 59
Saxton, Leroy, 59, 77–78, 79, 82
Scorsese, Martin, 253
Scott, Yasmin, 13
Shoemaker, Kate, 184–86, 241
Silfa, Francisca, 59–60, 90
Singleton, Caressa
    Three-year-old Journey program and,
      200–201, 202–4
    zero-to-three movement and, 57, 58
SLANT system, 160, 226
Sly and the Family Stone, 236
Smith, Eric, 210, 211–12
Smith, Jamel, 138, 139–40
Snyder, Sarah, 142
Socioeconomic status
    class transmission research, 48–51
    cognitive ability and, 190, 191
    "concerted cultivation," 49–51
    continuum vs. distinct classes, 48–49
    home language use and, 42–43, 208
    parenting abilities/child outcomes and,
      44–45, 51–52
    skills gap and, 191
Sondheim, Stephen, 25
Sparzak, Ryan
    background, 224–25
    field trips, 226

    parents and, 225, 226, 229
    statewide tests and, 222, 223–24, 227
    as teacher, 223–24, 225–27, 244
*Starting Points: Meeting the Needs of Our
    Youngest Children,* 56
Superhero approach
    conveyor belt concept vs., 196–97
    non-Promise strategy as, 262, 263–65
    TRUCE as example, 263, 264

TerraNova tests, 132–33, 136, 144, 153–54,
    216
Thernstrom, Abigail/Stephan
    charter schools and, 130, 157
    education vs. home environment
      debate, 129–30, 131
Three-Bag Assessment, 44
Three-year-old Journey program
    Bracken test and, 201–4
    conveyor belt concept and, 195–96
    description, 195, 200–204
    supermarket field trip, 203–4
Title I money, 211
Today show, 153
Tolbert, Mona-Lisa, 66
Torgesen, Joseph
    early intervention results, 209–10, 263
    reading spiral investigations, 209–10
TRUCE, 263, 264
Tumma, Jasmine, 59, 64–66, 84–85, 95

Ukoidemabia, Efiom
    citywide tests and, 138–41, 142, 145–47,
      148–50, 150–51
    description, 139
Unemployment rate (1990s), 37, 38
Unequal Childhoods (Lareau), 49
Utley, Virainia/children, 13–14, 16, 17
Uzzell, Nashakeem, 253

Vargas, Tiffany, 150, 152
Vasquez, Angelique/Bria, 76, 79, 82, 92
Vasquez, Sharlynn, 151
Vietnam War, 26

Waite, Cheryl
    Baby College and, 59–61, 71, 72, 73–74,
      75, 79, 84, 87–88, 90–91, 92, 94, 257
    background, 59–60, 72–74, 88–90, 92
    as mother/wife, 257–58, 260
    Victor's proposal, 90–91, 257

Wal-Mart, 136
War on Poverty
    description, 26
    Murray on, 28–29
    See also Welfare system
Washington, Denzel, 146
Weissbourd, Richard, 94–95
Welfare system
    as poverty "cause," 24–25, 28–29
    poverty "solution" and, 29, 32–33, 37
    Reagan-era cuts in, 32–33
Welsh, Natasha, 59, 76–77
West Side Story, 25
What Money Can't Buy (Mayer), 24
Williams, Chastity, 146–47, 148, 149, 152
Williams, Jason, 226
Williams, Leonard/Lydia
    grandchildren and, 53, 54, 112–15
    history of, 99–100

Williams, Mary, 99–100
    See also Canada, Mary
Wilson, William Julius
    on Moynihan report, 27–28
    on poverty causes, 29–32, 33
    on poverty solutions, 32, 33, 37, 38
Wyatt, Alfonso
    background, 14–15
    at eighth-grade graduation, 255
    at lottery, 15–16
    middle school changes and, 249

Young Disciples and Union Avenue, 110–12
Young Dro, 235

Zero-to-three movement, 56–58